Critical Essays on

ERNEST HEMINGWAY'S
A FAREWELL TO ARMS

CRITICAL ESSAYS
ON
AMERICAN LITERATURE

James Nagel, General Editor
University of Georgia, Athens

Critical Essays on

ERNEST HEMINGWAY'S
A FAREWELL TO ARMS

edited by

GEORGE MONTEIRO

G. K. Hall & Co. / New York
Maxwell Macmillan Canada / Toronto
Maxwell Macmillan International / New York Oxford Singapore Sydney

G. K. Hall & Co. Maxwell Macmillan Canada, Inc.
Macmillan Publishing Company 1200 Eglinton Avenue East
866 Third Avenue Suite 200
New York, New York 10022 Don Mills, Ontario M3C 3N1

Library of Congress Cataloging-in-Publication Data

Critical essays on Ernest Hemingway's A Farewell to Arms / edited by
  George Monteiro.
p.   cm. — (Critical essays on American literature)
  Includes bibliographical references and index.
  ISBN 0-7838-0011-8
1. Hemingway, Ernest, 1899–1961. Farewell to arms. 2. World War,
  1914–1918—Literature and the war. 3. War stories, American—
  History and criticism. I. Monteiro, George. II. Series.
  PS3515.E37F3533   1994
  813'.52—dc20   94-19102
                                                              CIP

---

10   9   8   7   6   5   4   3   2   1

Printed in the United States of America

for Ed Monteiro

Contents

◆

CRITICISM

General Editor's Note

◆

This series seeks to anthologize the most important criticism on a wide variety of topics and writers in American literature. Our readers will find in various volumes not only a generous selection of reprinted articles and reviews but original essays, bibliographies, manuscript sections, and other materials brought to public attention for the first time. This volume, *Critical Essays on A Farewell to Arms*, is the most comprehensive collection of essays ever published on one of the most important novels of the twentieth century. It contains both a sizable gathering of early reviews and a broad selection of more modern scholarship as well.

Among the authors of reprinted articles and reviews are John Dos Passos, Michael S. Reynolds, James Nagel, Scott Donaldson, Judith Fetterley, Philip Young, Carlos Baker, and Millicent Bell. In addition to a substantial introduction by George Monteiro, there is also an original essay commissioned specifically for publication in this volume, a new study by Peter Griffin (on the concept of "home" for Ernest Hemingway and Frederic Henry). We are confident that this book will make a permanent and significant contribution to the study of American literature.

JAMES NAGEL
University of Georgia, Athens

Publisher's Note

◆

Producing a volume that contains both newly commissioned and reprinted material presents the publisher with the challenge of balancing the desire to achieve stylistic consistency with the need to preserve the integrity of works first published elsewhere. In the Critical Essays series, essays commissioned especially for a particular volume are edited to be consistent with G. K. Hall's house style; reprinted essays appear in the style in which they were first published, with only typographical errors corrected. Consequently, shifts in style from one essay to another are the result of our efforts to be faithful to each text as it was originally published.

Introduction

GEORGE MONTEIRO

I

Looking back at the books of 1929, the English novelist Horace Walpole marveled at the year's "odd and perplexing phenomenon"—"the dominance of the War Book." "Why, after almost complete silence for ten years, this sudden flood?" he asked.

> Because, I suppose, the distance is just sufficient for the war to be bearable for those who shared in it and exciting for those who did not. Remarque's "All Quiet on the Western Front," Sherriff's play, "Journey's End," have been the driving sensations of the year. Remarque's book has, I think, been over-praised. Place it beside Zweig's "Grischa" or Hemingway's "A Farewell to Arms" and it is surely not creative literature. But it is not as creative literature that it has been read. It has had the effect of reality for many who were never at the Front and the effect of reminiscence for many who were. After this Richard Aldington's "Death of a Hero" and Robert Graves's autobiography "Good-bye to All That" have caused the widest interest. The first is peevish in tone, the second a little selfish in its honesty, but Graves's book has, I fancy, as large a possibility of enduring as any book of the year.[1]

Walpole's listing remains useful for its identification of the principal works published in 1929 with which Hemingway's war novel would compete for popularity and critical acclaim. Walpole had already decided, as he said in the same piece, that Hemingway's novel, "a most moving and beautiful story," was "the finest novel of the year."[2] Walpole's personal choice anticipated general critical consensus over time.

Yet the grounds for the high critical valuation of A Farewell to Arms have varied over the last 65 years. Hemingway's novel has been many different books to different readers at different times. It has been read as a work of pure naturalism marked by philosophical determinism, exemplifying in its narrator-hero true patterns of behaviorism. It has been singled out as a novel that is sociologically realistic in its treatment of war and wartime love. Many readers have hailed it, and many readers have taught it, as a trenchant antiwar novel. It has been described as a realistic work, striated, nevertheless, by structural motifs and religious and spiritual symbols. It has been praised (and scorned) as a young man's dream—not of war, as Hemingway described Crane's *Red Badge of Courage*—but of love. Still other readers have seen Frederic Henry's narrative as a misogynist's dehumanizing idealization of one woman. To many readers, the book is more about words and their political devaluation and public debasement than about war or love. And then, too, it has been called a poem, from beginning to end, and studied as such.

A *Farewell to Arms* is also one of those works that evoke strong opinions. Even fictional and pseudonymous characters have weighed in with judgements. Whether or not they express their authors' views, Van Wyck Brooks's Oliver Allston and J. D. Salinger's Holden Caulfield are less than awed by Hemingway's novel. A similar story of "true love lost," A *Farewell to Arms* is "much the same tale as [Henry Wadsworth Longfellow's] *Evangeline*," huffs Allston. Holden, whose creator had once written to Hemingway that as a young soldier he, too, was looking for a nurse like Catherine Barkley, decides that Hemingway's much-revered war story is a "phony book" with, in Lieutenant Henry, a "phony" hero.[3] The nonagenarian justice of the United States Supreme Court, Oliver Wendell Holmes, offered a less hostile judgement. He found that *Farewell* had "some thrilling power" that "moved" him "moderately," though "not to the superlative degree."[4] But it is generally to writers that one must turn for the most meaningful and lasting professional assessments, and their views of *Farewell* are almost always favorable. Even the rather harsh treatment Hemingway accorded Irwin Shaw did not prevent him from acknowledging that A *Farewell to Arms* is a "great" book.[5] Reynolds Price praised its Horatian and Biblical styles.[6] T. S. Eliot saw evidence in *Farewell* that its author was a "writer of tender sentiment, and true sentiment," adding that he "seems to me to tell the truth about his own feelings at the moment when they exist."[7] In an unfinished review Hemingway's young contemporary Thomas Wolfe praised the novel's "superb concision." Hemingway "says one thing and suggests ten more," he marveled, "his words not only pull their own weight in a sentence, they also pull a very rich weight of profound and moving association and inference."[8] And it was to Hemingway's novel that Wolfe's *Look Homeward, Angel* was compared when Sinclair Lewis wanted to praise it: "It and *Farewell to Arms* seem to me to have more spacious power in them than any books for years, American OR foreign."[9] A young poet serving as editor of his school newspaper, Winfield Townley Scott, printed an unsigned review (probably his own) calling Hemingway's book "one of the finest novels—one of the three best—that 1929 has seen come from the presses." Hemingway "puts style experimenters to shame," he concluded with an undergraduate's assurance, for "he has something to say, and he is succeeding in putting it down in glowing prose."[10] A decade after recording his reservations about the book he read in typescript, F. Scott Fitzgerald decided that like "the Joyce of *Dubliners*, the Keats of 'The Eve of St. Agnes' [and] 'The Grecian Urn,'" the Mark Twain of the great central parts of *Huckleberry Finn*, the *Daisy Miller* of Henry James, the Kipling of *The Drums of Fore and Aft*"—"the Hemingway of *Farewell to Arms*" was one of the "great English classics."[11]

Not everyone agreed with Wolfe, Lewis or Fitzgerald, of course. The author of *From Here to Eternity*, James Jones, thought otherwise. Hemingway had sentimentalized "this old affair . . . all out of reality by wishful and romantic thinking about what it *could* or *should* or might have been." The true story of the young Hemingway's "'tragic' losing of the nurse" in Italy in 1918, decided this canny reader, had already been told in the sketch "A Very Short Story."[12] William Faulkner criticized *Farewell* in another way, when in 1939 he published *The Wild Palms*, an ironic treatment of the theme of "all for love" done in "Hemingwaves" (Faulkner's expression).[13]

In 1929, however, the great news that Hemingway's novel brought to the poets was not so much thematic as stylistic. His preeminence was assured for Allen Tate, who called him "unquestionably one of the great stylists of English prose."[14] Even before the novel had completed its pre-publication run in *Scribner's Magazine*, Archibald MacLeish had decided that with *Farewell* Hemingway had established himself as "the great novelist of our time": "The world of this book is a complete world, a world of emotion as well as of feeling. To subject the whole experience of a man's soul to the pure & perfect art of your prose is a great, a very great, achievement."[15]

II

At 30, Ernest Hemingway was the author of four trade books when Charles Scribner's Sons brought out *A Farewell to Arms*. He had begun his commercial career with Boni & Liveright in 1925 with a collection of short stories, *In Our Time*, following it in 1927 with a parodic novel, *The Torrents of Spring*, and *The Sun Also Rises*, both of them brought out by Scribners, which, from that date, would be Hemingway's sole American publisher. *The Sun Also Rises* gave him his first taste of commercial success. In 1929, he published *Men Without Women*, his second collection of stories, following it, later in the year, with *A Farewell to Arms*.

A Farewell to Arms was banned in Boston. The first installment of the novel's serialization in the May issue of *Scribner's Magazine* was barred from the bookstands on 19 June 1929.[16] Scribners seems to have anticipated this act of censure and censorship, for the July issue of the magazine (in press before the Boston banning) carried a letter from Owen Wister, author of *The Virginian* and at the time a friendly acquaintance of Hemingway's. "This book is full of beauty and variety, and nobody in it is garbage," he wrote presciently.[17] The editors followed Wister's letter with quotations from newspapers across the country hailing the publication of Hemingway's new novel. But this presumptive strike (if that is what it was) proved worthless when the Boston police continued to pull the magazine from the news-stands.[18] Scribners had met the initial ban with a statement defending the book's morality and—curiously, considering the reactions of its first (and subsequent) readers—defending it against the charge that it was an antiwar book.[19] Others joined in the good fight against censorship. For example, the writer-critic Mary Colum, a friend of Hemingway's editor at Scribners, Maxwell Perkins, entered the fray with a letter to the *New York Times*.[20] She took the high road of praising the novel's moral and aesthetic value, arguing:

> The question [of] what constitutes either high literature or high morality is a very complicated one even for people who have devoted a lifetime to the study of such matters—far too complicated for a Police Superintendent who has to think of traffic laws and bootleggers. Literature is the history of life and human relations, and if there are high moral and literary reasons why people should read the Old Testament, why cannot the same people have the stomach to read an account of life at the front during wartime by one of the most distinguished modern writers, whose object is certainly not to corrupt anybody in Boston or out of it? And what form of morality is served by bamboozling people as to what goes on at a wartime front? And one may ask for the hundredth time why are publications which deliberately exploit disreputability, falseness and abnormality allowed in piles man-high on the news stands, and why is a high-class magazine banned from the same places for publishing a sincere piece of literature?[21]

Oscar Cargill would later claim, somewhat exaggeratedly, that the actions of the Boston police "aroused something like national resentment."[22] The situation in Boston did amuse the *Daily Oklahoman*, which contributed some doggerel: *"Scribner's* may have a large circulation / Since Boston with its codfish and its beans / Deems Hemingway a menace to the nation."[23] Under any circumstances, the novel would certainly have found its own critical way with discerning readers, but its journey to commercial success might have been longer.

If the Boston banning of *Farewell* boosted sales, it also had the less salutary effect of exacerbating Hemingway's prepublication difficulties with his editor. Hemingway quarreled with Perkins over the hard, if not entirely objectionable, language of his text. The actions taken by the Boston police strengthened Perkins' editorial hand regardless of Scribners' publicly stated position, as he pushed Hemingway to eliminate offensive words and revise several untoward references. Under pressure, Hemingway agreed to most of the suggested changes. Sometimes the revised text did the trick, for the *Portland Evening News* found the "book worth buying, than which no more need be said, unless it is a general warning that unprintable expressions abound and only unimaginable expressions, that will cause the curious to pause and guess, are deleted for Boston's sake."[24] Boston was not so readily mollified. The *Boston Transcript*, for instance, turned the subject of Hemingway's "hard words" into a broader question of literary aesthetics and public morals, warning, "it might be well to say, that it is hard to believe that many intelligent and liberal-minded readers of any age can be very much in sympathy with Mr. Hemingway's use of hard words. It is not that such usage would tend to corrupt the youth, for practically every boy of twelve knows all of them, but it is rather that such usage lowers the tone of literature in general. The best writing is not necessarily the most realistic; indeed, in order to be a really fine work, a book should have some little idealism to it."[25]

A smattering of similar reviews, however, induced no tempest, especially when favorable reviews began to accumulate and sales mounted. On one list of the week's "most discussed books," Hemingway's novel started out in fifth place on 16 October, climbed to fourth over the next two weeks, and achieved first place on 6 November. It stayed there for six weeks, dropping only to number three at Christmas time.[26] The *Daily Oklahoman* was right. The ban had helped to fill Scribners' coffers. Other writers were envious. Wolfe, with *Look Homeward, Angel* about to appear, revealed privately that he yearned for a Boston ban on his own work, sure that it would aid its commercial success. "Scribners do not want to have my book 'Banned in Boston'—they are a very fine and dignified firm, and did not like the Hemingway ban, although it helped the sale of the book," he complained. "But—this is between *us*—if it does get banned, I hope it makes a loud noise—for God's sake try to get some publicity out of it for me."[27] And Scott Fitzgerald kept close watch on the effect the Boston banning of *Farewell* was having on sales. "[T]here was a certain amount of controversy over the 'Farewell' out of which we seem to have come very successfully," he reminded Perkins, the editor he shared with Hemingway and Wolfe.[28] For Hemingway, the financial aspects of publication had turned out well, starting with the $16,000 that he was paid for serialization, an unprecedented sum.[29]

Farewell also faced censorship abroad. In Mussolini's fascist Italy, it was seen as vilifying Italian character and distorting recent Italian history. Hemingway's picture of an Italian army in total disarray, especially in retreat from Caporetto, earned a ban on the book for years.[30] So effective was Mussolini's interdiction that *Farewell* was not published in Italy while he was in power. Only in 1945, with the collapse of Mussolini's government, was Hemingway's novel published—appropriately enough, in Milan.[31]

III

Scribners has never allowed *A Farewell to Arms* to go out of print. Officially published on 27 September 1929, in both trade and limited editions, the book was advertised by Scribners as "a farewell to war as useless and hateful," one that "might be grim reading if it were not illumined with the beauty of the world, of the characters, and by love; and if it were not also lively with incident and often extremely amusing."[32] The publicity did not oversell the book, though readers may search in vain through the reviews that greeted the book's publication or in subsequent commentary and interpretation accumulated over six decades, for any acknowledgement of those "extremely amusing" elements. By November, when it was brought out in England by Jonathan Cape, the book was in its sixth American printing. By mid-February sales totaled 79,251 copies. In June 1930, the Leipzig publisher Bernard Tauchnitz was permitted to add *Farewell* to his list. In May 1932, it became volume 19 of "The Modern Library of the World's Best Books." The value of having his books appear in this popular series was clear to Hemingway, who years later protested (unsuccessfully) Scribners' decision, after he had been awarded the Nobel Prize, to rescind Modern Library's right to reprint. At Hemingway's death, in 1961, sales had reached 1,383,000 copies.

Besides making his novel available at 95 cents a copy, the Modern Library edition brought Hemingway another boon: Ford Madox Ford's introduction. Its effect on Hemingway's literary reputation is incalculable, for it served to educate a generation of readers and scholars on the way to read Hemingway's style. Calling Hemingway one of "the three impeccable writers of English prose" that he had "come across in fifty years or so of reading in search of English prose"—the other two were Joseph Conrad and W. H. Hudson—Ford wrote:

> Hemingway's words strike you, each one, as if they were pebbles fetched fresh from a brook. They live and shine, each in its place. So one of his pages has the effect of a brook-bottom into which you look down through the flowing water. The words form a tessellation, each in order beside the other.
>
> It is a very great quality. It is indeed the supreme quality of the written art of the moment. It is a great part of what makes literature come into its own at such rare times as it achieves that feat. Books lose their hold on you as soon as the words in which they are written or demoded or too usual the one following the other. The aim—the achievement—of the great prose writer is to use words so that they shall seem new and alive because of their juxtaposition with other words. This gift Hemingway has supremely. Any sentence of his taken at random will hold your attention. And irresistibly. It does not matter where you take it. "I was in under the canvas with guns. They smelled cleanly of oil and grease. I lay and listened to the rain on the canvas and the clicking of the car over the rails. There was a little light came through and I lay and looked at the guns."

You could not begin that first sentence and not finish the passage.

That is a great part of this author's gift. Yet it is not only "gift." You cannot throw yourself into a frame of mind and just write and get that effect. Your mind has to choose each word and your ear has to test it until by long disciplining of mind and ear you can no longer go wrong.

That disciplining through which you must put yourself is all the more difficult in that it must be gone through in solitude. You cannot watch the man next to you in the ranks smartly manipulating his side-arms nor do you hear any word of command by which to time yourself.

On the other hand a writer holds a reader by his temperament. That is his true "gift"—what he receives from whoever sends him into the world. It arises from how you look at things. If you look at and render things so that they appear new to the reader you will hold his attention. If what you give him appears familiar or half familiar his attention will wander. Hemingway's use of the word "cleanly" is an instance of what I have just been saying. The guns smelled cleanly of oil and grease. Oil and grease are not usually associated in the mind with a clean smell. Yet at the minutest reflection you realise that the oil and grease on the clean metal of big guns are not dirt. So the adverb is just. You have had a moment of surprise and then your knowledge is added to. The word "author" means "someone who adds to your consciousness."[33]

It is a tribute to Ford that the best of Hemingway's critics were influenced by his view of Hemingway's diction. His description of Hemingway's words as "pebbles fetched fresh from a brook" was expanded by Malcolm Cowley to reveal something about the way the author's temperament shaped the substance of his fiction. Interested above all in theme and authorial intentions, Cowley begins his introduction to the Viking Portable Library *Hemingway* in 1944 with an unacknowledged homage to Ford:

Going back to Hemingway's work after several years is like going back to a brook where you had often fished and finding the woods as deep and cool as they used to be. The trees are bigger, perhaps, but they are the same trees; the water comes down over the black stones as clear as always, with the same dull, steady roar where it plunges into the pool; and when the first trout takes hold of your line you can feel your heart beating against your fishing jacket. But something has changed, for this time there are shadows in the pool that you hadn't noticed before, and you have a sense that the woods are haunted.[34]

Against such a portentous and haunting background, Cowley later takes up Hemingway's characteristic rain motif, which in *Farewell* "becomes a conscious symbol of disaster." " 'Things went very badly,' the hero tells us in the first chapter," writes Cowley.

"At the start of the winter came the permanent rain and with the rain came the cholera." Catherine Barkley is afraid of the rain because, she says, "sometimes I see me dead in it." Rain falls all during the retreat from Caporetto; it falls while Catherine is trying to have her baby in a Swiss hospital; and it is still falling when she dies and when Frederic pushed the nurses out of the room to be alone with her. "It wasn't any good," he says. "It was like saying goodbye to a statue. After a while I went out and left the hospital and walked back to the hotel in the rain."[35]

To introduce *A Farewell to Arms* to a new generation of readers after World War II, Scribners chose Robert Penn Warren, the poet, critic, and novelist. His novel, *All the King's Men*, had appeared in 1946. Warren's introduction, adapted from his 1947 essay in the *Kenyon Review*, was more informative than Ford's. Using critical writing that was unavailable to Ford, Warren provided an up-to-date introduction that was biographical, historical, and thematic. Above all, he provided an historical and literary context for Hemingway's revolutionary style. Publication of this edition coincided with the twentieth anniversary of the first publication of *Farewell*.

Only one other trade edition of *A Farewell to Arms* in English has carried an introduction. An illustrated edition published in mid-November 1948 (obviously aiming at the Christmas trade) carries an introduction by Hemingway. He wrote it to oblige Charles Scribner, Jr., whose first task as a Scribners editor was to bring out this edition.[36]

Several dramatizations form part of the larger story of *A Farewell to Arms*. The novel's immediate critical acclaim and newsworthy popularity captured the attention of New York theater producers. Laurence Stallings, who was the author, along with Maxwell Anderson, of *What Price Glory?* (a war play that had been a Broadway hit during the 1924 season), was asked to "arrange" (his word) a script from Hemingway's text. *A Farewell to Arms* opened in New York's National Theater on 22 September 1930 (after satisfying Philadelphia censors in its out-of-town run) and ran for 24 performances. A different dramatic version of *Farewell*, in German, premiered on 1 September 1931. Relying heavily on Annemarie Horschitz's translation, "Kat" was the work of Carl Zuckmayer and Heinz Hilpert. Hemingway attended opening night but seems not to have known German well enough to follow the play.[37]

Despite its short run in New York, Stallings' script provided the starting point for Frank Borzage's Hollywood version of *Farewell*, although Borzage soon modified it considerably. Starring Gary Cooper as Lieutenant Henry, Helen Hayes as Catherine Barkley, and Adolphe Menjou as Rinaldi, the movie was more commercially successful than the play. Hemingway would have nothing to do with the making of the movie—"They'll have Catherine give birth to the American flag and rename the movie *The Star Spangled Banner*," he complained—and refused to see the finished product. His refusal was vociferous enough to attract the transatlantic attention of T. S. Eliot, who expressed admiration for Hemingway's stand.[38] (Predictably, Mussolini extended his ban on the novel to include Borzage's film.) Hemingway also rejected Hollywood's second version of his novel, the 1957 remake produced by David O. Selznick. Based on Ben Hecht's script, directed by Charles Vidor, and starring Jennifer Jones (the producer's 40-year-old wife) as Catherine, Rock Hudson as Frederic Henry, and Vitorio de Sica as Rinaldi, this movie was not as well received as Borzage's. It is true that Hemingway despised Selznick's *Farewell* even more than he had Borzage's. But there is no documentation, beyond A. E. Hotchner, for the anecdote that Hemingway's reaction to Selznick's offer to pay him $50,000 if and when the film made a profit was to advise Selznick to "have all $50,000 changed into nickels at his local bank and shove them up his ass until they came out of his ears."[39]

A *Farewell to Arms* was dramatized at least twice for radio broadcast, further evidence of its popularity. Orson Welles cast Katharine Hepburn as the lead in his version, while in 1937 "Lux Theater" presented a one-hour version starring Clark Gable, Josephine Hutchinson, and Adolphe Menjou.

IV

Almost from the beginning, many of its readers assumed that *Farewell* was a fictionalized, if artistically arranged, version of its author's wartime experiences. Frederic Henry on the Italian front, his wounding and subsequent desertion, his flight to Switzerland with his pregnant lover—all followed the author's emotional reality and, if not always the actual incident, at least the essence of his wartime fate. It took considerable scholarly spade work to uncover the evidence necessary to overturn this well-entrenched canard. Strong evidence was accumulated to support contrary arguments that would direct readers away from such naively biographical interpretations of Hemingway's novel. In 1976, combining a close look at manuscripts with assiduous research on Hemingway's own reading (of maps as well as books), Michael S. Reynolds demonstrated conclusively that behind A *Farewell to Arms* lay a great deal more reading and study that any reader had previously suspected, and very much less transcribed biography.[40] Besides studying closely the author's revisions in his manuscript and the circumstances surrounding the book's publication, Reynolds looked into those works of history and literature that fed Hemingway's imagination and suggested ways in which Hemingway's interest in travel literature throws light on his novel's technique and structure. In *Hemingway in Love and War* (1989), Henry Serrano Villard and James Nagel's presentation and close study of the wartime diary of Agnes von Kurowsky—Hemingway's nurse—proved conclusively that not only did *Farewell* contain more poetry than naked biographical truth, but also that much that has passed for unassailable biography simply was not so. Several varnished and distorted "facts," often initiated and sustained by Hemingway himself, are investigated by Nagel, who straightens out the record on matters such as the extent of Hemingway's wounds, the nature of his romance with Agnes, the medals he was awarded, and whether he was ever in the Italian Army.[41]

Yet while there is little one-to-one correspondence between the events of *A Farewell to Arms* and Hemingway's wartime biography, the novel bears reading within the context of the author's life during the years in which he wrote it. By the time Hemingway began to write his war novel, a decade after the war had ended, it had long been preceded by several formidable books. In fact, in 1916, even before Hemingway had volunteered for service as an ambulance driver, Henri Barbusse had published *Le feu*, a novel translated as *Under Fire* in 1917. Shortly after the war's end, in the United States, John Dos Passos's highly influential *Three Soldiers* appeared in 1921, and E. E. Cummings' autobiographical account of incarceration in France, *The Enormous Room*, appeared in 1922. In 1929, the year that *Farewell* appeared, Hemingway was anticipated by Frederic Manning, whose novel *The Middle Parts of Fortune* was published anonymously, and Erich Maria Remarque, whose *Im Westen nichts Neues* was translated as *All Quiet on the Western Front*. Remarque's novel, appearing just weeks before *Farewell*, became a measure of comparison for Hemingway's work.[42]

Manning's novel, re-issued shortly thereafter as *Her Privates We*, became a Hemingway favorite. He reread the book, he affirmed, "each year in July, the anniversary of the month when I got the big wound."[43] That wounding he placed at Fossalta di Piave around midnight on 8 July 1918, less than a month after he arrived in Italy. His first letter, written from a hospital in Milan on 21 July 1918, was not published until 1981, that is, half a century after the publication of *A Farewell to Arms* and long after the novel had accumulated its heavy burden of biographical criticism.

To the great surprise of many readers, in this first letter home the young Hemingway is both buoyant and boastful. He is the first American soldier wounded in Italy, he informs his family, but his wounds are being well cared for in this "peach of a hospital." To prove to his family that he is being very professionally attended, this doctor's son affects the clinician's concern with those precise details that could only please his father:

> [O]ne of the best surgeons in Milan is looking after my wounds. There are a couple of pieces still in, one bullet in my knee that the X-Ray showed. The surgeon, very wisely, is after consultation, going to wait for the wound in my right knee to become healed cleanly before operating. The bullet will then be rather encysted and he will make a clean cut and go in under the side of the knee cap. By allowing it to be completely healed first he thus avoids any danger of infection and stiff knee. That is wise don't you think Dad? He will also remove a bullet from my right foot at the same time. He will probably operate in about a week as the wound is healing cleanly and there is no infection. I had two shots of anti tetanus immediately at the dressing station. All the other bullets and pieces of shell have been removed

and all the wounds on my left leg are healing finely. My fingers are all cleared up and have the bandages off. There will be no permanent effects from any of the wounds as there are no bones shattered. Even in my knees. In both the left and right the bullets did not fracture the patella; one piece of shell about the size of a Tinker's roller bearing was in my left knee but it has been removed and the knee now moves perfectly and the wound is nearly healed. In the right knee the bullet went under the knee cap from the left side and didn't smash it a bit. By the time you get this letter the surgeon will have operated and it will be all healed, and I hope to be back driving in the mountains by the latter part of August.[44]

Having answered his practitioner-father's anxious questions, the young son turns to talk that might come from any young soldier still new to battle, still excited by war's adventure despite his wounds. He has collected many interesting photographs and souvenirs, he says. "I was all through the big battle and have Austrian carbines and ammunition. German and Austrian medals, officer's automatic pistols, Boche helmets, about a dozen Bayonets, star shell pistols and knives and almost everything you can think of. The only limit to the amount of souvenirs I could have is what I could carry for there were so many dead Austrians and prisoners the ground was almost black with them. It was a great victory and showed the world what wonderful fighters the Italians are."[45] What is missing from this brave letter is that characteristic Hemingway irony. The young Hemingway is not only pleased with his surgeon's ministrations but approves of his decision to delay the operation. The observation that the battlefield is "almost black" with the enemy dead is singularly devoid of tone. Even Mussolini could have approved of this letter, especially in its praise of the Italians as "wonderful fighters." The young Hemingway, except for his having been wounded, hardly fore-shadows the fictional Frederic Henry, that former lieutenant who would emerge as the subdued and doleful author of a retrospective narrative of ill-fated love amidst chaotic war on the Italian front in 1917.

Before 1928 Hemingway had used his own war materials sparingly in a handful of untitled sketches and in stories such as "Soldier's Home" and "In Another Country."[46] He had tried his hand at the sketch later retitled "A Very Short Story," which (as the novelist James Jones detected) reimagines in just 644 words the entire ironic story of his love for the American nurse Agnes von Kurowsky in the summer of 1918 and its (for him) unsatisfactory outcome. But by late 1927 or early 1928, Hemingway finally made a genuine start on the war novel that would do justice to his private experience as well as the extensive materials on the Great War that he had gathered through reading and research, especially in histories of fighting on the Italian-Austrian front. What made this creative breakthrough possible was his discovery of an elegiac narrative voice that would carry him through his extended retrospective story. This voice emerged out of his personal pain in 1927–28 when he separated from and then divorced Hadley Richardson, to live with and then marry Pauline

Pfeiffer. Something deeply and intensely valued was coming to an end, and—he would confess in *A Moveable Feast*—there was no way to get it back. His depression, sometimes bordering on despair, led him to the one fictional voice that enabled him to turn his personal pain into a long "poem" about war and love. That discovery enabled him—to borrow Maxwell Perkins' words 15 years after the book was published—to show "how everything is conditioned, and indeed contaminated, by war—and how a purely physical attempt at seduction grew, in spite of everything, into love."[47] It also enabled him to discover the sweeping metaphor that would fuse into a single whole his twin stories of war and love—the world seen as hospital.[48]

V

Beyond *Farewell*'s putative biographical sources, the historical accuracy of its account of the Italian retreat from Caporetto, and its imagistic and symbolic deployment of rain, three or four other matters have caught the interest of Hemingway's critics: Catherine's delivery scene, Frederic Henry's denunciation of abstract patriotic words, and the novel's conclusion. The first of these, the death-in-childbirth scene, has even been dismissed as little more than a cliché. Episodes from earlier novels—Dreiser's *The "Genius"* and Tolstoy's *Anna Karenina*, for example—have been adduced as sources.[49] Of the baby's birth in the Swiss hospital, English novelist Arnold Bennett wrote, "I have read nothing in that line so graphic, so beautiful, so harrowing. It need not fear comparison with the coming into the world of Anna Karenina's child."[50] For the symbolic conjunction of rain with childbirth, Hemingway seems to have had recourse to Chekhov's short story "The Party."[51] For many recent readers, Catherine's death in childbirth has become the locus of what they consider to be Hemingway's misogyny, a notion hinted at more than 50 years ago, when it was suggested that "the death of Catherine can better be justified on sadistic than aesthetic grounds. The author put his own need ahead of his reader's."[52]

Critics continue to show interest in Frederic Henry's philippic against what Malcolm Cowley called the "big words" of war.[53] Engaged in a discussion over winning and losing at war, Frederic Henry reacts silently to his companion's brave assertion that "what has been done this summer cannot have been done in vain." His thoughts are expressed, not in the voice of the young lieutenant who fought in the war, but in that of the older Frederic Henry who is the book's narrator:

> I was always embarrassed by the words sacred, glorious, and sacrifice and the expression in vain. We had heard them, sometimes standing in the rain almost out of earshot, so that only the shouted words came through, and had read

them, on proclamations that were slapped up by billposters over other proclamations, now for a long time, and I had seen nothing sacred, and the things that were glorious had no glory and the sacrifices were like the stockyards at Chicago if nothing was done with the meat except to bury it. There were many words that you could not stand to hear and finally only the names of places had dignity. Certain numbers were the same way and certain dates and these with the names of the places were all you could say and have them mean anything. Abstract words such as glory, honor, courage, or hallow were obscene beside the concrete names of villages, the numbers of roads, the names of rivers, the numbers of regiments and the dates.[54]

This passage's centrality looms large in Robert W. Lewis' 1992 book-length introductory interpretation of Hemingway's novel, a multi-faceted study that reads the novel in terms of characters, mode of presentation (including voice and point of view), and themes of games, craziness, and appearance versus essence, yet carries as its subtitle "The War of the Words."[55] At stake, above all, is the nature and fate of Frederic Henry's idealism. Delmore Schwartz, writing in 1955, suggested that behind Frederic Henry's words stands Hemingway: "although the hero deserts from the army, and although the abstract words have become obscene, it is nevertheless precisely glory, honor, courage, and sacrifice which are the true ideals and aims of conduct in all of Hemingway's writing."[56] Arguably, it is Hemingway's hidden but never expunged idealism that provides the basis for a true understanding of Frederic Henry's denunciation.

The third matter that has interested Hemingway's critics is the novel's conclusion. Carlos Baker's publication in 1962 of what he then called "the original conclusion to *A Farewell to Arms*"[57] proved to be the tip of the iceberg when Hemingway's papers and manuscripts were opened to scholars. The survival of numerous variant endings belies the author's own statement (perhaps made tongue-in-cheek) in something he called "Ernest von Hemingstein's Journal." "Thursday.—Commenced writing a new novel," he writes. "It is to be called A Farewell to Arms and treats of war on the Italian front which I visited briefly as a boy after the death of Henry James. A strange coincidence. Some difficulty about deciding how the book will end. Solved it finally."[58] How he finally solved it after much effort has been the subject of considerable study by several Hemingway scholars, including, preeminently, Reynolds (1976) and Bernard Oldsey (1979). Oldsey has catalogued those endings in nine categories: (1) the "*nada*" ending; (2) the "Fitzgerald" ending; (3) the "religious" ending; (4) the "Live-Baby" ending; (5) the "Morning-After" ending; (6) the "Funeral" ending; (7) the "Original *Scribner's Magazine*" ending or the "Combination" ending; (8) variants of "*The*" ending; and (9) "Miscellaneous" endings.[59]

Critics have also considered the titles Hemingway devised for the novel and then abandoned, for the light they shed on interpretations of the novel.

Reynolds, Oldsey, Paul Smith, and the present author have written on the titles.[60]

VI

The notoriety of A Farewell to Arms before its publication in book form was such that by the time Scribners brought out Hemingway's second novel in early fall 1929, reviewers everywhere were poised to react. On both sides of the Atlantic, the novel was praised for its authentic reporting of the fighting in Italy (a domain which Hemingway had made his own, since most Anglo-American war writing dealt with the Western front), for the author's spare, understated style, and for the pathos and tragedy of the love story of Catherine Barkley and Frederic Henry. One British reviewer noted astutely that A Farewell to Arms gave a trenchant account of what happened to the soldier between the two emblematic acts depicted in the familiar World War I illustrations entitled "The Soldier's Farewell" and "The Soldier's Return." Hemingway's novel, concluded B. E. Todd, deserved a place on the wall between the two illustrations, "so that it can be used as an antidote to the sickly poison of glory and glamour."[61] It is true that faced with censorship, Scribners had hastened to dissociate Hemingway's novel from "antiwar propaganda," but, as John Dos Passos explained, while the great commercial success of the novel might itself be attributed to the "military propaganda going on in the schools and colleges," it was not possible that the military would profit from the vogue for the book.[62] Since the prevailing view turned out to be, in H. L. Mencken's words, that "the virtue of the story lies in its brilliant evocation of the horrible squalor and confusion of war—specifically, of war à la Italienne,"[63] Scribners soon dropped its disclaimer that Farewell was not antiwar propaganda. Concerned that the book's depiction of the Italian military might cause Italians to stop sales of the book, Hemingway wrote to his editor that his "only fear" was that there might be "some Italian action" to discredit the book. "How would it be," he suggested, "to run in the front matter that statement I wrote that was published in the magazine when the first number of A Farewell appeared?"[64] Indeed, in its second printing Scribners did run Hemingway's statement that "none of the characters in this book is a living person, nor are the units or military organizations mentioned actual units or organizations" (later the statement was dropped).[65] The historical authenticity of Hemingway's account of the Italian retreat at Caporetto would be disputed occasionally, but, by and large, it has stood up over time.

Whether A Farewell to Arms was a war story or a love story was a frequent theme in the contemporary reviews. Some reviewers merely asserted that the war was an appropriate backdrop for Hemingway's theme of sentiment and love, while others saw the story of Frederic and Catherine's love as a telling microcosm of the war that gives it its meaning. Cowley simply bypassed the issue by declaring the book to be Hemingway's "first love story . . . also his first long story about the war, his first novel in the strict sense."[66] Incidentally, given Cowley's importance in many subsequent interpretations of the novel, it is notable that he praised the "description of the Italian retreat." He would include it in his influential Viking Portable *Hemingway*, a copy of which the young soldier and future Hemingway scholar Philip Young carried with him during World War II. Cowley compared it to Stendhal's account of the retreat from Waterloo.[67] Cowley is also the only reviewer to touch on Hemingway's strength as a "symbolic" writer, calling his title symbolic of Hemingway's "farewell to a period, an attitude, and perhaps to a method also." He said nothing then, however, about the specific symbols—such as the rain—that pervade the novel. Cowley's emphasis was on what Kenneth Burke disapprovingly called "the test of naturalness in writing"—which "leads too inexorably to Hemingway, whom I hate," he explained a week after the publication of *Farewell*, "as though sent upon earth to hate him." This idea would be expanded to embrace the thematics of naturalism in one of the most influential early essays on *Farewell*, Ray B. West, Jr.'s study of "the biological trap" as the key to the novel's meaning (1945, 1949), and would be further extended in Dewey Ganzel's 1971 essay, published, as was West's first piece, in the *Sewanee Review*.[68] Cowley was not concerned with that pervasive symbolism in *Farewell* that, oddly enough, Burke himself later discovered (1950) and that Carlos Baker featured so prominently in his studies of Hemingway as artist (1951, 1952).[69]

The contemporary reviewers were primed by the public reaction to Hemingway's work to praise, criticize, describe and measure Hemingway's already famous style. Most of them found it, once again, perfectly suitable to the author's general outlook and fictional intentions. The style in *Farewell* was described as clipped, terse, objective or subjective. It was judged—favorably or unfavorably—to be brilliant, banal, inventive, unimagined, understated, unintellectual or ungrammatical. Even the novel's opening paragraph, which has been so much favored, especially in the classroom, had its detractors. Prominent among them was Henry Seidel Canby, whose two pieces on *Farewell* (a mixed review and an ambivalent defense) raised most of the issues surrounding Hemingway's style. Many of those issues were not adequately addressed until Walker Gibson, in 1966, defended Frederic Henry's rhetoric. By comparing the first paragraph of *Farewell* with a paragraph from William Dean Howells' nineteenth-century novel *A Modern Instance*, he defined what makes Hemingway's style both innovative and effective.[70]

There was, of course, much interest in the nature, personality and character of Hemingway's personages. Some reviewers insisted that the principals Catherine and Frederic Henry paled in characterization before the minor characters—Rinaldi, the priest, nurse Ferguson, Count Greffi, and even Lieutenant Henry's subordinates in the field. One reviewer found it remarkable that Hemingway was able to accomplish his complex characterizations almost entirely through the use of dialogue since he limits the narration to a single point of view. Rinaldi, "drawn entirely in dialogue," ventures the *London Times*, is "the most brilliant achievement in a brilliant book."[71] Clifton Fadiman agreed, finding the relationship between Frederic Henry and Rinaldi to express the second of *Farewell*'s two central "strong and simple feelings: love for a beautiful and noble woman, affection for one's comrades."[72] Catherine is also drawn in dialogue, of course, though, in her case, the *Times Literary Supplement* saw her only as a "stupid girl," a charge echoed by other reviewers.[73] Yet Orlo Williams found Catherine to be "the most striking achievement" of the book, even if she was "a silly girl without an idea in her head," for "her creator makes her beautiful through her courage and the intensity of her devotion."[74] A different reviewer, anticipating academic interpretations of the late 1970s and 1980s, admires Catherine's strength. Unlike Brett Ashley of *The Sun Also Rises*, he decided, Catherine is the "principal instrument" through that "selfless faith" she gives her lover, and which "may seem to come from a knowledge very like despair," in the author's own conversion away from the "note of hopelessness we hear so much as the undertone of courage."[75]

That Hemingway intended to characterize Catherine as "stupid" or "silly" was a position shared in part by the reviewer who claimed that Catherine is represented from "purely a man's view" (foreshadowing the starting point of feminist criticism in the 1970s and 80s), but that the view is as such "unfalteringly delineated." As for the book's message, this reviewer decided: "so drink deep and go a-whoring while you may is the very plainly illustrated motto, and love truly, as Henry and Catherine loved, if you can; but the world will get you in the end, as it got Catherine, who died in childbirth with her child at Lausanne, leaving Henry with nothing, on a rainy night."[76] The occasional reviewer found Frederic Henry and Catherine Barkley to be equally harmless, dull, and somewhat bovine, but, as one of them argues, such characterization is entirely intentional, for the author "wants to show what a shocking mess humanity is in when even a perfect pair of animals like these cannot love and propagate undisturbed to grow mellow and bored and old together."[77]

Cowley approvingly describes what he called Hemingway's "subtractive" style.[78] However, the characteristics of that same style are judged quite differently in a review entitled "Perfect Behavior." The Southern fugitive critic Donald Davidson attributed to Hemingway the intentions of the would-be scientific novelist. Watsonian behaviorism explains Hemingway's characters. For them there is nothing moral or immoral. There is just behavior—stimulus, response. Even his fellow agrarian Allen Tate's vigorous contestation of this view—"there is nothing scientific about Hemingway," argued Tate; "if you think he is a realist, then realism must be redefined"—

failed to dissuade Davidson.[79] Others were just as critical of Hemingway's style without adopting Davidson's explanation. Henry Hazlitt described its dialogue as "brilliantly authentic," but found the book's overall stylistic simplicity carried too far, becoming, finally, "palpably artificial." "One feels," he complained, "like a thirsty man compelled to drink a high ball with a teaspoon."[80] Others, such as Fanny Butcher, welcome Hemingway's "coldly unsentimental" and "purely subjective" technique, tracing it, shrewdly, to Gertrude Stein's example in *Three Lives*. Butcher went too far, perhaps, when she concluded that Hemingway's work is "the direct blossoming of Gertrude Stein's art."[81]

Many reviewers described Hemingway's novel as tragic, either for its portrayal of a terrible war or for its devastating enactment of the fate of two lovers. Lionel Trilling went further by identifying the genre of the book as tragedy. Hemingway is "probably our most skilful writer of tragedy," he wrote, which "has always been humanistic, asserting the worth of man in the face of all unhuman forces." Hemingway's story, a tragedy of "a love fulfilled and destroyed," is set down by a protagonist who "feels to the war as he feels to all life: receptive, willing, observant, but not very articulate. He is neither a sensitive young man eager for experience nor is he weary and disillusioned. He feels and sees a great deal, but not from any central core of interest."[82] Here is quite a different hero from the "dumb ox" Wyndham Lewis extolled in a much misinterpreted essay collected in his *Men Without Art* (1933), or the man in search of an identity in the studies of Gerry Brenner (1983) and Gwen L. Nagel (1987).[83] He is a far cry, too, from the guilt-ridden anti-hero Delbert E. Wylder (1969) discovered in the young American architect-lieutenant, that "rather selfish, rather casual" young man described by Jackson J. Benson (1969) as "somewhat indifferent to the consequences of his actions, wilfully a victim of his own self-indulgence and completely unconvinced of the possibility of his own death," or the "selfish lover," who is "one of those first-person narrators whose opinions are not to be trusted," according to Scott Donaldson (1977).[84] But Trilling's view of Hemingway's protagonist is compatible with that of Wirt Williams, who described Frederic Henry as compelled to inhabit a world in which "all systems of the book have been converging" to bring about "doom—of catastrophe unleavened and untranscended" (1981). It is also compatible with the Frederic Henry described by Millicent Bell as still unable, years after his tragedy, to divest himself of a paralyzing morbidity (1984).[85]

Several studies that shed light on Frederic Henry's character have focused on the principles and effects of Hemingway's narration in *Farewell*. A pioneering early piece by Forrest D. Robinson (1972) has been followed by important essays by Robert E. Fleming (1983), James Nagel (1987), and James Phelan (1989).[86] Essays devoted to the many "endings" that Hemingway tried out in his search for an efficient, satisfactory closing to *Farewell* form a subset of this group.

Hemingway's contemporary reviewers broached several other themes that have reemerged as concerns for later scholars. T. S. Matthews, for example, decided that *Farewell* is not "essentially a war story," but a "love-story" and suggested that at the conclusion the author has transformed his action into the "dramatics of a sentimental dream." (He also said that Catherine is "one of the impossibly beautiful characters of modern tragedy—the Tesses, the Alyoshas, the Myshkins.")[87] One wonders if Hemingway was obliquely answering Matthews when he later called Stephen Crane's *The Red Badge of Courage* "that great boy's dream of war."[88] Be that as it may, at least one later interpreter has rigorously analyzed the entire novel as a structuring dream.[89] Of course, this interpretation takes us far from the naturalness that Cowley originally favored and that Burke objected to, with the result that subsequent critics have studied the novel as if it were pure poetry. But this notion was only one of the direct results of the New Critical triumph in academe in the 1940s and 1950s. With Robert Penn Warren's essay in 1947 and Carlos Baker's in 1951, the critical conversion of Hemingway from realist-naturalist to symbolic realist caught fire.[90] Studies of *Farewell* that emanated from Warren's or Baker's work (including Baker's own very successful book) investigated Hemingway's modernist use of allusion (Charles R. Anderson, 1961), the novel as pure lyric—its organization through recurring imagery, language, and motif (Daniel J. Schneider, 1968)—and as testament to a religion-of-death marked by liturgical language and spiritual imagery (James F. Light, 1961).[91] Behind most of the major essays of this period lay the critic's unexpressed quest for the work's "figure in the carpet," a way to reach the novel's essential organicism. But the New Critics, following the heady lead of John Crowe Ransom, also highly valued the irony in the "pity and irony" joke shared by Jake Barnes and Bill Gorton in *The Sun Also Rises*. So even an essay such as E. M. Halliday's "Hemingway's Ambiguity: Symbolism and Irony" (1956), which pointed to serious limitations and inconsistencies in Baker's rather unyielding Wordsworthian reading of *Farewell* as a controlled interplay of images (notably, plains and mountains) built around "the opposed concepts of Home and Not-home," must finally be read as a "new critical" corrective fine-tuning of a flawed "organic" reading.[92] If Lausanne, where Catherine meets her death, is not situated on the plains as demanded by Baker's scheme, the fault lay with the critic rather than the author, whose symbolism at its best emerged from the naturalness of his vision and whose ethic called for authenticity over literary effect. Yet, Baker's reading of the symbolic artistry of Hemingway's novel has always had its adherents, as William C. Slattery's 1980 analysis of Chapter 20 suggests.[93]

In 1930, before he had entirely subjugated himself to Marxist ideology, Granville Hicks published a study of Hemingway's work that has never been granted its primacy. Anticipating Edmund Wilson (1939), Malcolm Cowley

(1944), and Philip Young (1952), Hicks pointed out that the study of "the world of Ernest Hemingway" should begin "with Nick Adams, the first of his heroes." "There is an actual reworking of material that links Nick both with Jake Barnes of *The Sun Also Rises* and with Frederic Henry of *A Farewell to Arms*, but the temperamental resemblances of the three men are more important," he wrote. "These lead to the conclusion that there is a certain kind of person with whom Hemingway chooses to concern himself. We can, indeed, trace, after a fashion, the spiritual history of a Hemingway hero."[94] Here, in short, is a major source for those interpretations that link Hemingway directly to his heroes—the man who was there and who suffered. Add the motif of the traumatic war wound, as did Wilson, Cowley, and (especially) Philip Young—though already in the mid-1930s, Canby had referred to "the hero of *A Farewell to Arms* whose mind is a wound"—and one has the essence of biographical readings of *Farewell* that continue to thrive in classrooms and textbook headnotes.[95]

VII

There have been several notable earlier collections of criticism devoted entirely, or in part, to *A Farewell to Arms*. Carlos Baker's highly influential 1962 *Ernest Hemingway: Critiques of Four Major Novels* (A Scribner Research Anthology) collected Ray B. West's 1940s "biological trap" essay, James F. Light's "The Religion of Death" (1961), "The Mountain and the Plain" chapter from Baker's own book *Hemingway: The Writer as Artist* (1952), E. M. Halliday's criticism of that chapter, "Hemingway's Ambiguity: Symbolism and Irony" (1956), and what Baker called "The Original Conclusion to *A Farewell to Arms*."

The first collection devoted entirely to *A Farewell to Arms* was the Prentice-Hall Twentieth Century Interpretations volume edited by Jay Gellens in 1970. It reprinted several excerpts from work by such critics as Louis L. Martz, D. S. Savage, Leslie Fiedler, Frederick J. Hoffman, and Maxwell Geismar, the well-known essay by Ray B. West, Jr., as well as chapters from Philip Young's 1952 book, Earl Rovit's chapter from his Twayne study in 1963 (on *Farewell* as a novel of epistemology and self-discovery), Robert W. Lewis, Jr.'s 1965 chapter (on *Farewell* as a chivalric novel within the context of a "tough" war), and Wyndham Lewis's "The Dumb Ox."

Harold Bloom's 1987 volume on *A Farewell to Arms* in the Modern Critical Interpretations series published by Chelsea House collected previously published essays by Daniel J. Schneider, William Adair, Judith Fetterley, Scott Donaldson, Robert Merrill, and Millicent Bell, a chapter from Michael S. Reynolds' *Hemingway's First War: The Making of "A Farewell to Arms,"* and an original essay by Sandra Whipple Spanier. In "Catherine Barkley and the Hemingway Code," Spanier redefined a strong heroine who in the course of the novel comes to exemplify the author's code and ethos.

According to its editor Scott Donaldson, *New Essays on "A Farewell to Arms"* (published in 1990 in the American Novel series by Cambridge University Press) presented four articles representative of "the most interesting of current studies."[96] In the first article Paul Smith updated the study of Hemingway's partial use, in journalism and fiction, of the material provided by his war experience while his big novel lay fallow. In the second essay James Phelan applied current narrative theory to the sometimes difficult and subtle narration Hemingway conceived for what is arguably his greatest novel. Sandra Whipple Spanier, in the third essay, once again defended Catherine as a strong and powerfully realized character, this time by locating her within the overall context of the Great War. In "A Sliding Discourse: The Language of *A Farewell to Arms*," Ben Stoltzfus offered a highly speculative psychoanalytic (Lacanian) reading. He concluded: "The discourse of the self, which is always a discourse of desire, seeks to retrieve the lost object. For Frederic, on the conscious level, it is Catherine, whereas on the unconscious level, for him as for all of us, it is the mother. Our language is our mother's tongue, and in using language, as Roland Barthes points out, we unwittingly recover the loss of the mother."[97] The changes that Freudian readings of Hemingway have undergone over the years can be measured by reading Stoltzfus' piece against Richard B. Hovey's two-part essay on *Farewell* (subtitled "Hemingway's Liebestod"), first published in the *University Review* in 1966–67 and collected in 1968 in *Hemingway: The Inward Terrain.*

To commemorate the sixtieth anniversary of the novel's publication, the *Hemingway Review* dedicated its Fall 1989 issue to essays on *A Farewell to Arms.*

The present collection of critical and scholarly materials on *A Farewell to Arms* is divided into four parts: Composition, Censorship, Reviews, and Criticism. Section 1 gathers together materials relating to the writing and revision of the novel. Included here is material from two books devoted to the novel's composition: Michael S. Reynolds' *Hemingway's First War: The Making of "A Farewell to Arms"* (1976), and Bernard Oldsey's *Hemingway's Hidden Craft: The Writing of "A Farewell to Arms"* (1979).[98] In both instances the novel's genesis and its composition are approached through surviving manuscripts.

The second section presents two pieces relating to the censoring of *A Farewell to Arms.* Even before a single word was in print, the novel was censored in various ways. First, Hemingway's editors at Scribners objected to various matters, and they did so weeks before the June issue of *Scribner's Magazine* serializing the book was banned in Boston. Hemingway's letter to his editor Maxwell Perkins, dated 7 June 1929, protested that his so-called "tough" language must not be excised or toned down. Scott Donaldson's essay draws on the Scribners files at Princeton University to shed new light on the different, sometimes indirect, ways in which the novel was censored. Given the textual problems arising from editorial compromise—the use of dashes and the silent suppression of objectionable references—it is obvious that what is now needed is an unexpurgated edition of the "original" novel— one that would incorporate the author's original intentions before he reached his uneasy agreement with the publisher on how to handle objectionable words and references.[99]

The third section presents five reviews of *A Farewell to Arms* by Hemingway's contemporaries, culled from the generous supply of reviews and notices accorded this novel. As an established writer's second novel, well-publicized over the course of an entire summer, *A Farewell to Arms* was understandably given for review to several knowledgeable critics and well-known writers. Included here are reviews by critics such as Clifton P. Fadiman, Donald Davidson, and B. E. Todd, and one novelist, John Dos Passos. The poet critic Davidson warned against Hemingway's novel as a work of pure and unremitting behavioristic psychology. The last of the five reviews considered Laurence Stalling's 1930 dramatization of Hemingway's novel. Stark Young shrewdly accounted for the difficulties the dramatist faced in attempting to translate Hemingway's war novel into good theater.

The fourth and final section of this collection contains eight works of scholarship and criticism, presented chronologically by date of publication. Such ordering, rather than by theme or critical approach, has the advantage of enabling readers to discover the way in which the most influential scholarship on Hemingway's novel has evolved over the last five decades.

The principles of formalist criticism are strongly evident in a good deal of the earlier scholarship presented here, such as Carlos Baker's essay. Philip Young's strongly biographical interests are turned informatively in the direction of psychology. Charles R. Anderson's tack in "Hemingway's Other Style" is to unravel some of Hemingway's surprisingly complex intertextuality (though the term was not then in use).

Form and genre, as might be expected, are centers of concern for readers raised on the New Criticism. Many scholars of the 1950s and 1960s marched under this banner. From a large number of insightful and useful articles, I have chosen Anderson's essay, which has had considerable influence.

Each of the major characters in Frederic Henry's retrospective narrative of love and war (as well as certain secondary characters, such as the priest and nurse Ferguson) has attracted a respectable body of specific criticism. Interest in Frederic Henry's narrative, often combining stylistic commentary with character analysis, bulks large in recent studies. The range of such work is represented by Millicent Bell's "Pseudoautobiography and Personal Metaphor" and James Nagel's "Catherine Barkley and Retrospective Narration."

Conceptions of Catherine Barkley—the narrator's, the author's, and the reader's—have been the focus of much critical activity, especially since Judith Fetterley first published her resistant reading of Hemingway's novel in 1976. The harsh words and style, and now notorious arguments of "Hemingway's 'Resentful Cryptogram' "—Catherine dies to fulfill Frederic Henry's unconscious wish, his need to kill her; her death is the logical consequence of "the cumulative hostilities which Frederic feels toward her," and the final expression of the link between the themes of love and war—evoked a myriad of responses and new assessments of Catherine's fictional character and novelistic role.[100] The final essay—Peter Griffin's—was written specifically for this collection, and appears in print for the first time. "The Search for 'Home' " sheds light on the way Hemingway's novel grows out of a young returning-soldier's deepest concerns of displacement.

Notes

1. Hugh Walpole, "The Best Books of 1929," *Saturday Review* 148 (21 December 1929), 747.
2. Walpole, "Best Books," 748.
3. Van Wyck Brooks, *Opinions of Oliver Allston* (New York: E.P. Dutton, 1941), 173; Karen L. Rood, "Writers Who Went to War and Wrote About It, From The Civil War to Vietnam," in *American Literary Almanac from 1608 to the Present*, ed. K. Rood (New York and Oxford: Facts on File, 1988), 297; and J.D. Salinger, *The Catcher in the Rye* (Boston: Little, Brown, 1951), 182.
4. *Holmes-Laski Letters: The Correspondence of Mr. Justice Holmes and Harold J. Laski, 1916–1935*, ed. Mark De Wolfe Howe (Cambridge, MA: Harvard University Press, 1953), 2:1209; and *The Holmes-Einstein Letters: Correspondence of Mr. Justice Holmes and Lewis Einstein, 1903–1935*, ed. James Bishop Peabody (New York: St. Martins, 1964), 308.
5. Quoted in Denis Brian, *The True Gen: An Intimate Portrait of Ernest Hemingway by Those Who Knew Him* (New York: Grove, 1988), 203.
6. Reynolds Price, "For Ernest Hemingway," in *Things Themselves: Essays & Scenes* (New York: Atheneum, 1972), 202–5. Price tells of delivering an oral report on *Farewell* in the eleventh grade: "I remember standing on my feet before forty healthy adolescents—it was only 1949—and saying that Hemingway had shown me that illicit love could be pure and worth having. I don't remember remarking that, like water, it could also kill you—or your Juliet—but I must have acquired, subliminally at least, the welcome news that it made Frederic Henry, a would-be architect, into a highly skilled novelist" (194).
7. T. S. Eliot, "A Commentary," *Criterion* 12 (April 1933), 471. Eliot also says, "[Hemingway] has, at the moment, a popularity which I think (it is a high compliment) is largely undeserved" (471).
8. Quoted in Andrew Turnbull, *Thomas Wolfe* (New York: Scribners, 1967), 194.
9. *Letters of Thomas Wolfe*, ed. Elizabeth Nowell (New York: Scribners, 1956), 270–71; quoted in Turnbull, *Thomas Wolfe*, 166. In a generally unfavorable review of *To*

Have and Have Not, Lewis refers to "the rich and exhilarating *A Farewell to Arms*" (*Newsweek* 10 [18 October 1937], 34).

10. [Winfield Townley Scott?], "War and Love," *Brown Daily Herald* (Brown University) (14 November 1929), 3.

11. *The Letters of F. Scott Fitzgerald*, ed. Andrew Turnbull (New York: Scribners, 1963), 593. For Fitzgerald's prepublication reactions to Hemingway's novel, see Charles Mann, "F. Scott Fitzgerald's Critique of *A Farewell to Arms*," *Fitzgerald/Hemingway Annual 1976*, ed. Matthew J. Bruccoli (Englewood, CO: Information Handling Services, 1978), 141–52.

12. James Jones to R.P. Adams, 30 August 1955, in *To Reach Eternity: The Letters of James Jones*, ed. George Hendrick (New York: Random House, 1989), 224.

13. William Faulkner, *The Wild Palms* (New York: Random House, 1939), 97. See also *Selected Letters of William Faulkner*, ed. Joseph Blotner (New York: Random House, 1977), 334–35.

14. *The Literary Correspondence of Donald Davidson and Allen Tate*, ed. John Tyree Fain and Thomas Daniel Young (Athens: University of Georgia Press, 1974), 244.

15. *Letters of Archibald MacLeish, 1907 to 1982*, ed. R.H. Winnick (Boston: Houghton Mifflin, 1983), 230. Late in life MacLeish reaffirmed his view of Hemingway's work: "One thing is now clear, and will be clearer when the present vogue of denigration ends— as it will. Ernest was the one great prose stylist this century has produced. He is part of the tongue and of few writers—very few—can that be said" (quoted in Brian, *True Gen*, 305).

16. "Boston Police Bar *Scribner's Magazine*," *New York Times* (21 June 1929), 2.

17. Owen Wister, "What You Think About It," *Scribner's Magazine* 86 (July 1929), 27.

18. "Boston Bans *Scribner's* for July," *New York Times* (29 June 1929), 8.

19. Quoted in "Boston Police Bar *Scribner's Magazine*," 2.

20. See "The Phoenix Nest," *Saturday Review of Literature* 6 (5 October 1929), 222.

21. Mary M. Colum, "Literature and Morals: Questions and Observations Aroused by Boston Police Action," *New York Times* (5 July 1929), 16.

22. Oscar Cargill, *Intellectual America: Ideas on the March* (New York: Macmillan, 1941), 360.

23. Quoted in Roger Asselineau's notes to Hemingway's *L'Adieu aux Armes (A Farewell to Arms)*, in *Oeuvres Romanesques: Poèmes de Guerre et d'Après-Guerre* (Novels: Poems of War and After the War) (Paris: Éditions Gallimard, 1968), 1:1384.

24. Jo Pattangall, "Hemingway On Love and War," Portland (Maine) *Evening News* (15 October 1929), 10.

25. A.C., "Echoes from the Great War in Ernest Hemingway's Novel," *Boston Transcript* (19 October 1929), Book Section, 2.

26. *Outlook and Independent* 153 (16, 23, 30 October; 6, 13, 20, 27 November; 4, 11, 18, 25 December 1929). Audre Hanneman reported that *A Farewell to Arms* "appeared on 'The Bookman's Monthly Score' of best-sellers for the first time in February 1930, in seventh place. From April through June 1930, it was in third place; and it appeared for the last time in July, in ninth place" (*Ernest Hemingway: A Comprehensive Bibliography* [Princeton, NJ: Princeton University Press, 1967], 24).

27. *Letters of Thomas Wolfe*, 206.

28. *Dear Scott/Dear Max: The Fitzgerald-Perkins Correspondence*, ed. John Kuehl and Jackson R. Bryer (New York: Scribners, 1971), 158.

29. Jeffrey Meyers, *Hemingway: A Biography* (New York: Harper & Row, 1985), 219.

30. Asselineau, *Oeuvres Romanesques*, 1:1385.

31. Hanneman, *Comprehensive Bibliography*, 188.

32. Advertisement in *Scribner's Magazine* 86 (October 1929), unnumbered page.

33. Ford Madox Ford, "Introduction," *A Farewell to Arms* (New York: Modern Library, 1932), ix, xvi–xvii.

34. Malcolm Cowley, "Introduction," *Viking Portable Library Hemingway*, ed. Malcolm Cowley (New York: Viking, 1944), vii.

35. Cowley, *Viking Portable Hemingway*, xvi.

36. Publication details come from Hanneman, *Comprehensive Bibliography*, 23–31.

37. See Wayne Kvam, "Zuckmayer, Hilpert, and Hemingway," *PMLA* 91 (March 1976), 194–205.

38. Madelaine Hemingway Miller, *Ernie: Hemingway's Sister "Sunny" Remembers* (New York: Crown, 1975), 127; "Refuses to See Film of His Novel," *New York Times* (6 December 1932), 27; and T.S. Eliot, "A Commentary," 471.

39. A. E. Hotchner, *Papa Hemingway: A Personal Memoir* (New York: Random House, 1966), 218.

40. Michael S. Reynolds, *Hemingway's First War: The Making of "A Farewell to Arms"* (Princeton: Princeton University Press, 1976).

41. James Nagel, "Hemingway and the Italian Legacy," in Henry Serrano Villard and James Nagel, *Hemingway in Love and War: The Lost Diary of Agnes von Kurowsky, Her Letters, and Correspondence of Ernest Hemingway* (Boston: Northeastern University Press, 1989), 197–269.

42. See, for example, Robert Herrick, "What is Dirt?" *Bookman* 70 (November 1929), 258–62; and Scott, "War and Love," 3.

43. Ernest Hemingway, "Introduction," *Men at War* (New York: Crown, 1942), xvi.

44. *Ernest Hemingway: Selected Letters, 1917–1961*, ed. Carlos Baker (New York: Scribners, 1981), 12.

45. *Hemingway: Selected Letters*, 12.

46. Paul Smith has surveyed Hemingway's earlier uses of his war experiences in "The Trying-out of *A Farewell to Arms*," *New Essays on "A Farewell to Arms"*, ed. Scott Donaldson (Cambridge: Cambridge University Press, 1990), 27–52.

47. *Editor to Author: The Letters of Maxwell E. Perkins*, ed. John Hall Wheelock (New York: Scribners, 1950), 251.

48. Gerry Brenner, "A Hospitalized World," *Concealments in Hemingway's Works* (Columbus: Ohio State University Press, 1983), 27–41; reprinted in this volume. See also George Monteiro, "The Limits of Professionalism: A Sociological Approach to Faulkner, Fitzgerald, and Hemingway," *Criticism* 15 (Spring 1973), 145–55.

49. Robert M. McIlvaine, "A Literary Source for the Caesarean Section in *A Farewell to Arms*," *American Literature* 43 (November 1971), 444–47; and Arnold Bennett, review of *A Farewell to Arms* in the London *Evening Standard* (14 November 1929), 5.

50. Bennett, 5.

51. George Monteiro, "Chekhov's Rain, Hemingway's War," *Estudos Anglo-Americanos* (forthcoming in 1994).

52. Cargill, *Intellectual America*, 361.

53. Malcolm Cowley, "American Writers and the First World War," *Proceedings of the American Academy of Arts and Letters and the National Institute of Arts and Letters*, 2d ser., no. 18 (New York: 1968), 40–43.

54. Ernest Hemingway, *A Farewell to Arms* (New York: Scribners, 1929), 196.

55. Robert W. Lewis, *A Farewell to Arms: The War of the Words* (New York: Twayne, 1992).

56. Delmore Schwartz, "The Fiction of Ernest Hemingway: Moral Historian of the American Dream," in *Selected Essays of Delmore Schwartz*, ed. Donald A. Dike and David H. Zucker (Chicago and London: University of Chicago Press, 1970), 261. Schwartz's insight into the way Hemingway's idealism infuses his work has not received the attention it merits. Neither, for that matter, has his related observation that "Hemingway asserts traditional moral values often by an action which seems an inversion or violation of them—e.g., the

desertion in *A Farewell to Arms*" (*Portrait of Delmore: Journals and Notes of Delmore Schwartz 1939–1959*, ed. Elizabeth Pollet [New York: Farrar, Straus, and Giroux, 1986], 375).

57. *Ernest Hemingway: Critiques of Four Major Novels*, ed. Carlos Baker (New York: Scribners, 1962), 75.

58. *Hemingway: Selected Letters*, 768.

59. Bernard Oldsey, *Hemingway's Hidden Craft: The Writing of "A Farewell to Arms"* (University Park and London: Pennsylvania State University Press, 1979), 101–10.

60. Reynolds, *Hemingway's First War*, 295–97; Oldsey, *Hemingway's Hidden Craft*, 11–34; Paul Smith, "Almost All is Vanity: A Note on Nine Rejected Titles for *A Farewell to Arms*," *Hemingway Review* 2 (Fall 1982), 74–76; William Gargan, " 'Death Once Dead': An Examination of an Alternative Title to Hemingway's *A Farewell to Arms*," *Notes on Modern American Literature* 4 (Fall 1980), item 26; and George Monteiro, "Ernest Hemingway, Psalmist," *Journal of Modern Literature* 14 (Summer 1987), 83–95.

61. "Farewell and Return," *Spectator* 143 (16 November 1929), 727; reprinted in this volume.

62. "Boston Police Bar *Scribner's Magazine*," 2; and John Dos Passos, "Books," *New Masses* 5 (December 1929), 16; reprinted in this volume.

63. H.L. Mencken, "Fiction by Adept Hands," *American Mercury* 19 (January 1930), 127.

64. *Hemingway: Selected Letters*, 317.

65. Hanneman, *Comprehensive Bibliography*, 24.

66. Malcolm Cowley, "Not Yet Demobilized," *New York Herald Tribune Books* (6 October 1929), 1.

67. Stendhal's influence on Hemingway is considered by Robert O. Stephens in "Hemingway and Stendhal: The Matrix of *A Farewell to Arms*," *PMLA* 88 (March 1973), 271–79. See also Stirling Haig, "Hemingway and Stendhal," *PMLA* 88 (October 1973), 1192–93.

68. *The Selected Correspondence of Kenneth Burke and Malcolm Cowley, 1915–1981*, ed. Paul Jay (New York: Viking, 1988), 190; Kenneth Burke, *A Rhetoric of Motives* (New York: Prentice-Hall, 1950), 327; Ray B. West, Jr., "Ernest Hemingway: The Failure of Sensibility," *Sewanee Review* 53 (Winter 1945), 120–35; West, "Ernest Hemingway: *A Farewell to Arms*," in *The Art of Modern Fiction*, ed. West and Robert Wooster Stallman (New York: Rinehart, 1949), 622–33; Dewey Ganzel, "*A Farewell to Arms*: The Danger of Imagination," *Sewanee Review* 79 (Autumn 1971), 576–97.

69. Carlos Baker, "The Mountain and the Plain," *Virginia Quarterly Review* 27 (Summer 1951), 410–18 (reprinted in this volume); and Baker, *Hemingway: The Writer as Artist* (Princeton, NJ: Princeton University Press, 1952), Chapter 5.

70. Walker Gibson, *Tough, Sweet & Stuffy: An Essay on Modern American Prose Styles* (Bloomington & London: Indiana University Press, 1966), 28–42.

71. "The War and After," London *Times* (15 November 1929), 20.

72. Clifton P. Fadiman, "A Fine American Novel," *Nation* 129 (30 October 1929), 497; reprinted in this volume.

73. "*A Farewell to Arms*," London *Times Literary Supplement* (28 November 1929), 998.

74. Orlo Williams, "Books of the Quarter," *Criterion* 9 (July 1930), 728.

75. T. S. Matthews, "Nothing Ever Happens to the Brave," *New Republic* 60 (9 October 1929), 208.

76. *Times Literary Supplement*, 998. In a joint review of *A Farewell to Arms* and the Canadian war novel *All Else Is Folly*, H. J. Davis draws no inference for Hemingway's novel from his own apt explanation that the Canadian writer has taken his title from the sentence "Man shall be trained for war, and woman for the recreation of the warrior; all else is folly" ("War," *Canadian Forum* 10 [February 1930], 171).

77. Lyn Ll. Irvine, "New Novels," *Nation and Athenaeum* 46 (30 November 1929),

319. Critical attitudes toward Catherine are surveyed by Sandra Whipple Spanier, "Hemingway's Unknown Soldier: Catherine Barkley, the Critics, and the Great War," *New Essays*, 75–108.

78. Cowley, "Not Yet Demobilized," 1.

79. Donald Davidson, "Perfect Behavior," *Nashville Tennessean* (3 November 1929), Magazine section, 7 (reprinted in this volume); *Literary Correspondence of David Donaldson and Allen Tate*, 245. While Davidson continued to insist that Hemingway's book was "a misguided application of science (in this case, it seemed to be behavioristic psychology) to literature," he did admit that he had "sacrificed Hemingway (to some extent) in order to make a point against science" (248–49).

80. Henry Hazlitt, "Take Hemingway," *New York Sun* (28 September 1929), 38.

81. Fanny Butcher, "Here is Genius, Critic Declares of Hemingway," *Chicago Daily Tribune* (28 September 1929), 11.

82. Lionel Trilling, "Tragedy and Three Novels," *Symposium* 1 (January 1930), 106–14.

83. Brenner, *Concealments*, 27–41; Gwen L. Nagel, "A Téssera for Frederic Henry: Imagery and Recurrence in *A Farewell to Arms*," in *Ernest Hemingway: Six Decades of Criticism*, ed. Linda W. Wagner (East Lansing: Michigan State University Press, 1987), 187–93.

84. Delbert E. Wylder, *Hemingway's Heroes* (Albuquerque: University of New Mexico Press, 1969), 66–95; Jackson J. Benson, *Hemingway . . . The Writer's Art of Self-Defense* (Minneapolis: University of Minnesota Press, 1969), 82; and Scott Donaldson, *By Force of Will: The Life and Art of Ernest Hemingway* (New York: Viking, 1977), 151, 162.

85. Wirt Williams, *The Tragic Art of Ernest Hemingway* (Baton Rouge and London: Louisiana State University Press, 1981), 88; and Millicent Bell, "*A Farewell to Arms*: Pseudoautobiography and Personal Metaphor," in *Ernest Hemingway: The Writer in Context*, ed. James Nagel (Madison: University of Wisconsin Press, 1984), 107–28 (reprinted in this volume).

86. Forrest D. Robinson, "Frederick Henry: The Hemingway Hero as Storyteller," *CEA Critic* 34 (Fall 1972), 13–16; Robert E. Fleming, "Hemingway and Peele: Chapter I of *A Farewell to Arms*," *Studies in American Fiction* 11 (Spring 1983), 95–100; James Nagel, "Catherine Barkley and Retrospective Narration in *A Farewell to Arms*," in Wagner, *Six Decades*, 71–85 (reprinted in this volume); and James Phelan, "Evaluation and Resistance: The Case of Catherine Barkley," in *Reading People, Reading Plots* (Chicago and London: University of Chicago Press, 1989), 165–88.

87. Matthews, "Nothing Ever Happens to the Brave," 208–10.

88. *Men at War*, xvii.

89. William Adair, "*A Farewell to Arms*: A Dream Book," *Journal of Narrative Technique* 5 (January 1975), 40–56.

90. Robert Penn Warren, "Hemingway," *Kenyon Review* 9 (Winter 1947), 1–28; Baker, "The Mountain and the Plain," 410–18.

91. *Writer as Artist*; Charles R. Anderson, "Hemingway's Other Style," *Modern Language Notes* 76 (May 1961), 434–42 (reprinted in this volume); Daniel J. Schneider, "Hemingway's *A Farewell to Arms*: The Novel as Pure Poetry," *Modern Fiction Studies* 14 (Autumn 1968), 283–96; and James F. Light, "The Religion of Death in *A Farewell to Arms*," *Modern Fiction Studies* 7 (Summer 1961), 169–73.

92. E. M. Halliday, "Hemingway's Ambiguity: Symbolism and Irony," *American Literature* 28 (March 1956), 1–22.

93. William C. Slattery, "The Mountain, the Plain, and San Siro," *Papers on Language & Literature* 16 (Fall 1980), 439–42.

94. Granville Hicks, "The World of Hemingway," *New Freeman* 1 (22 March 1930), 40–42. See Edmund Wilson, "Ernest Hemingway: Bourdon Gauge of Morale," *Atlantic Monthly* 164 (July 1939), 36–46.

95.   Henry Seidel Canby, *Seven Years' Harvest: Notes on Contemporary Literature* (New York: Farrar & Rinehart, 1936), 123.

96.   Donaldson, "Introduction," *New Essays*, 21.

97.   Ben Stoltzfus, "A Sliding Discourse: The Language of *A Farewell to Arms*," *New Essays*, 133–34.

98.   The Oldsey chapter was first published in *Modern Fiction Studies* 23 (Winter 1977–78), 491–510. It is reproduced in this collection as it appeared in that journal.

99.   See James B. Meriwether, "The Text of Ernest Hemingway," *Papers of the Bibliographical Society of America* 57 (October–December 1963), 403–21; "The Dashes in Hemingway's *A Farewell to Arms*," *Papers of the Bibliographical Society of America* 58 (October–December 1964), 449–57.

100.   Judith Fetterley, "Hemingway's 'Resentful Cryptogram'," *Journal of Popular Culture* 10 (Summer 1976), 203–14; reprinted in this volume. For a cogent early response to Fetterley, see Joyce Wexler's "E.R.A. for Hemingway: A Feminist Defense," *Georgia Review* 35 (Spring 1981), 111–23.

COMPOSITION

◆

The Writing of the Novel

MICHAEL S. REYNOLDS

With few exceptions, the serialized version of *A Farewell to Arms* that appeared in *Scribner's Magazine* is identical with the hardcover publication. If we compare both novel and magazine to the holograph manuscript, we find the difference is not more than a dozen words or phrases, except for the final paragraphs. This would seem to indicate that the Kennedy Library manuscript is the final revised draft that Hemingway's typists used in Key West. A detailed examination of the manuscript reveals something of the development of the novel as well as Hemingway's working habits.

The remarkable part about the manuscript is its incredible smoothness. Although there are heavily rewritten passages, forty-five percent of the first draft appears unrevised. Another thirty percent of the manuscript has only minor revisions, sometimes as little as a single word on a page. Seventy-five percent of the holograph manuscript went straight to publication with insignificant changes. From a writer who reputedly worked slowly, revising heavily, this apparent smoothness of the working draft is puzzling.

This puzzle is simplified by a reconstruction of Hemingway's working habits, which account for the apparent smoothness. The first draft was written and numbered sequentially. As he was writing, he would sometimes make minor additions or deletions that are in the same pencil as the draft. The following morning, as he told Perkins, he would rework the previous day's production. Sometimes this could be done on the same page, using the margins or interlinear space. However, on those incredibly smooth pages, there is the possibility that the second-day changes became so heavy that he recopied the manuscript on a fresh page. The numbering on these recopied pages would still be in sequence, for he had not yet begun the second day's writing. Of course, some pages were exactly right on the first draft, but not 300 out of 650. The first draft of the recopied page was probably destroyed. Thus, forty-five percent of the working draft will not support any conclusions about stylistic changes or narrative problems. Fortunately, the remaining portion of the manuscript tells us a good deal.

In August, when he was in the final hundred pages of the manuscript,

Reynolds, Michael S., *Hemingway's First War: The Making of "A Farewell to Arms."* Copyright © 1976 by Princeton University Press. Used with permission.

Hemingway began rereading the novel from the beginning. On August 12, he made a note on the top of MS-109: "Seems fine so far." He was, perhaps, most concerned about the early portion, for it had been written before he knew exactly where the novel was going. Quite possibly as he read his way through the manuscript in August, he made some revisions, for the early chapters of the manuscript are the most heavily revised.

With the draft finished in August, Hemingway put it aside until sometime in late November, when the final revisions were begun. In the August draft, the pages were numbered sequentially; several major revisions during the rewrite period disrupted the first draft pagination. The first such revision occurs at MS-103. At that point Frederic is taking leave of Catherine for the front, where he will be wounded. Catherine gives Frederic a St. Anthony's medal, the patron saint of Italy. On the first draft, Hemingway had not made much of the medal. In the revision, he wrote an insert page of over twenty lines describing the medal and Frederic's conversation about it with his driver. First this page was marked "insert 102." Then it was changed to "103." The original MS-103 was changed to "104a" and MS-104 to "104b." The newly inserted page runs over on to the back side, something rare in the manuscript, but he did not want to have to insert yet another page. The last three lines of MS-103 are in three different pencils: *"I felt him in his metal box against my chest while we drove.* Then I forgot about him. After I was wounded I never found him. Some one probably got it at one of the dressing stations." Later on MS-162 when the priest is visiting the wounded Frederic (p. 68), there is a passage about the St. Anthony which Hemingway cut:

"~~See my Saint Anthony~~."

where it lay   "You see my Saint Anthony."
I pulled the metal capsule out from/on my chest./He looked

at the thin gold chain.

"Perhaps he saved your life."

"Passini saved my life," I said. "He was between me and the burst."

"Poor Passini. You might remember him in your prayers."

"All right."

"I don't want to make you sad."

MS-162

Since the inserted MS-103 appears to have been done at the revision stage, the last three lines of the page show Hemingway coming back to the passage twice, each time adding a slightly more ironic touch to the minor incident. It is this attention to the possibilities of detail that kept him working long hours during the revision stages.

A similar hiatus in the pagination occurs following MS-128, where Frederic has just been blown up at Plava. MS-129a appears to be the first draft of the explosion, for it is written on the same Grisom Mill paper as MS-128. MS-129b is on WAT/ALLS paper, indicating that it was written during the revision stage. By the time Hemingway had revised the passage in December, it looked like this:

(MS-128)
I ate the end of my piece of cheese and took a swallow of wine.

Through the noise I heard a cough, then came the chuh-chuh-chuh-chuh—then there was a ~~roar and a white hot~~ flash, as ~~when~~ a blast-furnace

door is swung open, and a roar that started white ~~hot~~ and went red and on

                    (MS-129A) my breath would not come
and on in a rushing ~~like~~ wind. I tried to breath but ~~my chest would not~~

        rush
open and I felt myself ~~go~~ out of myself and out and out and out

        passing
and all the time the wind ~~roaring~~. I went out and on and on and I knew

        Then I floated, hesitated and instead of going on
I was dead and that it had all been a mistake to think you just died. / I

        there was a long thin wire through the center of
felt myself slide back as though / my soul ~~was sliding down a long~~
The me that was gone out slid   twice it caught and stood still and once it
down that wire   nothing   turned completely over on the wire
~~tight-wire~~ / through ~~space~~ and the wind / and then
    jerked
it ~~slid suddenly~~ and stopped and
~~I breathed and~~ I was back.   ~~I took a breath~~.   The ground was

~~churned~~
torn up and in front of my head was a splintered beam of wood. ~~I heard~~
In the jolt of my head I heard   I thought somebody was screaming
somebody
~~somebody~~ crying. "~~Mamma mia! Mamma mia!~~" ~~Somebody screamed~~,

~~then stopped, then screamed again~~.

Through revisions on MS-129b and in galleys, Hemingway trimmed his excesses to read:

> I felt myself rush bodily out of myself and out and out and out and all the time bodily in the wind. I went out swiftly, all of myself, and I knew I was dead and that it had all been a mistake to think you just died. Then I floated, and instead of going on I felt myself slide back. I breathed and I was back. The ground was torn up and in front of my head there was a splintered beam of wood. In the jolt of my head I heard somebody crying. I thought somebody was screaming. (p. 54)

A year earlier, 1927, he had written of a similar experience in the short story, "Now I Lay Me": ". . . I had been living for a long time with the knowledge that if I ever shut my eyes in the dark and let myself go, my soul would go out of my body. I had been that way for a long time, ever since I had been blown up at night and felt it go out of me and go off and then come back."[1] Obviously, the experience is based on Hemingway's own wounding on the Piave river in 1918. What is interesting in the revisions is the writer's objective control. In the first revision, Hemingway had written a more detailed description of this seminal experience than he ever published. If the wounding was as traumatic as some believe,[2] it must have been a difficult passage to write honestly, but even more difficult to cut.

Another clear example of Hemingway's revisions can be seen at MS-168 bis. The first draft of these three pages was separated from the manuscript but saved by the author. In the deleted section Frederic and the priest discuss love, but the emphasis falls more on Frederic's values than the priest's. Returning to this passage when the novel was complete, Hemingway was able to focus their conversation more precisely on the nature of love and the importance of the high country—a crucial touchstone for the novel.

In the revision, it is the priest's definition of love that comes through so clearly: *"When you love you wish to do things for. You wish to sacrifice for. You wish to serve"* (MS-169). Ultimately it is Catherine, not Frederic, who fulfills these criteria. When Hemingway rewrote the conversation, he knew that Frederic was not the hero of the novel. Here he gives greater impact to Catherine's role, reinforcing her sacrifice in the name of love, and at the same time he underlines the basic failure of Frederic Henry.

When the priest leaves, Hemingway adds the idyllic description of the Abruzzi, where there was fine hunting and a less complicated way of life. Basing his description on a feature story he had done five years earlier,[3] Hemingway establishes the values that Frederic associates with the high country. The total impact of this passage on the focus and themes of the novel make it one of the most important revisions in the manuscript.

The next irregularity in the manuscript occurs in Chapter 12, when

Frederic is in the field hospital before being evacuated to Milan. There is a long deleted passage on MSS-174–175 that reads:

> I do not like to remember the trip back to Milan. ~~The train got into the station early in the morning.~~ if you have never travelled in a hospital train there is no use making a picture of it. This is not a picture of war, nor really about war. It is only a story. That is why, sometimes, it may seem there are not enough people in it, nor enough
>
>   unless it was quiet
> noises, nor enough smells. There were always people and noises / and
>
>   always
> always smells but in trying to tell the story I cannot get them all in / but
>
>   keeping
> have a hard time ~~just sticking~~ to the story alone and sometime it seems
>
>   But it wasn't quiet
> as though it were all quiet ~~and nothing going on but what happened~~ If you try and put in everything you would never get a single day done and ~~then the one who made it might not feel it so I will try to tell it~~ (MS-175) straight along and hope that the things themselves will give the feeling
>
>   Also when   a little out of your head
> of the rest. ~~Besides when~~ you are wounded or ~~a little crazy~~ or in love with someone the surroundings are sometimes removed and they only come in at certain times. But I will try to keep the places in and tell what happened. It does not seem to have gotten anywhere and it is not much of a love story so far but it has to go on in the way it was although I skip everything I can.

    This entire passage was cut for obvious reasons. It is out of character; it sounds more like Hemingway talking to himself then anything we might expect Frederic to say. Although the novel is a first-person narrative, the reader seldom sees Frederic-as-author. This cut was probably made the day after it was written, when Hemingway reread and revised the previous day's work. In making the cut, he left one paragraph at the top of MS-174 and one paragraph at the bottom of MS-175. Because of the extensive cut, it would appear that the typists at Key Wet jumbled the pages. The published novel separates the paragraph on MS-174 from the paragraph on MS-175 with the entire MS-173. As a result, there is a minor break in continuity between pp. 74–75 in the novel.

The next disruption of the manuscript is the result of eight pages Hemingway cut and revised at Key West. MSS-202 to 209 describe the first time Catherine goes to bed with Frederic in the Milan hospital. At Key West Hemingway realized his first draft was overwritten. His first revision attempt left the passage ambiguous. Finally he wrote the five page insert (MSS-201b-205), picking the first draft back up at MS-210. The revision makes the sexual relationship implicit in the dialogue without graphic description. The revised pages are completely clean, with only one additional line added at the galley-proof stage.

Again this is a crucial scene in the novel, which had to convince the reader of the spontaneous love of Frederic and Catherine. Critics of Catherine have frequently said that the scene is unbelievable, that it is a fantasy for Catherine to leap into bed with Frederic the first time he asks. Although psychological motivation has been provided earlier for Catherine's behavior, the first draft does not make the sexual relations clear. Hemingway's final choice was to convey the sexuality of the scene by eliminating everything but the lovers' dialogue.

The next major revision made at Key West occurs when Frederic has returned to the front in October, 1917. On the evening of Frederic's first night back with his ambulance unit, Chapter 25 closes (MS-337) with Frederic saying good-night to the major in charge. In the manuscript there followed a lengthy (MSS-337, 337 bis, 338) description of how the Italian major looked and felt the next morning when waking. Although it is an effective character sketch of the sort that Hemingway did so well, it added nothing to the novel unless the major were to reappear later, which he did not. Moreover, the sketch created a point-of-view problem: the description is outside Frederic's knowledge. Hemingway wisely cut out a piece of effective writing that did not contribute to the total effect of the book. The cut must have been made at Key West. Had it been made the day after it was written, he would not have kept the pages in the manuscript.

Two other breaks in the manuscript are the result, not of revisions, but apparently of Hemingway's misnumbering. It appears that he went from MS-396 to MS-399 from misreading his own numbering. Frederic and his enlisted men are in the middle of the Caporetto retreat. The last line of MS-

396 reads: " 'We would do best to start,' the first one said." The first line of MS-399 reads: " 'We are starting,' I said." This same sort of page mistake occurs between MS-477 and MS-480. The last line on MS-477 is: "I found a man in the station and asked him if he knew what hotels were open. The Grand-Hotel & des Isles Borromees." The sentence is completed on MS-480: "was open and several small hotels that stayed open all the year."

The next break occurs after MS-425. Hemingway added MS-425 bis, which is a smooth copy of the previous page, perhaps done for the benefit of the typist. Another irregularity occurs when Hemingway deleted several lines of dialogue from MS-470. He added a page marked "insert 470." The change involves Frederic's problems upon reaching Milan after his desertion. In the deleted passage, he arranges for false leave papers, but at Stresa it is important that Frederic not have proper papers, not even phony ones. Hemingway probably made this change during the first draft, when he realized it would be easier to motivate Frederic's flight up the lake if he were more vulnerable to arrest.

The only other irregularity in the pagination occurs on the final pages of the manuscript. MSS-650 bis to 652 is an alternate ending to the novel that does not appear in the published novel.

Of the major disruptions in the manuscript pagination, most are the result of material added during the Key West rewrite. The disruption at MS-173 resulted from a lengthy deletion that confused his typists. There are four other significant deletions that did not alter the pagination and that were also made at Key West. The first major deletion begins on MS-231, describing Frederic's operation:

When I was awake after the operation I had not been away. You do not go away. They only choak you. *It is not like death's other kingdom,*[4] *nor is it like death* and afterward you might as well have been drunk except that when you throw up nothing comes but bile instead of alcohol and you do not feel better afterward. I saw sandbags at the end of the bed. They were on pipes that came out of the cast. *My legs hurt so that I tried to get back into the choaked place I had come from but I could not get back in there but threw up again and again and nothing came. They gave me water to rinse out my mouth and then I lay still and waited for the pain to reach the top and go down but there was no limit to the pain and it had long passed the point where pain had always stopped. I thought how our Lord would never send us more {than} we could bear and I had always believed that* [MS-232] *meant me, became unconscious when it became too bad, hence the success of martyrs, but now it was not so but the pain went way beyond what I could bear in the bone and everywhere there was and then inside my chest it started to jerk and jerk and then I cried and cried without any noise, only the diaphragm jerking and jerking and then it was better and I knew I could bear it but gave no credit to our Lord.* ~~When I was through~~ *I did not think about our Lord but only that the pain was less.* ~~Crying and only my diaphragm still jerking a little~~ *When I was through crying and lying still and trying to keep my diaphragm from jerking—it had gone on crying after I was through—I saw Miss Gage and said to her*

Only the portion emphasized went into the novel. This deletion, like so many of the major revisions and deletions in the manuscript, is directly related to Frederic's feelings. By deleting this and other passages Hemingway effaces Frederic to the point that he is one of the least visible people in the novel. Only at crucial points is the reader told the narrator's feelings or emotional responses. His conclusions are minimal. This particular section is overwritten and out of character. By deleting it, Hemingway does not let the reader see Frederic's pain, which is consistent with his theory of leaving out as much as possible while letting incident and dialogue carry the story.

The second major deletion is a similarly overwritten passage which follows the previous one. It begins on MS-233:

Nothing that you learn by sensation remains if you lose the sensation. Sometimes pain goes and you cannot remember it from the moment before but only have a dread of it again. When love is gone you cannot remember it but only remember things that happen and places. There is no memory of love if there is no love. All these things, however, return in the dark. In the dark love returns when it is gone, pain comes again and danger that has passed returns. Death comes in the dark. Countries that regret executions kill men in daylight when it is easier for them to go and often if the daylight is bright and there is a little delay in the execution so the sun is higher and the morning cool, [MS-234] the condemned man having been given rum, which often makes things right which are not right, there is not much horror. I have seen men shot, slumping quickly, and hanged, twirling slowly, and kneeling, arms behind the back, chest on a table, that tipped quickly forward the knife falling into a slot and thudding on wood while boy soldiers presented arms and looked sideways at the basket that had been empty and now had a head in it. If there was daylight it was not bad. But countries that believe in executions, where the men who execute and sentence to be executed think that they themselves will never be executed, and so have no pity, pity being the faculty of seeing yourself in the person of the pitied-one, in such countries they execute men at night. Such things will not be easily forgiven, nor will they, in the end, prevent the deaths of the executioners. They will all die, of course, and many of them, not knowing about death will be greatly surprised, and those who die at night will have lived to wish they had killed in daylight. [MS-235] I do not know just when night began to be bad for me but I suppose it must have been around this time. When I had first gone to war it had all been like a picture or a story or a dream in which you know you can wake up if it gets too bad. Also I had a feeling that other people died but that I did not die. I had the belief in physical immortality which is given fortunate young men in order that they may think about other things and that is withdrawn without notice when they need it most. After its withdrawal I was not greatly worried because the spells of fear were always physical, always caused by an imminent danger, and always transitory. I was in the second healthy stage, that of not being afraid when I was not in danger. I suppose the third stage, of being afraid at night, started about this point. I did not notice it start because I was rarely alone at night. Fear grows

[MS-236] *through recognition. It is not good for a fear to talk about it and we talked about everything. But it was not much of a fear at this time and I may have used it and built it up as an argument for not being alone although on the nights when I was alone I was so tired that I slept heavily.*

This passage is curious for a number of reasons. The digression on executions, only peripherally relevant to Frederic's later desertion, distorts Frederic's character and was wisely cut. In it Hemingway obliquely refers to two inter-chapters from *in our time*: Chapter Five, the execution of the Greek ministers, and Chapter Fifteen, the hanging of Sam Cardinella. Written in 1923, neither of the two executions were based on firsthand experience.[5] Nor had Hemingway seen a guillotine execution, although he was well read on the French Revolution. He is attributing to Frederic firsthand knowledge that he had only imagined. The diatribe on those who execute at night without pity has no immediate relevance to the novel. Hemingway wrote this passage in May, 1928, at Key West, where John Dos Passos, among others, fished and drank with him when he was through with his morning writing. Dos Passos, whose socialist conscience was finely tuned to what had been happening to America in the Twenties, may well have discussed the Sacco-Vanzetti executions, which had taken place the previous August.[6] The two Italian immigrants died in the electric chair shortly after midnight, August 23, 1927. Even without Dos Passos, Hemingway must have been aware of the massive protest by American writers, particularly against Judge Thayer, who sentenced the two men to death. Regardless of the reference, Hemingway was correct in cutting Frederic's philosophy of execution. Alternately maudlin and preachy, the entire passage has no place in the novel. By eliminating it, Hemingway left only residual indications of Frederic's nighttime fears, which were clues enough to his psychological state of mind.

There are no more major deletions in the manuscript until after Frederic and Catherine are secure in Switzerland. On August 14, 1928, he finished Chapter Thirty-nine, with two pages of dialogue in which Frederic and Catherine discuss the unborn baby. On August 15, he wrote three pages of manuscript, all of which he later cut at Key West:

We had a fine life; the things we did were of no importance and the things we said were foolish and seem even more idiotic to write down but we were happy and I suppose wisdom and happiness do not go together. Although there is a wisdom in being a fool that we do not know much about and if happiness is an end sought by the wise it is no less an end if it comes without wisdom. It is as well to seize it as to seek it because you are liable to wear out the capacity for it in the seeking. To seek it through the kingdom of heaven is a fine thing but you must give up this life first and if this life is all you have you might have remorse after giving it up and the kingdom of heaven might be a cold place in which to live with remorse. They say the only way you can keep a thing is to lose it and this may be true but do not admire it. The only thing I know is that if you love anything enough they take it away from you. This may all be done in infinite wisdom but whoever does it is not my friend. I am afraid of god at night but I would have [MS-587] admired him more if he would have stopped the war or never have let it start. Maybe he did stop it but whoever stopped it did not do it prettily. And if it is the Lord that giveth and the Lord that taketh away I do not admire him for taking Catherine away. He may have given me Catherine but who gave Rinaldi the syphillis at about the same time? The one thing I know is that I do not know anything about it. I see the wisdom of the priest at our mess who has always loved god and so is happy and I am sure that nothing will ever take God away from him. But how much is wisdom and how much is luck to be born that way? And what if you are not built that way? What if the things you love are perishable. All you know then is that they will perish. You will perish too and perhaps that is the answer; that those who love things that are immortal and believe in them are immortal themselves and live on with them while those that love things that die and believe in them die and are as dead [MS-588] as the things they love. If that were true it would be a fine gift and would even things up. But it probably is not true. All that we can be sure of is that we are born and that we will die and that everything we love that has life will die too. The more things with life that we love the more things there are to die. So if we want to buy winning tickets we can go over on the side of immortality; and finally they most of them do. But if you were born loving nothing and the warm milk of your mother's breast was never heaven and the first thing you loved was the side of a hill and the last thing was a woman and they took her away and you did not want another but only to have her; and she was gone, then you are not so well placed and it would have been better to have loved God from the start. But you did not love God and it doesn't do any good to talk about it either, nor to think about it.

In cutting this entire passage, Hemingway saved only the opening sentence: "We had a fine life."

Although this is one of the more massive deletions from the manuscript, it is not unlike several minor false starts that characteristically occur immediately after a piece of finished action. Structurally it is as if Hemingway had written five tightly interrelated short stories. In the sequence prior to the above deletion, the action began at Stresa and ended at Montreux, following the classic short-story formula: conflict (the threat of arrest), rising action (the flight up the lake), climax (safe arrival in Switzerland), falling action (problems with customs), denouement (settling for the winter at Montreux). This pattern repeats itself five times with five separate climaxes: Frederic's wounding, Catherine's pregnancy, Frederic's threat of execution, the lovers eluding the lake patrol, and the onset of Catherine's labor pains. The first four climaxes either lead to a denouement that relieves the physical threat or, as with Catherine's pregnancy, postpones the threat. The final climax leads to the catastrophe that in one form or another has threatened one or both of the lovers from the beginning. Each time Hemingway builds the tension a little higher only to relieve it; but after each relief the tension remains higher than its previous level. Thus a graph of the action would be a jagged rising slope with five peaks. This structure is further confirmation that Hemingway plotted the book episodically, not knowing precisely where the next episode was going. Many of the letters he wrote during this period are dated at the end of such episodes, as if he took a break from the fiction for his correspondence. The manuscript shows that following each denouement Hemingway had difficulty beginning the next chapter, which frequently is characterized by a false start.

In the rejected philosophical passage above, he is once more attempting, through a modified stream-of-consciousness technique, to tie together loose ends and prepare the reader for Catherine's death. The central idea—those who choose the happiness of this world—finds its way back into the chapter later. Hemingway must have realized that there was no need to telegraph Catherine's death with such a heavy hand. Moreover, Frederic's wandering thoughts lack the impact that they have later when Catherine is actually dying. Here Frederic is full of self-pity with which the reader cannot identify. When Catherine is suffering in the hospital, Frederic's thoughts on the way of this world hit the reader much harder and ring truer.

It is interesting to see Hemingway once more trying to get Catherine, Rinaldi, and the priest into a kind of triad. He had attempted this once before at the beginning of Chapter Ten on a false start that he cut. Later in one of the false endings, he comes back to the same problem. Critics have long realized that these are the three "code" characters from whom Frederic learns about behavior under pressure. Because Hemingway had not plotted the novel through to its conclusion when he developed the characters of Rinaldi and the Priest in Book One, he had no way to bring them back into the conclusion except in Frederic's thoughts. Each time he tried to do this, it proved awkward. Finally he must have realized that Rinaldi and the priest were implicitly present at the conclusion, for Catherine embodies both flesh and spirit. Frederic's internal argument about the spirit and the flesh in the closing chapters is directly related to what he had learned from those two in Book One.

The Biblical style and allusions of this passage may be an indication that Hemingway was beginning his usual search through the Bible for a title. He had found *The Sun Also Rises* in the Old Testament. It is not unlikely that he began reading through the New Testament for this novel's title. The several references to "the kingdom of heaven" support this argument. It is primarily in the Gospel of Matthew that this phrase appears. In the other three Gospels, the phrase is characteristically "the kingdom of God." When Frederic says: "They say the only way you can keep a thing is to lose it," he is paraphrasing Matthew X: 39: "He that findeth his life shall lose it and he that loseth his life for my sake shall find it."[7] Throughout Matthew the central choice is between the things of this world and the Kingdom of Heaven. If a man chooses the Kingdom of Heaven, he must put aside the pleasures and objects of this life. This is the choice that Frederic is arguing in his head. Neither Frederic nor Hemingway found much solace in the Gospel of Matthew.

At crucial points throughout the novel, the possibility of prayer has been discussed. In Switzerland, Count Greffi, too old to pray, has asked Frederic to pray for him if he ever becomes devout. It is only when Catherine is dying that Frederic resorts to prayer, but the form runs contrary to the advice found in Matthew. Frederic prays: "Don't let her die. Oh, God, please don't let her die. I'll do anything for you if you won't let her die. Please, please, please, dear God, don't let her die. Dear God, don't let her die. Please, please, please don't let her die. God please make her not die. I'll do anything you say if you don't let her die. You took the baby but don't let her die. That was all right but don't let her die. Please, please, dear God, don't let her die."[8] In Matthew's version of the Sermon on the Mount, Christ tells the multitude that this is the improper form of prayer: "But when ye pray, use not vain repetitions, as the heathen do: for they think that they shall be heard for their much speaking. Be not ye therefore like unto them: for your father knoweth what things ye have need of, before ye ask him." (Matthew VI: 7–8.) Frederic prays for the wrong thing in the wrong way. As he tells himself in this deleted passage, "those who love things that die and believe in them die and are as dead as the things they love."

The manuscript pages of the novel's final chapter are carefully dated and almost entirely clean of revision, indicating that Hemingway probably recopied each day's production after the following morning's revisions. With the exception of the final paragraphs, the only portion that bears heavy Key West revisions involves the birth of the baby. The paragraph describing Catherine's sutures got much of its detail in the revision. The emphasized portions were Key West additions:

> *I thought Catherine was dead. She looked dead. Her face was gray,* the part of it I could see. *Down below, under the light, the doctor was sewing up the great long,* forcep-spread, *thick-edged, wound.* Another doctor in a mask gave the anaesthetic. Two nurses in masks handed things. It looked like a drawing of the Inquisition. *I knew as I watched I could have watched it all, but I was glad I hadn't.* I do not think I could have watched them cut, but *I watched the wound closed into a high welted ridge* with quick skilful-looking stitches like a cobbler's, and was glad. When the wound was closed *I went into the hall* and walked up and down again. *After a while the doctor came out.*
>
> MS-636 / p. 325

The most curious deletion involves the baby himself. On MS-638, a nurse tells Frederic that the baby was born dead, choked on the umbilical cord. On MS-642, written the same day, the same nurse tells Frederic: " 'The baby is alive you know.' 'What do you mean?' 'It's alive that's all.' 'You want to be careful what you tell people.' 'I'm glad,' the nurse said. 'Did you see the doctor?' 'Yes,' I said. 'I'm glad.' " The baby apparently remained alive until

Key West. There Hemingway cut this piece of dialogue and changed Frederic's prayer from: *"Take the baby* [my emphasis] but don't let her die" to: *"You took the baby* but don't let her die." A live baby would have been another loose end that Hemingway did not want. More importantly, a live baby would have been a sign of hope—life would go on. *A Farewell to Arms* is a massive defeat; there could be no sentimental hope left at the end.

The final paragraphs of the novel gave Hemingway more difficulty than any other single passage. The manuscript contains two endings that are similar but bear repeating:

There are a great many more details starting with my first meeting with an undertaker and all the business of burial in a foreign country and continuing on with the rest of my life—which has gone on and seems likely to go on for a long time. I could tell how Rinaldi was cured of the syphilis and lived to find that the technique acquired in wartime surgery is not much practical use in peace. I could tell how the priest in our mess lived to be a priest in Italy under Fascism. I could tell how Ettore became a Fascist and the part he took in that organization. I could tell what kind of singer whatisname became. I could tell how Piani got to be a taxi driver in New York. ~~*I could tell you how I made a fool of myself going back to Italy.*~~ *But they are all parts of something that was finished.* ~~*I suppose it was finished at the Tagliamento.*~~ *I do not know exactly where but certainly finished. Piani was the least finished but he went to another country. Italy is a country every man should love once. I loved it once and lived through it. You ought to love it once. There is less loss of dignity in loving it young. I suppose loving it or at least living in it is something like the need for the classics.*

I could tell you what I have done since March nineteen hundred and eighteen and when I walked that night in the rain alone, and always from then on alone, through the streets of Lausanne back to the hotel where Catherine and I had lived and went upstairs to our room and undressed and got into bed and slept, finally, because I was so tired—to wake in the morning with the sun shining; then suddenly to realize what it was that had happened. I could tell what has happened since then but that is the end of the story.

END

Many things have happened. Things happen all the time. Everything blunts and the world keeps on. You get most of your life back like goods recovered from a fire. It all keeps on as long as your life keeps on and then it keeps on. It never stops. It only stops for you. Some of it stops while you are still alive. You can stop a story anytime. ~~*Where you stop it is the end of that story.*~~ *The rest goes on and you go on with it. On the other hand you have to stop a story. You have to stop it at the end of whatever it was you were writing about.*

MSS-650–652

(FIRST REVISED ENDING)

There are a great many more details, starting with my first meeting with an undertaker and all the business of burial in a foreign country and going on with the rest of my life—which has gone on and seems likely to go on for a long time.

I could tell how Rinaldi was cured of the syphilis and lived to find that the technique learned in wartime surgery is not of much practical use in peace. I could tell how the priest in our mess lived to be a priest in Italy under Fascism. I could tell how Ettore [MS-651 bis] became a fascist and the part he took in that organization. I could tell how Piani got to be a taxi driver in New York and what sort of a singer Simmons became. Many things have happened. Everything blunts and the world keeps on. You get most of your life back like goods recovered from a fire. It all keeps on as long as your life keeps on and then it keeps on but you do not know about it. It never stops. It only stops for you. Some of it stops while you are still alive. The rest goes on and you go on with it. [MS-652 bis]

I could tell you what I have done since March nineteen hundred and eighteen when I walked that night in the rain back to the hotel where Catherine and I had lived and went upstairs to our room and undressed and got into bed and slept, finally, because I was so tired—to wake in the morning with the sun shining in the window; then suddenly to realize what it was that had happened. I could tell what has happened since then but that is the end of the story.

The first of these two drafts is heavily revised on the page, with sentences added on the margin and interlinearly. The second draft has nothing crossed out or revised—a smooth copy that improves some changes from the first draft. Both were written sometime after the manuscript had been completed. With the exception of walking back to the hotel in the rain, neither contributed significantly to the ending that Hemingway finally wrote the following June. Both have the wrong tone. They lack immediacy, and once more they show Frederic-as-author, an exposure that Hemingway had attempted earlier and judiciously cut. Once again he is attempting to bring back Rinaldi and the priest. They were loose ends of the novel that he had developed almost too well in Book One, when he did not know precisely where the story was going. In the first ending he is tempted to draw on his 1922 and 1927 trips to Italy, when nothing had been the same, but he scratched that as a bad idea. He also gives a further clue to his original intentions when Frederic says, "I suppose it was finished at the Tagliamento." "It" obviously wasn't finished at the Tagliamento, but that may well have been where Hemingway had earlier intended to end the novel.

Both false endings attempt to reduce the tension built by Catherine's death. After this emotional peak, Hemingway wanted to let the reader back down softly—to allow the catharsis to work, as he was able to do later at the end of *The Old Man and the Sea*. In *A Farewell to Arms* he could not find this release, although he continued to search for several months.

At the Kennedy Library, Mary Hemingway has collected the numerous false endings of *A Farewell to Arms*. Although they are not arranged in chronological order and several are merely fragments, there appear to be thirty-two variant endings, plus two more in the holograph manuscript and one more in the *Scribner's Magazine* corrected galleys. Most of the variants are based on the first ending of the manuscript. However, one variant has the baby alive. In the first draft of the manuscript, Hemingway had left the baby alive; by the time he wrote the first ending, he had rejected this idea. Sometime in May, 1929, he wrote an insert for MS-641, once more reviving the baby. Ultimately, of course, the baby appeared still-born.

One curious variant is the result of Scott Fitzgerald's suggestion when he critiqued the typescript: "Why not end the book with that wonderful paragraph on p. 241. It is the most eloquent in the book and could end it rather gently and well."[9] Fitzgerald was referring to the philosophical passage in which Frederic describes how the world eventually kills everyone impartially—the good, the gentle, and the brave. "If you are none of these you can be sure it will kill you too but there will be no special hurry" (p. 249). Hemingway liked the idea well enough to type it up, giving the pages the proper numbers to fit them into the typescript he had sent Scribner's. The suggestion was not a bad one, but it, too, ended up in the pile of rejected endings. Either Hemingway did not want to end the book on a moralizing note, or he did not want Fitzgerald to be given the credit. Fitzgerald had shaped the opening chapter of *The Sun Also Rises* by urging Hemingway to cut the first three galleys.[10] Hemingway's pride must have bridled at the thought of his fellow writer being responsible for the ending of his second novel.

While he was still working on the ending, he received the galleys for the novel's last installment in *Scribner's Magazine*. The galleys, dated June 4, 1929, have the second variant ending printed above. On Galley 19, Hemingway revised heavily in pencil but was unable to substantially change his initial concept. It was not until June 24, 1929, ten months after completing the first draft, that Hemingway got the ending that went into print. One can sense the surge of power on the manuscript page. The handwriting expands; the pencil width broadens as if he were trying to push it through the paper. There is a rush to get the words down; one can almost feel the relief and pleasure there on the page.

Falling back on his best technique, Hemingway wrote the terse dialogue between Frederic and the surgeon with only one final tight narrative paragraph: "But after I had got them out and shut the door and turned off the light it wasn't any good. It was like saying good-by to a statue. After a while I went out and left the hospital and walked back to the hotel in the rain" (p. 332). Frederic Henry, like so many twentieth-century fictional heroes, finds no catharsis. His failures have been inconsequential to everyone but himself; his personal loss has been massive, and he is left with no place to go.[11]

Notes

1. *The Short Stories of Ernest Hemingway* (New York: Scribner's, 1953), p. 363.

2. See Philip Young, *Ernest Hemingway: A Reconsideration* (University Park: Pennsylvania State University Press, 1966).

3.   Hemingway, "More Game to Shoot in Crowded Europe than in Ontario," *Toronto Star Weekly*, November 3, 1923, p. 20.

4.   A further indication that Hemingway while writing the novel was consciously aware of T. S. Eliot's crippled survivors: "Those who have crossed / With direct eyes, to death's other Kingdom / Remember us—if at all—not as lost / Violent souls, but only / As the hollow men / The Stuffed men." "The Hollow Men," 1925.

5.   Carlos Baker, *Ernest Hemingway: A Life Story* (New York: Scribner's, 1969), p. 113.

6.   See Dos Passos, "Camera Eye 50," *U.S.A.*

7.   Hemingway took two titles from Matthew later in the Thirties: "The Light of the World," and *To Have and Have Not:* "Ye are the light of the world. A city that is set on a hill cannot be hid" (Matthew V: 14.), and "For unto everyone that hath shall be given, and he shall have abundance: but from him that hath not shall be taken away even that which he hath" (Matthew XXV: 29).

8.   Hemingway, *A Farewell to Arms* (New York: Scribner's, 1929). Scribner Library Edition, p. 330. All further references to the novel will be from this edition and will appear parenthetically in the text.

9.   Fitzgerald critique, handwritten, undated, 1929.

10.   See Philip Young and Charles W. Mann, "Fitzgerald's *Sun Also Rises:* Notes and Comment," *Fitzgerald / Hemingway Annual* (Washington: NCR, 1970), pp. 1–9.

11.   Sheldon N. Grebstein's examination of the *A Farewell to Arms* MS in an appendix to his book, *Hemingway's Craft* (Carbondale: Southern Illinois University Press, 1973), appeared in print after my study had been completed. Certain conclusions of mine have been anticipated by Professor Grebstein; on other points we disagree. Where our observations overlap, footnotes will invite comparison.

The Sense of an Ending

BERNARD OLDSEY

"How much re-writing do you do?"

"It depends. I re-wrote the ending of *Farewell to Arms*, the last page of it, thirty-nine times before I was satisfied."

"Was there some technical problem there? What was it that had you stumped?"

"Getting the words right."

> —From George Plimpton's interview with
> Ernest Hemingway in the *Paris Review*, 1958

I

The final act of enclosure in *A Farewell to Arms* consists of less than one page of print, just under two hundred words. In its own way, however, as a dramatic piece of tightly rendered fiction, it proves to be as structurally sound and effective as the evocative "overture" (Chapter 1) with which the novel opens.[1] Long admired critically, this conclusion has become one of the most famous segments in American fiction—having been used in college classrooms across the land as a model of compositional compression and as an object lesson in authorial sweat, in what Horace called "the labor of the file." The undocumented story of how hard Hemingway worked to perfect the ending of *A Farewell to Arms* approached the level of academic legend. Some tellers of the tale said he wrote the conclusion fifty times, some as high as ninety; others used the safer method of simply saying Hemingway wrote it, rewrote it, and re-rewrote it. Carlos Baker, in his otherwise highly detailed biography, says of the matter only that "Between May 8th and 18th [1929] he rewrote the conclusion several times in the attempt to get it exactly right."[2] In their inventory of the papers available to them at the time, Philip Young and Charles Mann mention only one alternate conclusion separately and a rather small, indeterminate number of others attached to

From *Modern Fiction Studies*, 23 (Winter 1977–78): 491–510. © 1977 Purdue Research Foundation, West Lafayette, Indiana 49707. Reprinted by permission of the author and *Modern Fiction Studies*.

the galleys for the periodical publication of the novel.[3] One of these is the version Baker published, in a collection called *Ernest Hemingway: Critiques of Four Major Novels*, under the heading of "The Original Conclusion of *A Farewell to Arms*."[4] For reasons that will become clear later, this version should be referred to more precisely as "The Original *Scribner's Magazine* Conclusion," for although it was indeed the first to be set in galleys for that publication, it was preceded in composition by at least one other version in handwritten form, and probably more.[5]

As the papers now indicate, Hemingway deserved to be taken pretty much at his word when he told George Plimpton he had written the conclusion thirty-nine times. Depending upon a number of small variables and upon what one is willing to call an attempt at conclusion, there are between thirty-two and forty-one elements of conclusion in the Hemingway Collection of the John F. Kennedy Library.[6] These appear in typescript and in handwritten form and run from one or two sentences in length to as many as three pages. Some of the short elements show up again in the fuller attempts, helping to produce combination endings that consist of fragments arranged in varying alignments. There is, of course, no guarantee that Hemingway did not write even more variations: some could have been lost, destroyed, forgotten. But those that exist in the Hemingway Collection represent a rich fund of critical information capable of revealing the process of rejection-selection that the author went through to reach "the sense of an ending."[7] Not only can we see in this scattered process the thematic impulses which run through the novel and which the author was tempted to tie-off in many of these concluding attempts, but we find in it the figurative seven-eighths of Hemingway's famous "iceberg" that floats beneath the one-eighth surface of the art object. In one sense, most of the concluding attempts that are to be examined here may be considered as artistically subsumed under what finally became *the* ending of *A Farewell to Arms*. Understanding them should lead to a better understanding of it, and the novel as a whole.

All of the conclusions in the Hemingway Collection presuppose Catherine's death. Hemingway chose to present the actual death in understated, summary fashion at the very end of the penultimate section of the last chapter: "It seems she had one hemorrhage after another . . . and it did not take her very long to die."[8] Presumably, that summarization did not take much writing effort. In itself Catherine's death, although beautifully prepared for in the first three quarters of the last chapter, is not one of Hemingway's moments of artistic truth—like the flat cinematic projection of Maera's death in *In Our Time* or the elaborate mythic flight of Harry in "The Snows of Kilimanjaro." It contains none of the asyntactical eloquence of Frederic's near-death, when he feels his soul slip out of his body like a handkerchief from a pocket and then return to corporeal life (p. 57). This is, after all, Frederic Henry's story, and it is his reaction to Catherine's death that had to be depicted with revelatory force. All of the variant conclusions that Hemingway wrote for the novel are attempts to epitomize Henry's traumatized perception—from which, years later, the story unfolds.

Most of the variant attempts fall into natural clusters that can be referred to as: (1) The *Nada* Ending, (2) The Fitzgerald Ending, (3) The Religious Ending, (4) The Live-Baby Ending, (5) The Morning-After Ending, (6) The Funeral Ending, (7) The Original *Scribner's Magazine* Ending, and (8) *The* Ending (Mrs. Mary Hemingway has allowed the use of some examples of these endings). But a final grouping of (9) Miscellaneous Endings is needed initially to accommodate five brief attempts that have little in common with each other or any of those in the previously mentioned categories.

These five are all single-page holographs, four mere fragments. Two echo material in Chapter I by mixing rain with the thought of many men and women dying in war time, and they conclude that knowing about the death of many is no consolation to someone mourning the death of a specific person. Another reaches back to Henry's nearly fatal wounding, as he compares the traumatic effect of Catherine's death on him with that produced by the physical wound: in both instances the numbness wears off and only pain remains. Still another of these miscellaneous attempts makes use of the old saying "See Naples and die," concluding bitterly that Naples is a hateful place, a part of that unlucky Peninsula which is Italy. The last, and most interesting, of these attempts briefly entertains the notion of suicide: the narrator realizes he can end his life just as arbitrarily as he writes finis to his narrative, but he decides not to and later is not "sorry" about his decision. Through the first four of these attempts, and a number of others later, we can observe Hemingway trying to find the right linear motif with which to tie off the novel—climatological, psychological, or geographical. With the introduction of suicide in the fifth, however, we are reminded that the end of any novel, not just this, is in a sense a prefigurement of the novelist's death. All of the attempts to conclude a novel mirror the life choices of the creator, and the conclusion of a life can be as arbitrary and / or artistically appropriate as the conclusion of a novel.

"The *Nada* Ending" is represented by three fragmentary attempts to express Henry's sense of being-and-nothingness after Catherine's death. His mind is stunned and produces only a negative response, a form of *nada*. He senses that everything is gone—all their love—and will never be again. But at the bottom of one of these handwritten fragments an added note declares, with some of the ambiguity found at the end of "A Clean, Well-Lighted Place," that "nothing" is lost. The bluntest of the three attempts simply states that there is nothing left to the story and that all the narrator can promise is that we all die.[9] This nihilistic attitude echoes Henry's earlier statement made to a hungry animal nosing around a garbage can: "There isn't anything, dog." And it is this same negative tonality, expressed dramatically, which dominates the ending Hemingway eventually devised for the novel.

Although related to the *nada* group, "The Fitzgerald Ending" deserves separate discussion because of the peculiar editorial circumstances surrounding it. As is now well known, F. Scott Fitzgerald helped Hemingway considerably in choosing the proper opening of *The Sun Also Rises*. What has not been well known is that he also advised Hemingway editorially on a number of matters in *A Farewell to Arms*: Item 77 in the Hemingway Collection consists of nine handwritten pages of Fitzgerald's comments on the typescript of the novel.[10] He so admired one passage in the book that he noted it in the typescript as being "One of the most beautiful pages in all English literature"; and later, in his last note on the novel to Hemingway, he wrote: "Why not end the book with that wonderful paragraph on p. 241 [pp. 258–259 in print]. It is the most eloquent in the book and would end it rather gently and well." The passage referred to is that in which Henry, in Chapter XXXIV, contemplates how the world "kills the very good and the very gentle and the very brave" and concludes "If you are none of these you can be sure it will kill you too but there will be no special hurry." Hemingway did try to use the passage as an ending, once by itself in holograph and once with other elements in polished typescript. As we know, he rejected both possibilities and kept the passage intact within the novel. In a letter to Hemingway (dated June 1, 1934), defending his own *Tender is the Night*, Fitzgerald shed much light on his own sense of an ending, as well as Hemingway's and Joseph Conrad's:

> The theory back of it I got from Conrad's preface to *The Nigger*, that the purpose of a work of fiction is to appeal to the lingering after-effects in the reader's mind. . . . The second contribution . . . was your trying to work out some such theory in your troubles with the very end of *A Farewell to Arms*. I remember that your first draft—or at least the first one I saw—gave a sort of old-fashioned Alger book summary . . . and you may remember my suggestion to take a burst of eloquence from anywhere in the book that you could find it and tag off with that; you were against this idea because you felt that the true line of a work of fiction was to take a reader up to a high emotional pitch but then let him down or ease him off. You gave no aesthetic reason for this—nevertheless, you convinced me.[11]

"The Religious Ending" represents one of Hemingway's least negative variants and perhaps the most potentially incongruous. Had any form of this conclusion been retained, *A Farewell to Arms* would have emerged with a much different emphasis in theme—one depending heavily upon a passage (in Chapter III) that has puzzled many readers. This is the place where Henry tries to express the evanescent wisdom of the priest: "He had always known what I did not know and what, when I learned it, I was always able to forget. But I did not know that then, although I learned it later" (p. 14). What is the *it* which Henry learns, and when does he learn it? The usual interpretation stresses *it* as love: the priest's love of God, Frederic's love for

Catherine, and the connection between *agape* and *eros*. But Hemingway's experiments with religious conclusions for the novel reveal the *it* of the priest as transcending any mundane love, which can be snuffed out by death. Under these circumstances, the *it* that Henry learns "later" is that everything will be all right if, as these fragments indicate, "you believe in God and love God." No one, the narrator concludes, can take God away from the priest, and thus the priest is happy. With such a conclusion the priest would have emerged as the supreme mentor of this *Bildungsroman*, not Rinaldi, Count Greffi, or even Catherine. However, a question imbedded in two of these religious attempts helps to explain why this kind of conclusion was rejected. Henry wonders how much of what the priest has is simply luck, how much is wisdom—and how do you achieve what the priest has if you are not "born that way"? It is, eventually, a question of deterministic grace.

Another fairly positive ending that Hemingway dropped is one in which Frederic and Catherine's child lives, instead of dying as it does in the novel. Two of these "Live-Baby Endings" were written to be inserted into the penultimate section of the last chapter, to precede Catherine's death. But the third makes it clear that Hemingway attempted to provide an ending in which the fact of birth, of new life, mitigates death. In this version Henry finds it difficult to talk about the boy without feeling bitter toward him, but concludes philosophically that "there is no end except death and birth is the only beginning." Stoic as these words may sound, they, nevertheless, tend to mitigate the deeper gloom produced in the novel by the death of both mother and child. In several senses "The Live-Baby Ending" would have meant another story; and with a touch of editorial wisdom reflecting that of the author, Henry realizes "It is not fair to start a new story at the end of an old one. . . ."

The concluding element Hemingway worked on longest and hardest was one built on a delayed reaction, "The Morning-After Ending." In holograph and typescript form, ten variations on this conclusion exist as more or less discrete elements; five are incorporated into combination conclusions, including "The Original *Scribner's Magazine* Ending," as published by Baker, and both the "original" and "first-revised" conclusions, as represented in Michael Reynolds' *Hemingway's First War*.[12] In all of these Frederic returns, after Catherine's death, to the hotel where they had been staying: after some time he falls asleep because he is so tired; waking to a spring morning, he sees the sun shining in through the window and for a moment is unaware of what has happened. The moment of realizing Catherine is gone—something of a dull, truncated epiphany—is rendered in two ways. In most versions, including those published by Baker and Reynolds, Henry merely experiences a delayed response—"then suddenly to realize what had happened." But in other versions his recognition of his predicament is stimulated by a burning light bulb: seeing it still lit in the daylight brings double illumination. Through this simple device, Hemingway placed Frederic

Henry among those other protagonists of his who, like children, have trouble with the dark—including the Old Man in "A Clean, Well-Lighted Place," the Lieutenant in "Now I Lay Me," and Nick Adams in "A Way You'll Never Be," who confesses, "I can't sleep without a light of some sort. That's all I have now." His word could stand for Frederic Henry in these versions of the conclusion. He, too, earlier in the novel, gives utterance to nocturnal blues: "I know that the night is not the same as the day: that all things are different . . . the night can be a dreadful time for lonely people once their loneliness has started. But with Catherine there was almost no difference in the night except that it was an even better time" (p. 258). Without Catherine, all that is left is a light bulb burning in the night, announcing on the morning after that she is dead.

In one instance Hemingway employed "The Morning-After Ending" as a transitional device to achieve "The Funeral Ending." The initial material of this one-page holograph is essentially the same as that described in the Baker version, but this variant does not end with the flat statement of "that is the end of my story." Instead, Hemingway here makes one of his first attempts to conclude with an obverse-iteration method: Henry says that he could tell about his meeting with the undertaker and "the business of burial in a foreign country," but, the implication is, as the sentence trails off, he will not. The same kind of obverse iteration is incorporated into the two other attempts at this funeral conclusion: people die and they have to be buried, but the narrator does not have to tell about the burying, or the resulting sorrow. Henry tells us—somewhat reversing the earlier notion of suicide—that in writing "you have a certain choice that you do not have in life."

It is impossible to state with certainty what the exact order of composition was for all the variant elements of conclusion, since they are undated.[13] But there are good indications that the combining form of "The Original *Scribner's Magazine* Ending" was the penultimate version. For one thing, most of the variations in this group (five of eight) are highly polished typescripts. For another, these versions combine many of the previously mentioned attempts as contributing elements—including the "morning-after" idea, as well as the funeral, suicide, lonely nights, the Fitzgerald suggestion, and the obverse-iteration method of stating-but-not-stating what happened after that particular night in "March nineteen hundred and eighteen." Most significantly, one version of this combining conclusion very nearly became the ultimate one—to the extent of having been set in galleys for the serial publication of the novel.

Hemingway scribbled a note to hold matters on this conclusion, however, and then eventually supplanted it with the dramatic version that we now have. If he had not done so, *A Farewell to Arms* would have ended in the old-fashioned manner of tying up the loose narrative ends in summary fashion. For in the original galley version, Frederic Henry says that he could, if he wanted to, tell his reader many things that had happened since that night when Catherine died. He could tell how Rinaldi was cured of syphilis (answering the question of whether Rinaldi did indeed have the disease); how the priest functioned in Italy under Mussolini (indicating that this is a story being told years after its occurrence); how Simmons became an opera singer; how the loudly heroic Ettore became a Fascist; and how the loyal Piani became a taxi-driver in New York. A variant of this conclusion places Piani in Chicago instead of New York and hints that something unpleasant happened to the socialist-deserter Bonello in his home town of Imola. In all of the variants of this combining ending, however, Henry decides he will not tell about all of these people, or about himself, since that time in 1918, because all of that would be another story. This story ends with Catherine's death or, more specifically, with the dawn of his awakening to that fact on the morning after.

Hemingway reached this point in his search for an ending by August, 1928. He made some galley adjustments on this combination ending early in June, 1929. But he still was not satisfied; the last phase of his search began; and on June 24, 1929, almost ten months after completion of the first full draft of the novel, Hemingway reached "The Ending."[14] Tracing through all of the elements of conclusion for A Farewell to Arms in the Hemingway Collection is like accompanying the captain of a vessel who has been searching through uncharted waters for a singularly appropriate harbor: then suddenly after all this pragmatic probing there appears the proper terminus to his voyage, and yours, something realized out of a myriad number of possibilities. In less figurative terms, "The Ending" emerges suddenly as the product of what Mark Schorer has aptly called "Technique as Discovery."

Even in the very last phase of this process, Hemingway continued to write and rewrite to discover what should be said on the final page of the novel as a result of what had been said in the preceding three hundred and forty pages. Including the ultimate choice, there are extant five holographic variants of "The Ending." They are closely related, and they remind us that Hemingway once said the most difficult thing about writing was "getting the words right." With cross-outs, replacements, realignments, these final five efforts demonstrate technique as discovery in the most basic sense of getting the words right, which leads to getting the right message, the right form.

All five are basically alike in form and substance. They are all examples of the dramatic method of showing, rendering, rather than telling. They all contain the descriptive element of the rain, the dramatic action of clearing the hospital room and taking leave of Catherine's corpse, and the narrative reflection that none of it is any good. All include the most important sentence in the actual conclusion: "It was like saying good bye to a statue." But they all state these matters in slightly different ways, using different positions for various phrases and ideas, achieving different emphases and effects. For example, Hemingway moved the sentence about "saying good bye to a statue" around like a piece in a puzzle: in one instance he tried for maximum effect by making it the very last sentence of the novel but evidently thought that too obvious and placed it eventually in its penultimate position, where it is now followed by the line that runs—"After awhile I went out and left the hospital and walked back to the hotel in the rain."

Kenneth Burke reads that last line as a small masterpiece of understatement and meteorological symbolism: "No weeping here," he declares; "Rather stark 'understatement.' Or look again, and do you not find the very heavens are weeping in his behalf?" Burke finds here an echo of Verlaine's line "It rains in my heart as it rains on the town."[15] This critical hunch receives support from the most interesting variant of "*The* Ending," which takes from the heavens a touch of religious consolation. In this version, out of Frederic Henry's reflections, comes a brief line obviously modeled on the Beatitudes: "Blessed are the dead that the rain falls on . . ." It has poetic lilt and fits in beautifully with the weather imagery throughout the novel, and at first the reader is inclined to think Hemingway made the wrong decision in dropping it from the final ending. But further consideration reveals a sense of craft wisdom. Having previously rejected "The Religious Ending" that features the happiness of the priest, and having depicted the inefficacy of Henry's prayers for the dying Catherine, the author here remained artistically consistent. In eliminating this nub of religious consolation, he obtained the flat, nihilistic, numbing conclusion that the novel now has.

Here again, in this last instance of rejection as in all of the preceding instances, we are reminded that Hemingway's best fiction is the product not only of *what has been put in* but also of *what has been left out*. "Big Two-Hearted River" is perhaps the most obvious example of this propensity in Hemingway's work; it took critics years to fill in the deliberate gaps in that story, by borrowing information from other pieces of Hemingway's fiction, in order to get a full reading of what they sensed was a powerful work of suppressed drama. Hemingway intuitively understood that sublimated words form part of any message as uttered, providing as they do a psychological tension and an emotional context for that utterance. He spoke of trying to achieve "a fourth and even a fifth dimension" in his fiction and formulated a synecdochic theory for the-thing-left-out: "I always try to write on the principle of the iceberg. There is seven-eighths of it underwater for every part that shows. *Anything you know you can eliminate and it only strengthens your iceberg. It is the part that doesn't show.*"[16] Examining some forty attempts at conclusion for *A Farewell to Arms* provides a rare inside view of that theory: it reveals what the author knew, the submerged, suppressed part of the message. Moreover, it opens to critical view an auctorial process of exclusion-inclusion, an exercise of willed choice, that closely parallels the life-choices of the protagonist-narrator. Thus we can see that the published conclusion is possessed of an extraordinary tension and literary power because it sublimates,

suppresses, and / or rejects the same things that Frederic Henry does—
including religious consolation; hope for the future and the continuance of
life (as reflected in "The Live-Baby Ending" and in the summary of characters
in the combination endings); the eloquence of courage and beauty (expressed
in "The Fitzgerald Ending"); and even the negative solution of suicide
(suggested in one of the miscellaneous endings). In this instance, everything
that the author and the protagonist knew and eliminated went into strength-
ening this tip of the iceberg.

Conceived as it was in the spirit of rejection, the conclusion of *A
Farewell to Arms* is in and of itself a compressed exemplification of the process
of rejection and negation. The only thing that Hemingway retained from
all the preceding attempts at ending the novel is the core of "The *Nada*
Ending." He eventually wrote finis to the story by bringing its materials
down to a fine point of "nothingness" and thus left the reader with the same
kind of message Frederic Henry gives the hungry dog in the last chapter:
"There isn't anything, reader." Within the short space of the one hundred
and ninety-seven words that comprise the conclusion, Hemingway uses *nothing* three times and a series of some thirteen forms of negation, in various
phrases like "No. There is nothing to do," "No . . . There's nothing to
say," and simply "No. Thank you." In the process, Frederic Henry rejects
the attending physician's explanation of the caesarian operation, his offer of
aid, and the nurse's demand that he stay out of Catherine's room. But the
most powerful form of rejection occurs in the final paragraph of the book,
when Henry says his last farewell to arms: "But after I got them [the nurses]
out and shut the door and turned off the light it wasn't any good. It was
like saying good-by to a statue." He rejects the corpse; it rejects him.
Even in this ultimate scene of nullification Hemingway uses his principle
of omission in a subtle manner: he says nothing about Frederic's embracing
or kissing the statue-like corpse, although it is a rare reader who does not
interpolate some such act. Also, Hemingway does nothing here to remind
the reader that with Catherine Lt. Henry had come to accept the night, the
darkness, and found that with her it was an "even better time" than the
day. But now Henry deliberately turns off the light, as though to test his
alliance with Catherine, and finds that the warmth and companionship of
love are inoperative, defunct. We can thus understand why, in many of the
combination endings, Henry is described as sleeping with the light bulb turned
on in the hotel room. Night will never be "a better time" for him again.

II

To estimate the worth of the conclusion Hemingway finally composed for
A Farewell to Arms, and to get beneath its surface meaning, we should

consider some of the literary and philosophical propensities involved in the conclusions of novels in general. E. M. Forster, in his sensible and perceptive *Aspects of the Novel*, makes what may be the most commonly repeated statement on the subject: "If it was not for death and marriage I do not know how the average novelist would conclude."[17] Indeed, Forster believes that endings constitute "the inherent defect of novels," partly because authors simply tire and then force their characters to do and say things to bring about a specious conclusion, or because they behave like Henry James in forcing characters to fit a predetermined plot and conclusion. Forster proves to be an early advocate of what has recently been referred to as "open-end" forms of fiction: he recommends that novelists look not to the drama for complete-seeming endings, but to music and its trailing reverberations as a concluding analogue. "Expansion," he declares: "That is the idea the novelist must cling to. Not completion. Not rounding off but opening out."[18]

Forster was in partial agreement with the nineteenth-century English novelist George Eliot, or Mary Ann Evans. In correspondence, she confided that "Beginnings are always troublesome," but "conclusions are the weak point of most authors." She added, however, that in her estimation, "some of the fault lies in the very nature of a conclusion, *which is at best a negation.*"[19] Frank Kermode, who quotes Eliot's remarks in *The Sense of an Ending*, takes exception to them by declaring: "Ends are ends only when they are not negative but frankly transfigure the events in which they are immanent."[20]

This is an important, carefully worded statement, and *The Sense of an Ending* is an important contribution to the small critical circle of literary eschatology. Limited by thesis, it is an informative and illuminating treatise on literary conclusions as derived from apocalyptic bases. With considerable scholarly and rhetorical force, Kermode traces a line of descent from public apocalypse to private crisis in literary endings and demonstrates that some of our best modern poetry, drama, and fiction partake of this eschatological endgame. The line of descent runs roughly from St. John of Patmos through the Shakespeare who wrote *King Lear* to the Blake who wrote the visions to a host of twentieth-century writers like Yeats, T. S. Eliot, Beckett, Camus, Sartre, and Robbe-Grillet. What these writers have in common, according to Kermode, is a system of literary conclusions that stand as transfiguring revelations. These are Kermode's true endings, which "transfigure the events in which they were immanent." This definition demands a final convolution, the sense of a world ending with either a bang or a whimper, a universal metamorphosis. Although it certainly fits works which are basically apocalyptic, in Kermode's expanded sense, this definition of an ending as something which exists *only* when transfiguration takes place seems if not wilful at least overly stringent.

How do the conclusions of many excellent and well-known novels meet Kermode's concept of a true ending? He points to *Anna Karenina* as a novel with a proper sense of ending, by which he means the epiphanated conversion of Levin to some transcendent concept of man's ability to will goodness. But there are really two "endings" to Tolstoy's novel, just as there are two inter-crossing plots; and to discuss Levin's inner transformation without considering Anna Karenina's suicidal *negation* is to miss half the point of the novel, which is based on antithesis rather than simple peripety. *War and Peace*, which Forster selects for its musical after-effect, ends with no transfiguration in sight: it ends, in fact, with a somewhat dull essay on historical and theological necessity (part of the essayistic material in the novel which Hemingway advised readers to skip).

A brief review of the endings of some famous novels, chosen almost at random (closest to hand on a worthy bookshelf) may throw some light on the problem of concluding and upon the specific accomplishment of Hemingway in *A Farewell to Arms*. *Tom Jones* ends in marriage and an old-style summary of what happens to "the other persons who have made any considerable figure in this history." *Vanity Fair* ends with a welter of events, death and marriage, a summary of the characters, and a final word from the stage-managing narrator: "Come, children, let us shut up the box and the puppets, for our play is played out." *Madame Bovary* ends with funereal considerations in respect to Emma, followed by Charles' death, the disposition of the child, and the ironic triumph of viciousness, as represented in the last sentence of the book which simply says of M. Homais, "He has just received the cross of honor." After the death of Bazarov, *Fathers and Sons* ends with a summary of characters and a visit to the graveyard, and also with a considerable amount of sentimental consolation: "the flowers . . . tell us, too, of eternal reconciliation and of life without end." *Crime and Punishment* ends with the forced repentance of Raskolnikov in the arms of a reformed prostitute and under the wings of Russian Orthodoxy. Along with the long anti-climactic section of *Huckleberry Finn*, Dostoevsky's must be one of the most suspect and controversial endings in all of literature. (Hemingway, incidentally, showed critical concern about the conclusion of Twain's book, advising readers to stop reading at the place where Huck makes his decision to help Nigger Jim escape slavery.)

These great novels of the eighteenth and nineteenth century are certainly not the works of what Forster calls "the average novelist," but they do support his observation about the dependence upon death and marriage in reaching conclusions. Except in one instance, however, they contain none of the transfiguration which Kermode insists upon for a true ending. His apocalyptic description becomes more meaningful with such twentieth-century novels as Kafka's *The Trial* and Camus' *The Stranger*. Fitzgerald's conclusion of *The Great Gatsby*, with its green light effulgence and pervasive sense of continental ruination, also tends toward the apocalyptic. And in *The Sound and the Fury*, *The Bear*, and especially *Light in August*, Faulkner approaches transfiguration through the disruption of chronological time and blasts of discordant activity.

58 ◆ BERNARD OLDSEY

But not all modern novels utilize such concluding means. The long interior ramble of Molly Bloom which ends *Ulysses* is difficult to define as transfiguring—except in the sense that all great literary figures transcend the bounds of ordinary beings. There have to be other considerations of what constitutes the proper, the right, the true ending for a work of literature. To begin with, conclusions cannot be made or judged by some outside measure; it is self evident that they must fit the beginnings and middle of the works which they terminate. Concordance and decorum are as important considerations as claritas. It would be nonsensical, for example, to expect the conclusion of Steinbeck's *Grapes of Wrath* (not to mention one of Dickens' or C. P. Snow's works) to end in some great contortion of events leading to transfiguration. Even though *Grapes of Wrath* contains some of the materials for social apocalypse, its conclusion is true to the naturalistic body of the book and to its sociological sentiment, as Rose of Sharon quite literally provides a starving man with her own milk of human kindness.

Although, then, Kermode provides us with some excellent insights into the literary endgames of works that are essentially tragic in nature, cataclysmic in event, there are other legitimate ends besides these. *The Sense of an Ending* is an admittedly restrictive analysis, and what is needed to balance out Kermode's definition of an ending is some understanding of Martin Heidegger's "zero" (the quintessential "not" or "naught") and of Henry James' geometrical figure, the "circle" of artistic appearance. At the very least, they help account for the conclusion which a young American novelist intuited, through the exercise of his craft, for *A Farewell to Arms*.

It is doubtful that Hemingway read Heidegger's *Existence and Being*. Much more important than any possible influence is the parallel working of minds—the one philosophical, the other artistic—in seeking out answers to the question of nothingness. In *Existence and Being*, Heidegger argues the supremacy of philosophy over natural science, because philosophers can ask the prime metaphysical question that includes "Nothing," or "non-being," while scientists are stuck with the question of "what is." How, Heidegger asks, can we account for *something* issuing forth from *nothing*? And how are we to relate what-is to nothing? Science simply ducks the question. Classical metaphysicians dealt poorly with the same question, conceiving of "nothing," in Heidegger's words, as "unformed matter which is powerless to form itself into 'being' and cannot therefore present an appearance." Their dictum on the subject was *"ex nihilo nihil fit"*—nothing comes from nothing. But Christian theologians changed that concept by placing God outside the circle of nothingness and having Him create the entire universe from it.

Heidegger believes that we are projected to our fullest moments of truth, toward an understanding of "nothing" and its relation to being, by boredom (which brings us to the abyss of existence), by "the presence of the being—not merely the person—of someone we love," and by a dread that comes to us when "what-is" slips away and we are faced with "nothing." Thus "Dread reveals Nothing." This is what Heidegger means by *"Da-sein,"* which he defines in part as "being projected into nothing." It is interesting to compare Heidegger's language in the search for "nothing" and the words of the middle-aged waiter in Hemingway's "A Clean, Well-Lighted Place." Heidegger writes: "Where shall we see Nothing? Where shall we find Nothing? In order to find something must we not know beforehand that it is there? Indeed we must! First and foremost we can only look if we have presupposed the presence of a thing to be looked for. But here the thing we are looking for is Nothing. Is there after all a seeking without pre-supposition, a seeking complemented by a pure finding?"[21] Hemingway writes:

> What did he fear? It was not fear or dread. It was nothing that he knew too well. It was all nothing and a man was nothing too. It was only that and light was all it needed and a certain cleanness and order. Some lived in it and never felt it but he knew it all was nada y pues nada y nada y pues nada. Our nada who art in nada nada be thy name thy kingdom nada thy will be nada in nada as it is in nada. . . . Hail nothing full of nothing, nothing is with thee. He smiled and stood before a bar with a shining steam pressure coffee machine.
> "What's yours?" asked the barman.
> "Nada."
> "Otro loco mas," said the barman and turned away.

Had this particular barman been reading Heidegger he would most certainly have uttered the same words he uses on Hemingway's middle-aged waiter. "Another crazy one." The barman, however, has not been undergoing an experience in "Da-sein," has not been projected into nothingness.

Hemingway, like Heidegger, only in fictive terms, is dealing with the metaphysical question of all times; and the middle-aged waiter recapitulates much of Christian dogma, except that he places God within, rather than outside, the circle of nothingness: "Our nada who art *in* nada. . . ." This parodistic statement may or may not be atheistical, but it is heretical. The principal function of an atheistical universe is to *make itself* out of nothing (cosmologists have not yet solved the problem of how this was done). The principal function of Christian theology is to separate the idea of God from the idea of nothing and illustrate how that deity created the universe out of nothing. The principal function of a literary artist is to imagine and make felt the "nothing" which Heidegger seeks, and then out of that nothing create the something which is his art. The middle-aged waiter in "A Clean, Well-Lighted Place" speaks more for artists than he does waiters when he speaks of the it-ness of being: "It was a nothing that he knew too well. . . . It was only that and light was all it needed and a certain cleanness and order." "Light," indeed. "And God said, 'Let there be light'; and there was light." All that the literary artist needs to add to that is the idea that in the beginning was the word, and the word is with the writer, whose job is to "get the words right," with a "certain cleanness and order."

A *Farewell to Arms* ends with no apocalyptic bang or whimper, only words that dwindle away to nothing. Lt. Henry is left at the end with much the same nothing sensed by the middle-aged waiter in "A Clean, Well-Lighted Place," by Santiago in *The Old Man and the Sea*, and by the protagonists depicted by Hemingway in a book of short stories entitled, appropriately enough, *Winner Take Nothing*. Henry takes the nothing with which A *Farewell to Arms* ends and out of it performs the artist's task of making his tale, whose conclusion rings with his own words of advice: "There isn't anything, dog." If a cosmic boom-bust cycle is suggested here, so is the ploy of an intricate modernist writer like John Barth, who introduces his *Lost in the Funhouse* with the makings of a Mobius strip whose twisted continuous message reads—"ONCE UPON A TIME THERE WAS A STORY THAT BEGAN ONCE UPON A TIME THERE WAS A STORY THAT BEGAN ONCE . . . ." Hemingway's novel dwindles to the nothingness of Catherine's death and then springs to full life out of the disruptive force of that nothingness and then again dwindles to the point of nothing. . . . The mutual inclusiveness of this kind of cycle parallels Heidegger who declares: "The old proposition *ex nihilo nihil fit* will then acquire a different meaning, and one appropriate to the problem of Being itself, so as to run: *ex nihilo omne ens qua ens fit*: every being, so far as it is a being, is made out of nothing. Only in the Nothingness of *Da-sein* can what-is-in-totality . . . come to itself."[22]

The true conclusion of A *Farewell to Arms*, the one Hemingway sweated to conceive and perfect, consists of the fourth segment of the last chapter. This short segment is characterized by extraordinary dramatic compression, by a succinct recapitualization of leading motifs, by implicative understatement, by a high percentage of negating phrases, and by the final effect of dwindling away to nothing, with a seeming rupture of chronological time. (It should be said that the first three segments of the last chapter pay full attention to chronological and biological time, using Frederic Henry's three dull meals and Catherine's labor pains as metronomic devices.)

The action of this conclusion makes it as much a playlet as "Today Is Friday." The action begins with the surgeon's explanatory regrets and his offer, which is rejected, to take Henry to his hotel. The second part consists of Henry's forcible entrance into the room containing Catherine's body and his ejection of both nurses: " 'You get out,' I said. 'The other one too.' " In the third section he shuts the door, deliberately turns out the light, and makes his unsatisfactory, inexplicit farewell to arms. The final element of action, a kind of one-sentence coda, marks his exit from the hospital and his lonely walk in the rain toward the hotel. To manage all of this activity (in one hundred and ninety-seven words) without seeming to hurry it and mar the presentation, to compress the events in a manner consonant with the inherent emotional tension—these are considerable artistic achievements.

The supreme touch in the conclusion, however, is the provision of a single encapsulating image in the line "It was like saying good-by to a statue." This is an independent creation, based on nothing, which attempts to metaphorize beyond the bounds of knowing, to enclose being and nothingness. As mentioned before, Hemingway shifted that line around in the variants he wrote, trying to find its proper position, and finally deciding on penultimate placement. Out of the very last line of the novel—"After a while I went out and left the hospital and walked back to the hotel in the rain"—Kenneth Burke fashions a renewal reading, in which the rain signifies sorrow and rebirth. "Add to that," Burke says, "the fact that the hero is there returning in the rain to his hotel. Does not such a destination stand for the potentiality of new intimacies?"[23] Although that reading may have merit on its own, it receives no support from the variant conclusions Hemingway wrote.[24]

The image of the statue is more deserving of close attention than the rain in this instance. The truth about death and marriage (and E. M. Forster seems to find little difference between them) as subjects of novelistic conclusion is that, in a sense, all novels end in death. When the book is closed, all of the characters "die," no matter their fictive status. The magical advantage literature has over human life is that we can open the book again and all the characters will pop back into full-blown life. The truth is that all novelists create to murder, and in some instances murder to create. Hemingway reduces Catherine Barkley to the level of a cold piece of stone, but an artistically shaped stone. The Pygmalion myth is here acted out in reverse, and then put right again. For out of that "statue" of the penultimate line of A Farewell to Arms springs the entire warm and loving story that constitutes the novel, a story told years after its occurrence. Out of the dread nothingness of Catherine's death, which takes Frederic Henry and the reader to the edge of the abyss, is fashioned "what-is-in-totality" the novel.

The art wisdom implicit in the conclusion of A Farewell to Arms is critically revealed in Henry James's statement of the central problem of ending novels, which he made in the preface to Roderick Hudson: "He [the writer] is in the perpetual predicament that the continuity of things is the whole matter for him, of comedy and tragedy; that this continuity is never broken, and that, to do anything at all, he has at once intensely to consult and intensely ignore it." As the variant endings here examined indicate, Hemingway struggled mightily with the problem of breaking and yet not breaking continuity in his narrative design. His solution to the problem in A Farewell to Arms amounts to a latter-day exemplification of James's astute directive on literary conclusions: "Really, universally, relations stop nowhere, and the exquisite problem of the artist is eternally but to draw, by a geometry of his own, the circle within which they shall happily *appear* to do so."[25]

Example Endings

EXAMPLE: "The Religious Ending" from Letter of November 18

> You learn a few things as you go along and one of them is never to go back
> to places. It is a good thing too not to try [and] too much to remember very
> fine things [too much] because if you do you wear them out and you lose
> them.* A valuable thing too is never to let anyone know how [how] fine you
> thought anyone else ever was because they know better and no one was ever
> that splendid. You see the wisdom of the priest at [our] the mess who has
> always loved God and so is happy. And no one can take God away from him.
> But how much is wisdom and how much is luck to be [built] born that way?
> And what if you are not built that way?

EXAMPLE: "The Live-Baby Ending"—"I could tell about the boy. He did
not seem of any importance then except as trouble and God knows that I
was bitter about him. Anyway he does not belong in this story. He starts
a new one [story]. It is not fair to start a new story at the end of an old one
but that is the way it happens. There is no end except death and birth is
the only beginning."

EXAMPLE: "The Funeral Ending"—"After people die you have to bury
them but you do not have to write about it. You do not have to write about
an undertaker nor the business of burial in a foreign country. Nor do you
have to write about that day and the next night nor the day after nor the
night after nor all the days after and all the nights after while numbness
[becomes] turns to sorrow and sorrow blunts with use. In writing you have
a certain choice that you do not have in life."

EXAMPLE: The Original Basis for "The *Scribner's Magazine* Ending"

> There are a great many more details, starting with [the] my first meeting
> with an undertaker and all the business of burial in a foreign country and
> continuing on with the rest of my life—which has gone on and [will probably]
> seems likely to go on for a long time. I could tell how Rinaldi [recovered
> from] was cured of the syphilis and lived to [learn] find that the technique
> acquired in wartime surgery is [rarely employed] not of much practical use
> in peace. I could tell how the priest in our mess lived to be a priest in Italy
> under Fascism. I could tell how Ettore became a Fascist and the part he took
> in [Fascism] that organization. I could tell [what] the kind of singer whatsis
> name became. [I could tell how I made a fool of myself by going back to
> Italy.] I could tell about how Piani [became] got to be a taxi driver in [xxxxx]
> New York. But they are all parts of [an old story] something that was finished.

---

*Brackets and parentheses are used to indicate authorial deletions.

I [suppose it was finished at the Tagliamento] do not know exactly where but certainly finished. Piani was the least finished but he went to another country. Italy is a country that [a man] every man should love once. I loved it once and lived through it. You ought to love it once. There is less loss of dignity in loving it young or, I suppose, living in it [or at least live in it,] is something like the [utility] need for the classics. I could tell what I have done since March nineteen hundred and eighteen [and] when I walked that night in the rain [alone, and always from then on alone, through the streets of Lausanne] back to the hotel where Catherine and I had lived and went upstairs to our room and undressed and got into bed and slept, finally, because I was so tired—to wake in the morning with the sun shining; [and] then suddenly to realize what [had happened] it was that had happened. I could tell what has happened since then. [The world goes on but only seems to stand still for certain people] but that is the end of the story.

End

[Lots of] Many things have happened. Things happen all the time. [xxxxx] Everything blunts and the world keeps on. You get most of your life back like goods recovered from a fire. It all keeps on as long as your life keeps on and then it keeps on. It never stops. It only stops for you. [A lot] Some of it stops while you are still alive. [A lot] The rest goes on and you go on with it. [You can stop a story anytime. Where you stop it is the end of that] On the other hand you have to stop a story. You stop it at the end of whatever it was you were writing about.

EXAMPLE: Variant of "*The* Ending"

They went out and I shut the door and turned off the light. The window was open and I [could] heard it raining in the courtyard. [It wasn't any good. She was gone. What was there was not her.] After a while I said goodbye and went away. It was like saying goodbye to a statue. But I did not want to go. I looked out the window. It was still raining hard. Blessed are the dead that the rain falls on, I thought. Why was that? I went back. Good-bye, I said. I have to go I think. It wasn't any good. I knew it wasn't any good. I thought if I could get them all out and we could be alone we would still be together. But it wasn't [not like that] any good. It was like saying goodbye to a statue.

Notes

1.   For a discussion of the original opening of the novel and the subsequent composition of the published opening, see Bernard Oldsey, "The Genesis of A Farewell to Arms," *Studies in American Fiction*, 5 (Autumn 1977), 175–185.

2.   Carlos Baker, *Ernest Hemingway: A Life Story* (NY: Scribner's, 1969), p. 201. In his *Hemingway: The Writer As Artist* (Princeton, NJ: Princeton University Press, 1952). Baker declares, "There is a persistent tradition that the present ending was rewritten seventeen times before Hemingway got the corrected galley-proof aboard the boat-train" (p. 97).

3.   Philip Young and Charles W. Mann, *The Hemingway Manuscripts: An Inventory* (Univer-

sity Park: Pennsylvania State University Press, 1969), pp. 11–12. Item 5-F in this inventory describes a three-page manuscript ending in which the baby lives; Item 5-H mentions only that there are "Different versions of ending" attached to the foul galleys set for the *Scribner's Magazine* publication of the novel; and Item 5-J merely adds that "four more endings of the novel" are attached to two galleys dated June 4, 1929. If this information seems somewhat vague, it should be said in fairness to Young and Mann that their inventory was meant to be an "interim report," as they declare in their preface, "and not the much more elaborate catalogue . . . that should be made when the papers have reached their permanent repository."

    4. (NY: Scribner's, 1962), p. 75.

    5. See the Hemingway Collection, John F. Kennedy Library, specifically Items 64 and 70. The first item is the manuscript of the novel as first finished; the second is a series of drafts for an ending (some forty pages in manuscript and typescript). See also Michael Reynolds, *Hemingway's First War* (Princeton, NJ: Princeton University Press, 1977), pp. 46–48.

    6. These materials (found in Items 64, 65, 70, and 73 of the Hemingway Collection) are cited by permission of Mrs. Mary Hemingway and the Kennedy Library.

    7. Used with a slightly contradictory connotation in the title of this essay, this phrase is borrowed from Frank Kermode's challenging analysis of apocalyptic literary conclusions: *The Sense of an Ending: Studies in the Theory of Fiction* (NY: Oxford University Press, 1967).

    8. Ernest Hemingway, *A Farewell to Arms*, Modern Standard Authors ed. (NY: Scribner's, 1953), p. 343. (All subsequent references are to this easily available and reliable edition).

    9. This variant has been published by Reynolds in *Hemingway's First War*, p. 294.

    10. See Philip Young and Charles W. Mann, "Fitzgerald's *Sun Also Rises:* Notes and Comment," *Fitzgerald / Hemingway Annual 1970* (Washington, DC: NCR / Microcard Editions, 1970), pp. 1–9. See also Item 77 of the Hemingway Collection, which contains Fitzgerald's comments on an early form of the novel, probably Item 65, the original typescript and setting copy of *A Farewell to Arms*.

    11. As reprinted in George Perkins' *The Theory of the American Novel* (NY: Holt, Rinehart and Winston, 1970), p. 334.

    12. See note 5; Reynolds, pp. 46–48.

    13. There is a date established for Item 64, the manuscript copy of the novel (see note 14 below); but the great bulk of the variants, found in Item 70, are not dated.

    14. See Reynolds, pp. 50 and 285.

    15. Kenneth Burke, *A Grammar of Motives and A Rhetoric of Motives*, a double-volume ed. (Cleveland, OH: World Publishing, 1962); this material comes from the second volume, p. 850.

    16. In George Plimpton's interview with the author, "Ernest Hemingway: The Art of Fiction XXI," *The Paris Review*, 18 (Spring 1958), 84.

    17. E. M. Forster, *Aspects of the Novel* (NY: Harcourt, Brace, 1954, a reissue of the original 1927 edition), p. 95.

    18. Forster, pp. 168–169.

    19. As quoted by Frank Kermode in *The Sense of an Ending*, p. 174.

    20. Kermode, p. 175.

    21. Martin Heidegger, *Existence and Being* (Chicago, IL: Henry Regnery, 1960), p. 331; for other elements of his discussion paraphrased and quoted here, see pp. 326–344.

    22. Heidegger, p. 345.

    23. Burke, *A Rhetoric of Motives*, p. 851.

    24. As indicated throughout this essay, most of the concluding attempts are full of negation and rejection; and even those that indicate a continuance of life for the protagonist do so with the traumatized admission that "all that was gone now" and "it will never be that way again."

    25. Henry James, *Roderick Hudson* (1907; rpt. NY: Augustus M. Kelley, 1971), p. vii.

CENSORSHIP

♦

[To Maxwell Perkins, 7 June 1929]

ERNEST HEMINGWAY

Dear Max,

I got the proofs two days ago. They were held up at the Customs because the notation "Proofs for Correction" was made in such small type—without capitals—on the label that the Customs People did not notice it. I cleared them at the Customs and was on them all day yesterday and today.

I am sorry to have made you so much trouble having the corrections made on the original galleys copied.

I find many more suggested—some of them very good, others sad when it makes no difference. I am glad always to make it conventional as to punctuation. About the words—I have made a notation at the side about the bed pan. Originally I had about 2,000 words of that aspect of hospital life. It really *dominates* it. I cut it all out with the exception of the one reference to the bed pan.

It is the same with other words.

You say they have not been in print before—one may not have—but the others are all in Shakespeare.

But more recently you will find them in a book called All Quiet on the Western Front [by Erich Maria Remarque] which Scott gave me and which has sold in the 100s of thousand copies in Germany and is around 50,000 copies in England with the word shit, fart etc. never dragged in for coloring but only used a few times for the thousands of times they are omitted. Please read the statement on page 15 of that book.

The trouble is Max that before my book will be out there will be this All Quiet on the Western Front book and possibly at the same time the second volume of the man [Arnold Zweig] who wrote Sergeant Grischa—who knows his eggs also—and I hate to kill the value of mine by emasculating it. When I looked up in the Quiet on W. F. book to find the words to show you I had a very hard time finding them. They don't stand out.

There has always been first rate writing and then American writing (genteel writing). But you should not go backwards. If a word can be printed and is needed in the text it is a *weakening* to omit it. If it *cannot* be printed without the book being suppressed all right.

No one that has read the Mss. has been shocked by *words*. The words do not stand out unless you put a ring around them.

There is no good my pleading the case in a letter. You know my viewpoint on it. What would have happened if they had cut the Sun also? It would have flopped as a book and I would have written no more for you.

The first place you say you think a word must go is in galley 13. I can consider you leaving that a blank, but in galley 51 where the same word is used by Piani if that is cut out it is pretty ruinous—I don't consent and it's done over my head.

On galley 57 a word is used that is used again at the top of galley 60. If you think this word will cause the suppression of the book make it C——S——R. You see I have kept out all the words that are the constant vocabulary—but have given the sense of them by using once, twice or three times the real words. Using then only the most classic words. You know what General Cambronne said at the battle of Waterloo instead of "the old guard dies but never surrenders." He said *Merde* when they called on him to surrender.

In a purely conversational way in a latin language in an argument one man says to another "Cogar su madre!"

You see there is nothing wrong with any of the words I have used except the last—the one on galley 57—which is used as an expression of supreme insult and contempt. The others are common enough and I dare say will all be in print in U. S. A. before the year is out.

It's unsatisfactory to write this and I hope you don't think I'm getting snooty about it. I wish we could talk and you could tell me just how far you *can* go and what the danger is. I do not want trouble—But want everything that can be had without trouble. I thought you said that if I accepted certain blanks etc. for the serialization the book would be published as it was. I see in the 2nd installment cuts made without my knowledge but am of course in their hands.

Anyway am working all the time on this proof and will get it back to you as soon as possible—By a boat the first of the week.

I hope you got the signed sheets O.K. I mailed them about a week ago. Am enclosing the contract.

Yours always
Ernest Hemingway

P.S.

About the place in the galley 38 where F. H. is talking to the hospital matron—I don't know what to do—it is supposed to be the deliberate insult and rout-ing of a person through the use of direct language that she expected by her sex and position never to be exposed to—the final forced conflict between someone from the front and someone of the genteel base. Is the word so impossible of printing? If it is, the incident is killed. It was the one word I remember we omitted from the Sun. Maybe if it had been printed then we'd know now if it was printable.

If you decide that it is unprintable how bout b——ls. I think that's the only solution. I suppose on galley 57 C——S——RS and C——ks——r will do for the other too, galley 60. Certainly those letters cannot corrupt anyone who has not heard or does not know the word. There's no proof it isn't cocksure.

Censorship

Scott Donaldson

Most of Ernest Hemingway's books were banned in one place or another, at one time or another.[1] A *Farewell to Arms* was banned in Boston, or, rather, the second installment of a six-part serial version of the novel running in *Scribner's Magazine* was banned there on June 20, 1929, by police chief Michael H. Crowley, who brought his wide expertise in such matters to bear and pronounced the book "salacious." Though his ruling barred distribution of the magazine by Boston booksellers and newsstands for the run of the serial over the next four months, it had little or no effect on the overall circulation figures of the magazine and undoubtedly served to stimulate sales of the book when it was published on September 27. But the police chief's action did help resolve an incipient dispute between Hemingway and his publishers in the latter's favor and to shape the final version of the novel. The most idiotic censorships often have unfortunate consequences.

Maxwell Perkins rarely laid a glove on Hemingway's prose, once the author had become a property Scribners (the book publishers) could both market and be proud of. But in the early years he and Hemingway were often at odds over the language of his books. Perkins was thrust into the position of mediator between his old-guard conservative publishers, as personified by the strait-laced figure of Charles Scribner, and a young writer who took it as his duty to set down the way people talked, even if that led him into the realm of obscenity. If it is true that Perkins was an "editor of genius," as his biographer A. Scott Berg calls him, it was in this capacity of middleman, quieting the outraged sensibilities of old Scribner while soothing the outsized ego of young Hemingway. "Do ask him for the absolute minimum of necessary changes, Max," Fitzgerald had implored their editor in connection with *The Sun Also Rises*.[2] That was sound advice, for Hemingway early and late resisted any change in his copy. But at the same time, Perkins worked for a man who "would no sooner allow profanity in one of his books than he would invite friends to use his parlor as a toilet. . . ." Faced with this dilemma, Perkins first persuaded Scribners to publish *The Sun Also Rises*, dirty words and all ("We took it with misgivings," he reported

Originally published in *Studies in American Fiction*, 19 (Spring 1991), 85–93. Reprinted by permission of *Studies in American Fiction* and Northeastern University.

after the editorial conference) on the grounds that the firm would suffer if knowledge of their rejecting *Sun* got about among young writers.[3] Then he started working on Hemingway to eliminate some of the objectionable verbiage. Out came even the suggestion of *shitty*, in Bill Gorton's Irony and Pity jingle. Out came the bulls' *balls*, to be replaced by more acceptable *horns*. Out came the explicit reference to Henry *James'* bicycle.

It was some trick, this balancing act between author and publisher, and in the context it became clear that Perkins' own sensibilities often lay close to those of his employer. People were now attacking books on the grounds "of 'decency' which means *words*," he wrote Hemingway. "In view of this, I suggest that a particular adjunct of the bulls referred to a number of times . . . be not spelled out, but covered by a blank."[4] Hemingway might write openly of the bulls' balls, but Perkins could not bring himself to put the word on paper.

Three years later, editor and author were once more engaged in the same kind of charade. On a February 1929 visit to Key West, Perkins read the script of *A Farewell to Arms* between fishing excursions on the Gulf Stream. He liked the book very much, but recognized the problems it might pose. "BOOK VERY FINE BUT DIFFICULT IN SPOTS," he wired New York. Later, in a letter to Charles Scribner, he expanded on the point: "It is Hemingway's principle both in life and literature never to flinch from facts, and it is in that sense only, that the book is difficult. It isn't at all erotic, although love is represented as having a very large physical element."[5] Here Perkins began to sound for the first time, in house, like Hemingway's advocate; during their long days on the Gulf Stream, he must have succumbed to some of the writer's famous charm. A few weeks thereafter he offered Hemingway $16,000 for a serial of *Farewell* in *Scribner's Magazine*.

Along with the contract for the serial, however, came a catch. *Scribner's* was a family magazine. Schools used it for "collateral reading," and in those schools were girls as well as boys. Ernest would therefore understand that certain words "must be concealed by a white space" and that "several little passages" might have to be omitted later, though not in the first installment.[6] In the glow of the $16,000, the highest price yet paid by *Scribner's* for a serialization, he consented to understand, but he did insist on one *caveat*: "What I ask is that when omissions are made a blank or some sign of omission" appear to indicate the cut.[7]

Soon enough that proviso was ignored, to Hemingway's consternation. Early in March he read through the galleys of the second (June) installment and found that the magazine had made two significant cuts without consulting him and (in one case) without indicating the deletions by way of blank spaces or even dots. Blanks were used for the officers' "——— house" and for "son of a ———" and even for a randy dog "in ———," but no such space was left in the crucial passage of omitted dialogue between Frederic and Catherine where he successfully persuades her to make love. "I'd rather return the money and call it all off than have arbitrary eliminations made without any mention of the fact they are being made," Hemingway angrily wrote Perkins. He especially objected to this omission because "the result in dialogue does not make sense—two consecutive sentences are left as . . . both spoken by the same person," an observation that should be kept in mind when debating the confusion of voices in "A Clean, Well-Lighted Place."[8]

In smoothing things over, Perkins disingenuously maintained that the cut "was made for only the one reason of simplifying things and speeding them up. . . . There is, and was, and never will be, any idea of making any change without your approval; and I doubt if there will be any change except for a few blanks hereafter, anyhow." Besides, he promised, it would be different with the book. On April 16, Perkins wrote again to say that they were setting up *Farewell* for book publication and following the original copy exactly.[9]

Or almost exactly, anyway. Still at issue was Hemingway's use of barracks language, including—so legend has it—three words so offensive to Perkins that he could not jot them down for Charles Scribner.[10] The situation was complicated by the publication early in 1929 of Erich Maria Remarque's worldwide bestseller *All Quiet on the Western Front*. Remarque freely used just those words (or their German equivalents) most common among soldiers, including the ubiquitous "f" word. For Hemingway to do otherwise, he argued in a June 7 letter to Perkins, would only weaken his text. But he offered a way out, a way that the events in Boston two weeks later were to make available to his publishers: "If it [any given word] *cannot* be printed without the book being suppressed all right."[11]

As Paul S. Boyer observed in *Purity in Print*, "Massachusetts censorship came over on the *Mayflower*," and up to the mid-1920's it was a serious matter for a book to be banned in Boston. The suppression of undesirable books during the late nineteenth century and through the Progressive period was but one of the activities of the highly respected Watch and Ward Society. Supported by the city's Brahmins, the Society also functioned as an "agency of reform and uplift, fighting prostitution, narcotics, gambling, and municipal corruption." From 1918 to 1925, the Society ran its book censorship operation under the aegis of the "Boston Booksellers' Committee," a group made up of three booksellers and three Watch and Ward directors. They read current novels and determined which ones could and could not be sold by Massachusetts book dealers. From fifty to seventy-five books were banned in this way, usually without any objection or publicity whatever. But the old-settler Protestant Watch and Ward Society gradually lost power to the Irish Catholic majority, and after 1926 the task of censoring books fell to the police. That was the beginning of the end, for police suppressions, including that of Dreiser's *An American Tragedy*, invited both legal action and national scorn. On April 16, 1929, two months before the *Farewell* ban, the city's literati held their annual banquet and frolic at Ford Hall, a gathering "By Undesirables—For Undesirables," presided over by Harvard historian Arthur M. Schlesinger as "Master of Rebelry" and celebrating such recently suppressed writers as H. G. Wells, Conrad Aiken, John Dos Passos, Sherwood Anderson, Sinclair Lewis, Dreiser, and Hemingway himself, for *The Sun Also Rises*. By the time the police clamped down on *Farewell*, the phrase "Banned in Boston" had become something of a joke. "Their law is such that intelligent people in Massachusetts oppose it," as Perkins wrote Hemingway after the ban; ". . . Irish Catholics rule the town."[12]

The *Boston Evening Globe* paid little or no attention to the removal of *Scribner's Magazine* from the newsstands on June 20. The big censorship story of that week involved Edward J. Fitzhugh, Jr. of Boise, Idaho, a Harvard senior, editor of the *Advocate*, and author of a prize-winning class hymn "sung in all solemnity" on the Sunday before commencement. Someone belatedly noticed that the first letters in the sixteen-line hymn, read as an acrostic, "spelled out four words which were in themselves obscene and profane and which slurred the high sentiments expressed in the hymn." For this crime, the authorities, who had after all selected Fitzhugh's hymn as the best submitted, summarily dismissed the senior on the day before graduation.[13] That sort of nose-thumbing was not to be tolerated, and there were those who regarded Hemingway's novel as a similar attempt to shock the eminently respectable. "Naughty Ernest," Harry Hansen chided in his *New York World* column. And from across the Atlantic, some months later, J. B. Priestley tartly observed that "literature is not a matter of pleasing Aunt Susan. But we must also remember that it is equally not a matter of simply shocking Aunt Susan."[14]

The New York Times gave the Boston Ban page-two coverage and asked Scribner's to respond to the charge of salaciousness. Speaking for the firm, Alfred Dashiell declared its confidence in the integrity of the author and his work:

> The ban of the sale of the magazine in Boston is an evidence of the improper use of censorship which bases its objections upon certain passages without taking into account the effect and purpose of the story as a whole. "A Farewell to Arms" is in its effect distinctly moral. It is the story of a fine and faithful love born, it is true, of physical desire.
>
> If good can come from evil, if the fine can grow from the gross, how is a writer effectually to depict the progress of this evolution if he cannot describe the conditions from which the good evolved? If white is to be contrasted with black, thereby emphasizing its whiteness, the picture cannot be all white.[15]

"Vive Dashiell!" Hemingway commented. "That was a statement to ring men's hearts."[16] Yet despite the eloquence of the "if good can come from evil" argument, the statement hardly qualified as a ringing defense of civil liberties. It objected only to "the improper use of censorship," not to censorship itself. It insisted not on the right to publication of the novel but on its underlying morality. *The New York Herald Tribune* took a more appropriate stance: "Many readers had doubtless missed Mr. Hemingway's powerful story," the paper commented editorially, "and they will be grateful to the [Boston police] chief for calling their attention to it."[17]

As for Scribners, they had no legal recourse against the ban, Massachusetts law being the way it was, but were not unduly troubled by the action against the magazine. Probably Hemingway was more disturbed by word of the censorship than Perkins. For one thing, Perkins suspected that the intervention might be commercially advantageous to the book. Personally he hated the publicity, which "brought a frivolous and prejudicial attention to one aspect of a book which is deeply significant and beautiful," he wrote Hemingway, but he also realized that it might turn out to be "greatly helpful."[18] For another thing, the trouble in Boston gave him a bargaining chip in his ongoing discussion with the author about his use of objectionable words.

"This incident affects the possibility of book suppression," Perkins noted in a letter written one week after the Boston ban. "There are things in the book that were never in another . . . since the 18th century anyway. . . . All right then! But I don't think we can print those three words, Ernest. I can't find *anyone* who thinks so. That supreme insult alone might turn a judge right around against us, and to the post office, it and the others, I think, would warrant (technically) action. It would be a dirty shame to have you associated in a way with . . . people who write with an eye to tickle a cheap public." Two weeks later he took up the cause again. There remained "considerable anxiety for fear of the federal authorities being stirred up. They seem to take curious activity of late, and if the post office should object, we would be in Dutch."[19]

In fact there was some validity behind Perkins' assertions, expedient though they certainly were in dealing with his unruly author. Ever since the Tariff of 1842, United States Customs officials had been empowered to confiscate shipments of incoming books they regarded as obscene. Naturally the sensibilities of local Customs inspectors varied widely: "A classic is a dirty book somebody is trying to get by me," one vigilant examiner commented in 1930, adding that in the preceding two years he had barred "272 different titles." Some cases were brought on appeal to the United States Customs Bureau, which in mid-1929 ruled against admitting the unexpurgated British edition of *All Quiet on the Western Front* (Little, Brown published a sanitized version for American readers). But Customs censorship obviously threatened overseas books more than ones printed in the United States. Here the Post Office was more to be feared, especially in the light of an April

1929 court decision against Mary Ware Dennett's pamphlet *The Sex Side of Life: An Explanation for Young People.* Mrs. Dennett told where the sex organs were and what they did, denied that masturbation was necessarily harmful, and celebrated the pleasures of sexual intercourse. The Post Office not only banned the pamphlet from the mails but brought court action against Mrs. Dennett for continuing to mail it under first-class seal. At the trial a Brooklyn clergyman took vigorous exception to the pamphlet's assertion that sexual intercourse was "the very greatest physical pleasure to be had in all human experience." Nursing a baby was far more pleasurable, he declared. Challenged on the point (how could he possibly know?), he said he knew this to be true because his wife had told him so.[20]

In other words, the federal authorities *had* been busy censoring books in recent months, and Perkins made sure that Hemingway knew of his publisher's concern. The message got across. In a letter to Fitzgerald, Hemingway observed that "Max sounded scared. If they get scared now and lay off the book I'll be out of luck." He had not asked for an advance on the novel, but now he wished he had, since "it is more difficult to lay off a book if they have money tied up in it already."[21] Then in a July 26 letter to Perkins, he capitulated entirely in the three words in dispute. Scribners could go ahead and blank out the word *balls* as spoken to Miss Van Campen, the word *shit* spoken by Piani before leaving Gorizia, and the word *cocksucker*, the "supreme insult" spoken by Piani when Aymo is shot by the Italian rear guard and by Lieutenant Henry when arrested by the battle police. "I understand . . . about the words you cannot print—if you cannot print them—and I never expected you could print the one word (C——S) that you cannot and that lets me out."[22] As it happens, yet another word (*fuck*) was almost certainly blanked out (pp. 206, 207) along with several instances of *shit* (not one) on various pages, and Hemingway later substituted *scrotum* for *balls*, thus averting a blank space, but after the letter of July 26, it was clear that Perkins—and Scribners—had come to terms with Ernest Hemingway.[23]

Of course it was not merely barracks talk that troubled Scribners and was to trouble conservative readers and critics. The love affair between Frederic and Catherine, unsanctioned by the church ("All right then!"), probably aroused more sentiment against the book than its language and was unquestionably responsible for police chief Crowley's edict of suppression. Magazine readers canceled their subscriptions rather than risk exposure to such "venereal fiction." Right-thinking commentators lamented that a writer obviously capable of higher things should choose to depict such "lustful indulgence" and, worse yet, depict it in a sympathetic light. Still others were critical of Frederic's "separate peace," since desertion by any name could not be condoned. A few inveighed against the author's outspoken use of obstetrical details, for "a lot of this biological and pathological data is neither necessary nor particularly relevant." And as Hemingway had feared, many Italians were offended, possibly because they did not see his disclaimer in *Scribner's Magazine* that the novel was not autobiographical and no more intended as a criticism of Italy or Italians than *Two Gentlemen of Verona.*[24] There was something in *Farewell*, it seemed, to offend almost everyone.

Still, Perkins was right about the publicity generating sales. *Farewell* was published late in September in a first printing of 31,050 copies, more than five times the 6,000 first run of *The Sun Also Rises*, and by November it was on most of the bestseller lists. Much of the critical commentary was highly favorable, and several reviewers made a point of deploring the suppression of the magazine version in Boston. "Boston has banned the story, but the rest of the country seems to think it is pretty fine," as the *Tulsa Tribune* commented.[25] For whatever reason, the Boston censors took no action against the book, though it was more explicit about Frederic and Catherine's lovemaking than the serial. The Post Office caused no trouble, either. *Farewell* was banned as a book only in Italy.

But this was not an unambiguous happy ending to the censoring of *Scribner's Magazine* by the Boston police chief. Financially, no one was really hurt. Nor were readers deprived of the pleasure of reading *A Farewell to Arms*, the book by virtue of which—according to Hemingway's friend Archibald MacLeish, who had no difficulty obtaining the magazine serial in western Massachusetts—Hemingway became "the great novelist of our time."[26] But there are ways and ways that censorship, and beyond and beneath it the threat of censorship, can affect the final version of a work of art. For better or worse, Hemingway undoubtedly produced a somewhat different novel as a consequence of what happened in Boston and what he feared might happen elsewhere. Specifically, he backtracked on his conviction that fictional soldiers could only emerge as real on the page if they spoke and acted like real ones. Robert Herrick, in his diatribe against the novel entitled "What Is Dirt?" in November of 1929, concluded that in his view "no great loss to anybody would result if *A Farewell to Arms* had been suppressed."[27] He could not have known that in a very real sense, Hemingway's novel already had been.

Notes

1. For a partial listing of censorings, see Anne Lynn Haight, *Banned Books* (New York: Bowker, 1970), pp. 89–90.

2. Quoted in Scott Donaldson, "The Wooing of Ernest Hemingway," *AL*, 53 (1982), 705–06.

3. See A. Scott Berg, *Max Perkins: Editor of Genius* (New York: Dutton, 1978), pp. 95–98.

4. Quoted in Michael S. Reynolds, "Words Killed, Wounded, Missing in Action," *HN*, 6 (Spring, 1981), 4.

SCOTT DONALDSON ♦ 77

5. Berg, p. 141.
6. Maxwell Perkins to Ernest Hemingway, February 13, 1929, Firestone Library, Princeton.
7. Ernest Hemingway to Maxwell Perkins, c. February 16, 1929, Firestone Library, Princeton.
8. Ernest Hemingway to Maxwell Perkins, March 11, 1929, Firestone Library, Princeton. The significant cuts Hemingway objected to appear in the serialization in *Scribner's Magazine*, 85 (June 1929), 651, where Rinaldi expounds on the difference "between taking a girl who has always been good and a woman"—these cuts indicated by dots—and the same issue, p. 724, where eight short speeches by Frederic and Catherine are deleted without any indication of ellipsis.
9. Maxwell Perkins to Ernest Hemingway, March 15, 1929, and April 16, 1929, Firestone Library, Princeton.
10. Berg, p. 142.
11. Ernest Hemingway to Maxwell Perkins, June 7, 1929, *Ernest Hemingway: Selected Letters, 1917–1961*, ed. Carlos Baker (New York: Scribners, 1981), pp. 296–98; reprinted in this volume.
12. This summary is drawn from "Banned in Boston," Chapter 7 of Paul S. Boyer, *Purity in Print: The Vice-Society Movement and Book Censorship in America* (New York: Scribners, 1968), pp. 167–206. Maxwell Perkins to Ernest Hemingway, July 12, 1929, Firestone Library, Princeton.
13. Fitzhugh's sad story appeared on the front page of the *Boston Evening Globe*, June 18, 1929. Harvard graduation took place the following day, the ban against *Farewell* the day after.
14. Hansen reiterated his charge when the book was published: "The First Reader," *New York World*, 27 September 1929, Scribners files, Firestone Library, Princeton. J. B. Priestley, *Now and Then*, 34 (Winter 1929), 11–12, reprinted in *Hemingway: The Critical Reception*, ed. Jeffrey Meyers (London: Routledge & Kegan Paul, 1982), pp. 136–37.
15. "Boston Police Bar Scribner's Magazine," *New York Times* (June 21, 1929), p. 2.
16. Ernest Hemingway to Maxwell Perkins, July 31, 1929.
17. Quoted in Boyer, p. 195.
18. Maxwell Perkins to Ernest Hemingway, June 17, 1929, Firestone Library, Princeton.
19. Maxwell Perkins to Ernest Hemingway, July 12, 1929, Firestone Library, Princeton.
20. See Boyer, pp. 208–09, 238–41.
21. Ernest Hemingway to F. Scott Fitzgerald, July, 1929, Firestone Library, Princeton.
22. Ernest Hemingway to Maxwell Perkins, July 26, 1929, Firestone Library, Princeton.
23. The *scrotum* substitution appears in *A Farewell to Arms* (New York: Scribners, 1929), p. 144; see also Maxwell Perkins to Ernest Hemingway, August 14, 1929, Firestone Library, Princeton, in this connection. Significant blanks in place of objectionable words appear on pp. 189, 192, 206, 207, 213, 223.
24. John G. Neihardt, "Of Making Many Books," *St. Louis Post-Dispatch*, September 30, 1929; Review of *Farewell, Lexington* (Kentucky) *Herald*, December 1, 1929; Robert Herrick, "What is Dirt?" *Bookman*, 70 (November, 1929), 258–62, reprinted in part in *Ernest Hemingway: The Critical Reception*, ed. Robert O. Stephens (New York: Burt Franklin, 1977), pp. 86–89; George A. Anderson, "Chat About Books," Morgantown (West Virginia) *New Deal*, November 5, 1929; Review of *Farewell*, Tulsa *World*, December 1, 1929; "Scribner's," *Salt Lake Tribune*, May 26, 1929. All of these citations, except the Herrick

article in the *Bookman*, are drawn from clippings in the files of Scribners, Firestone Library, Princeton. Several of these clippings bear no page numbers.

25. Item in *Tulsa Tribune*, August 11, 1929, Scribners files, Firestone Library, Princeton.

26. Archibald MacLeish to Ernest Hemingway, September 1, 1929, *Letters of Archibald MacLeish, 1907 to 1982*, ed. R. H. Winnick (Boston: Houghton Mifflin, 1983), p. 230.

27. Robert Herrick, "What Is Dirt?" *Bookman*, 70 (November, 1929), 262, reprinted in *Ernest Hemingway: The Critical Reception*, p. 89.

REVIEWS
◆

A Fine American Novel

Clifton P. Fadiman

Recently there have been laid down a number of dicta anent what the modern novel may not do if it is to remain a modern novel. One of them is to the effect that a representation of a simple love affair is impossible in our day. Another tells us that it is difficult, if not impossible, to reproduce the emotion of male friendship or love, as the present shift in sex conventions tends to surround the theme with an ambiguous atmosphere. A third dictum concerns itself with the impossibility of true tragedy in contemporary literature. A fourth, not so much a stated law as a pervasive feeling, would insist on the irrelevance to our time of the "non-intellectual" or "primitive" novel. Now, none of these generalizations is silly; there is a great deal of truth in all of them. It just happens that Mr. Hemingway, quite unconsciously, has produced a book which upsets all of them at once and so makes them seem more foolish than they really are. Worse still, his book is not merely a good book but a remarkably beautiful book; and it is not merely modern, but the very apotheosis of a kind of modernism. Mr. Hemingway is simply one of those inconvenient novelists who won't take the trouble to learn the rules of the game. It is all very embarrassing.

Take the business of love, for example. Neither Catherine nor Henry in "A Farewell to Arms" is a very complicated person. They are pretty intelligent about themselves but they are not over self-conscious. There are few kinks in their natures. I don't suppose they could produce one mental perversion between them. They fall in love in a simple, healthy manner, make love passionately and movingly; and when Catherine dies the reader is quite well aware that he has passed through a major tragic experience. Their story seems too simple to be "modern"; yet it is as contemporary as you wish. It seems too simple to be interesting; yet it is gripping, almost heartbreaking. I don't think any complex explanations are in order. I offer the familiar one that Hemingway, almost alone among his generation, feels his material very deeply and that he never overworks that material. Understatement is not so much a method with him as an instinctive habit of mind. (It is more or less

Reprinted with permission from the *Nation* magazine 129 (30 October 1929), 497–98. © The Nation Co., Inc.

an accident that it also happens to harmonize with the contemporary anti-romantic tendency.) Consequently we believe in his love story.

Similarly with the second motif of the book: the emotion of male affection, exemplified in the relationship between Henry and Rinaldi. This is the most perilous theme of all. With some of us a fake Freudism has inclined our minds to the cynical. Others, simpler temperaments, inevitably think of comradeship in oozily sentimental terms, the Kipling strong-men-and-brothers-all business. Hemingway seems unaware of either attitude. Perhaps that unawareness partially explains his success. At any rate, without in any way straining our credulity he makes us feel that this very sense of comradeship—nordically reticent in Henry's case, blasphemously, ironically effusive in Rinaldi's—was one of the few things that mitigated the horror and stupidity of the war.

I have rarely read a more "non-intellectual" book than "A Farewell to Arms." This non-intellectuality is not connected with Hemingway's much-discussed objectivity. It is implicit in his temperament. He is that marvelous combination—a highly intelligent naïf. I do not mean that he writes without thought, for as a matter of obvious fact he is one of the best craftsmen alive. But he feels his story entirely in emotional and narrative terms. He is almost directly opposed in temper, for example, to Sherwood Anderson, who would like to give the effect of naïvete but can't because he is always thinking about his own simplicity. "A Farewell to Arms" revolves about two strong, simple feelings: love for a beautiful and noble woman, affection for one's comrades. When it is not concerned with these two feelings it is simply exciting narrative—the retreat from Caporetto, the nocturnal escape to Switzerland. The whole book exists on a plane of strong feeling or of thrilling human adventure. It is impossible to feel superior to Hemingway's primitiveness, his insensibility to "ideas," because he strikes no attitude. A large part of the novel deals with simple things—eating cheese, drinking wine, sleeping with women. But he does not try to make you feel that these activities are "elemental" or overly significant. They are just integral parts of a personality which is strong and whole. Therein lies their effect on us. It is impossible to be patronizing about Henry's, or Hemingway's, complete contemporaneity, his mental divorcement from the past, the antique, the classical, the gentlemanly, cultured tradition. "The frescoes were not bad," remarks the hero at one point. "Any frescoes were good when they started to peel and flake off." This is not merely humorous; it is the reflection of a mind reacting freshly, freely, with an irony that is modern, yet simple and unaffected.

"A Farewell to Arms" is not perfect by any means, nor, to me at least, interesting all the way through. I find the military descriptions dull, and for a paradoxical reason. Hemingway's crisp, curt, casual style, so admirably suited to the rest of his narrative, fails in the military portions because of these very qualities. It is too much like a regulation dispatch. Military reports have always been written in a sort of vulgar Hemingwayese; therefore they give no sense of novelty or surprise. But a detail like this does not matter much; the core of "A Farewell to Arms" remains untouched. It is certainly Hemingway's best book to date. There seems to be no reason why it should not secure the Pulitzer Prize for, despite the Italian setting, it is as American as Times Square. It is a real occasion for patriotic rejoicing.

Perfect Behavior

Donald Davidson

Ernest Hemingway's novel *A Farewell to Arms* is like a direct and most remarkable answer to the recent wish of Dr. Watson, prophet of behaviorism, that somebody would write a novel containing people who act in a lifelike and scientific manner. That is exactly what Mr. Hemingway does, with such astounding verity as to overwhelm, befuddle and profoundly impress all readers. Mr. Hemingway here is playing scientist, and he is watching people behave. It is a mistake to suppose that people behave morally or immorally, becomingly or unbecomingly. That is not the point at all: they merely behave. There is no good, no ill, no pretty, no ugly—only behavior. Behaviorism argues that there is stimulus and response, nothing else, and Mr. Hemingway's books contain (ostensibly, but not quite) nothing else. The novel is a bold and exceptionally brilliant attempt to apply scientific method to art, and I devoutly hope that all the scientists will read it and admire it immensely.

This comment on a book that is apparently taking the public by storm requires further demonstration, which I shall attempt to give.

Look first at the people of the book, who happen to be people, not cockroaches or mice, acting and reacting in wartime Italy rather than in a laboratory. But they are only people, not highly differentiated individuals. That is to say they are, in a manner of speaking, laboratory specimens. In the interest of the scientific "experiment" or observation, they must be as normal and average as possible, and so they are. It is regrettable, perhaps, that they are nice healthy creatures, not without animal charm (even if without souls), but we must presume that their occasional sufferings are in the interest of some scientific investigation which will eventually declare the "whole truth" about something, possibly war and love.

Thus we have first a Male with no characteristics other than might be noted in a description like this: Henry, Frederick; American; commissioned in Italian ambulance corps; speaks Italian (with accent); reactions, normally human. And then of course a Female: Barclay, Katherine; nurse; English; normally attractive and equipped with normal feminine reactions. The subordinate characters, too, are just as colorless: Rinaldi, Italian officer, inclined

Reprinted by permission of the *Tennessean* (3 November 1929), 7. Used with permission.

to be amorous; a priest, unnamed; other officers, soldiers, police, nurses, surgeons, bawdyhouse keepers and inmates, restaurant keepers, Swiss officials, family folk. All of these, notice, talk alike and all do nothing but behave, offering given responses to given stimuli.

Then we must have a situation. It is simply this. Put the Male and Female under the disorderly and rather uninviting conditions of war, including battle, wounds, hospitalization, return to the front, retreat and bring the Male and Female into propinquity now and then. What will happen?

I am tempted to describe what does happen—it is all, of course, "natural"—in such a catechism as James Joyce uses in one part of *Ulysses*. It would run something like this:

Question: What do soldiers do in war?

Answer: They fight, drink, eat, sleep, talk, obey commands, march, go on leave, visit brothels, are tired or sick or dead or alive, wonder when the next battle will be, sometimes meet respectable women, sometimes fall in love hastily.

Question: Was the same true in the case of Henry, Frederick?

Answer: It was invariably true.

Question: What do nurses do in a war?

Answer: They eat, sleep, drink, talk, obey commands, tend the wounded, are tired or sick or dead or alive, wonder when the next battle will be, sometimes meet attractive officers, sometimes fall in love hastily.

Question: Was the same true in the case of Barclay, Katherine?

Answer: It was invariably true.

Question: What not very special circumstances modified the case of Henry, Frederick?

Answer: He was wounded in the leg, and was thus entitled to prosecute a love affair with Barclay, Katherine.

Question: What wholly natural thing did Henry, Frederick do during the Caporetto retreat?

Answer: He retreated, was arrested, saw police shooting fugitives, jumped in the river, escaped, joined Katherine, quit the war, went to Switzerland.

Question: What not unnatural consequences to Barclay, Katherine, attended her love affair with Henry, Frederick?

Answer: Ineffective labor in childbirth, Caesarean operation, death.

Question: And what were the results for Henry, Frederick?

Answer: Results unknown. He merely walked back in the rain.

The application of the scientific method may be further demonstrated by a scrutiny of other features of the novel. A scientific report of events requires that there be no comment, no intrusion of private sentiments, no depreciation or apology. The "bare facts" must be given—or tabulated.

Therefore style (as style is generally known) is wiped out, or is reduced to its lowest, most natural, terms. It will take the form of simple, unelaborated predications, not unlike the sentences in a First Reader. For instance: The dog is black. The sky is blue. Katherine is pretty. I did not love Katherine at first but now I love Katherine. I drank the wine and it did not make me feel good. She was unconscious all the time and it did not take her very long to die.

And that, as I see it, is the gist of Mr. Hemingway's hypothetical case, which by the unthinking may be called an indictment of war or of civilization or an apology for free love or what you will. But its method does not justify any of these interpretations, however latently they may exist.

What of it, then? On the surface it is assuredly a most remarkable performance. To those who take pleasure in contemplating a world of mechanisms doing nothing but acting and reacting, it must be a nearly perfect book. Let us leave them with their admirations, which are no doubt justifiable under the circumstances.

But what of those who, without knowing exactly why, have an uneasy sense of dissatisfaction with Mr. Hemingway's book and ask for something more than a remarkably natural series of conversations, daydreams, and incidents? Mr. Hemingway's book will have plenty of defenders to fly up and condemn those who are dissatisfied. I want to supply a little ammunition to the dissatisfied, out of pure sympathy for the underdog if for no other reason.

First of all, don't complain about vulgarity or obscenity. There you lose the battle. For to a scientist, nothing is vulgar or obscene any more than it is genteel or pretty. And Mr. Hemingway apparently is trying to be a scientist. Attack him instead at the point where a fundamental contradiction exists. Can there be such a thing as a scientific work of art? The nature of the contradiction can be immediately seen. Mr. Hemingway could treat human affairs scientifically only in a scientific medium. That is, he would have to invent equations, symbols, vocabularies, hypotheses, laws, as scientists are in the habit of doing. By so doing he would achieve all the "reality" that science is capable of achieving—which might perhaps be of practical use, but could not be vended as a novel, even by so respectable a house as Charles Scribner's Sons.

Obviously Mr. Hemingway did not, could not, go to such a logical limit. He was forced to compromise by using the vocabulary and the forms of art. The minute he made the compromise, he failed fundamentally and outrageously. His novel is a splendid imitation, but only an imitation, of science. It is a hybrid beast, ill-begotten and sterile. It is a stunt, a tour de force, and no matter how blindingly brilliant, no matter how subtle in artifice, it is in effect a complete deception (possibly a self-deception) and can exist only as a kind of marvelous monstrosity.

Note that he falls short even of science. Committed to the form of the novel, he must be selective where science is inclusive. He cannot destroy his own personality and bias, for from his book we get the distinct impression that he wishes us to believe war is unheroic, life is all too frequently a dirty trick, and love may be a very deadly joke on the woman. Even in his effort to get away from style he creates a new style that is in effect a reaction against all decorative imagistic prose.

A Farewell to Arms, which is apparently intended to give us a perfect example of pure behavior, turns out after all to be only the behavior of Mr. Hemingway, stupendously overreaching himself in the effort to combine the role of artist and scientist and producing something exactly as marvelous and as convincing as a tragic sculpture done in butter.

Farewell and Return

B. E. TODD

There are two pictures, "The Soldier's Farewell" and "The Soldier's Return," reproductions of which may still be seen on the walls of inn-parlours. The first shows a young soldier saying good-bye to his relations, and the second his return as a wounded hero. They are both indicative of the glamour of war, and, though mildly pathetic, are in no way disturbing. There is, as a rule, a space on the wall between the two pictures—a space which seems to wait for a third one illustrating war. There is no such gap among our present-day word-pictures, as those who have read of the *quietness* of the Western Front will realize. And now, to assure us that there was no sweet hush on the Italian Front either, comes Mr. Hemingway's *A Farewell to Arms*. There is no glamour here, and few thrills: even the physical horrors described are not quite so ghastly as those in many war books. It is an epic of weariness.

The record of the young American who joined the Italian army is one of boredom, injustice, ineptitude, and waste. If more resentment or fury were shown by the victims of chaos the book would be correspondingly more bearable. But there is little of that in this tale of weariness, so laconically written. Even the conversations are those of men, stupefied and numbed by boredom:—"Listen. There is nothing so bad as war. We in the auto-ambulances cannot even realize at all how bad it is. When people realize how bad it is they cannot do anything to stop it because they go crazy. There are some people who never realize."

"I know it is bad, but we must finish it."

"It doesn't finish. There is no finish to a war." And so in the book there is no finish to the misery of the hero. When, after taking part in an authorized retreat, he is nearly shot for desertion, he abandons his arms and escapes into Switzerland, where he resumes a love-affair, begun at the front. All ends, as it began, in misery, and we are given a terrible glimpse of the horrors of birth worse than the previous ones of death by violence.

There may be cruder war books, but there are none gloomier than this very great one, which deserves a shelf of its own on that space on the wall, so that it can be used as an antidote to the sickly poison of glory and glamour.

Reprinted from *The Spectator* 143 (16 November 1929), 727.

[The "Best Written Book"]

John Dos Passos

Hemingway's *A Farewell to Arms* is the best written book that has seen the light in America for many a long day. By well-written I don't mean the tasty college composition course sort of thing that our critics seem to consider good writing. I mean writing that is terse and economical, in which each sentence and each phrase bears its maximum load of meaning, sense impressions, emotion. The book is a first-rate piece of craftsmanship by a man who knows his job. It gives you the sort of pleasure line by line that you get from handling a piece of well finished carpenter's work. Read the first chapter, the talk at the officers' mess in Goritzia, the scene in the dressing-station when the narrator is wounded, the paragraph describing the ride to Milan in the hospital train, the talk with the British major about how everybody's cooked in the war, the whole description of the disaster of Caporetto to the end of the chapter where the battlepolice are shooting the officers as they cross the bridge, the caesarian operation in which the girl dies. The stuff will match up as narrative prose with anything that's been written since there was any English language.

It's a darn good document too. It describes with reserve and exactness the complex of events back of the Italian front in the winter of 1916 and the summer and fall of 1917 when people had more or less settled down to the thought of war as the natural form of human existence when every individual in the armies was struggling for survival with bitter hopelessness. In the absolute degradation of the average soldier's life in the Italian army there were two hopes, that the revolution would end the war or that Meester Weelson would end the war on the terms of the Seventeen Points. In Italy the revolution lost its nerve at the moment of its victory and Meester Weelson's points paved the way for D'Annunzio's bloody farce at Fiume and the tyranny of Mussolini and the banks. If a man wanted to learn the history of that period in that sector of the European War I don't know where he'd find a better account than in the first half of *A Farewell to Arms*.

This is a big time for the book business in America. The writing, publishing and marketing of books is getting to be a major industry along

Reprinted from the *New Masses* 5 (December 1929), 16. Used with the permission of Elizabeth H. Dos Passos for the Estate of John Dos Passos.

with beautyshoppes and advertising. Ten years ago it was generally thought that all writers were either drunks or fairies. Now they have a halo of possible money around them and are respected on a par with brokers or realtors. The American people seems to be generally hungry for books. Even good books sell.

It's not surprising that *A Farewell to Arms*, that accidentally combines the selling points of having a lovestory and being about the war, should be going like hotcakes. It would be difficult to dope out just why there should be such a tremendous vogue for books about the war just now. Maybe it's that the boys and girls who were too young to know anything about the last war are just reaching a bookbuying age. Maybe it's the result of the intense military propaganda going on in schools and colleges. Anyhow if they read things like *A Farewell to Arms* and *All Quiet on the Western Front*, they are certainly getting the dope straight and it's hard to see how the militarist could profit much. Certainly a writer can't help but feel good about the success of such an honest and competent piece of work as *A Farewell to Arms*.

After all craftsmanship is a damn fine thing, one of the few human functions a man can unstintedly admire. The drift of the Fordized world seems all against it. Rationalization and subdivision of labor in industry tend more and more to wipe it out. It's getting to be almost unthinkable that you should take pleasure in your work, that a man should enjoy doing a piece of work for the sake of doing it as well as he damn well can. What we still have is the mechanic's or motorman's pleasure in a smoothrunning machine. As the operator gets more mechanized even that disappears; what you get is a division of life into drudgery and leisure instead of into work and play. As industrial society evolves and the workers get control of the machines a new type of craftsmanship may work out. For the present you only get opportunity for craftsmanship, which ought to be the privilege of any workman, in novelwriting and the painting of easelpictures and in a few of the machinebuilding trades that are hangovers from the period of individual manufacture that is just closing. Most of the attempts to salvage craftsmanship in industry have been faddy movements like East Aurora and Morris furniture and have come to nothing. *A Farewell to Arms* is no worse a novel because it was written with a typewriter. But it's a magnificent novel because the writer felt every minute the satisfaction of working ably with his material and his tools and continually pushing the work to the limit of effort.

A Farewell to Dramatization

Stark Young

For a long time it has been a platitude that turning novels into plays is a thankless job. It is something like lecturing to a university audience. If you are profoundly erudite they say you lack spirit, if you have any animation and life, they say you are, of course, not very scholarly. It is like playing the piano when you have a sore finger; well, people say, of course it was nice of him to play, and his finger was sore of course, but we don't think he could play much anyhow. When you dramatize a novel and somehow catch it surely into play form, what you do is merely taken for granted; the credit goes to the novelist. When you muff the novel, you are cursed for your pains, and to this is added the likelihood that many people who have never thought about the novel one way or another suddenly find that it was the most marvelous book they ever read.

Of Mr. Hemingway's novels, *A Farewell to Arms* let us say, it might early seem that they would be easy to turn into stage form. Not only easy; it might even seem that page after page, scene after scene, of that Hemingway dialogue stands ready for the stage, could merely be transferred bodily to the play. As a matter of fact nothing could be more misleading.

There are a good many pages where Mr. Hemingway is doing what we know as getting away with murder. Short statements saying pretty little presuppose a profound meaning in the silences, to which we are more or less persuaded—if we are persuaded—by those other passages, written in the same method, in which he achieves beautiful, unique and glowing effects. There are, furthermore, certain brilliant narrative passages, mannered, etched like a sparse drawing, but these can only suggest effects, and only halfway provide material for a play. There is, also, the somewhat adolescent brave obscenity, better than most of the stage kind because more sincerely used and more imaginatively placed in the revelation of character and event. And there are the fine spots where the silences effected are rich and full, the rhythm strange and lovely, the combinations startling, the transitions not mere holes but highly imagined connections in mood and inner current. But these passages in the novel, taken strictly as they stand, are not suited to the stage at all. Though they appear to be direct and actable, they are

Reprinted from the *New Republic* 64 (8 October 1930), 208–9.

in reality not so much dramatic as lyric. A kind of graphic lyricism. Their spell is in their glowing starkness, their pitiless powers of repetition, their sharp revelation of character now and then, their infectious cadence, their poetic reduction of the moment to its simplest line and passion of life. Much of this excellence belongs very little to the stage, the silences especially. Where, in the novel, you may go on fancying wonders, turning yourself into the writer's echo and amplifier, imagining that you are imagining all the warm wonders of passion and the heart, of frankness, naturalness and freedom, on the stage you must take into account the actors, who are the necessary vehicle by which the thing is conveyed, and are not the immaterial print plus the spell and conjuration that may arise in you. If the piece were something in the Maeterlinck manner, full of self-conscious, pregnant and boundless pauses for things unsaid, the case might be different. But the surface of Mr. Hemingway's style is always realistic, even though his work may be always at bottom poetic and distilled. On the stage a large portion of this effect is impossible. The personality of the player, the visible, definite scene, the assertion of reality, together with the stylized elimination of the method, cut down half one's chances of success.

Something more of this silence and inevitable point of Mr. Hemingway's novel Mr. Stallings might have wisely retained. As it was, he had a great deal more of it than his director, Mr. Mamoulian, with his hard driving, allowed to appear. For the first two of the three acts, Mr. Stallings preserves as much of the original material as you could ask. In the last act he leaves the book, and combines diverse parts of it, as faithfully as he can, into one. While the Italian retreat is in progress, the firing, bombing, trumpets, desertions and shooting going on, Catherine Barkley lies in the next room giving birth to her child, and is at the last brought in on a stretcher to die. This, of course, leaves out the hero's escape by jumping into the river, leaves out the escape with Catherine into Switzerland and many other events, but it is hard to see how he could have swum the swift current on the boards of the National Theater, or rowed, with dawn, mountains, water and vast suspense, across the lake into Switzerland. I do think, however, that more of the scene between the dying woman and her lover might wisely have been retained and a good share of the soldier scene, the parting orderlies and so on, left out. Some of these characters bob up all through the book, are dear to the author and interesting to us; but they have not been stressed enough in the play to become suddenly interesting at the very last and in the presence of the personal tragedy of the two lovers.

In the hospital scene of the second act Mr. Stallings achieved some brilliant play writing, every bit as good as the novel, and to my mind much better, as well as being much more difficult to contrive in theater terms than it was in fiction. To come down to tacks, I think it was an excellent bit of practice and exercise in dramaturgy for Mr. Stallings to labor at dramatizing A *Farewell to Arms*. It is, for example, an engaging problem as to what to do in making a scene out of some such passage as might say there was fighting up ahead, cries of wounded men, and I could hear the cannon. The dramatist cannot send somebody out in front of the curtain to say these selected words; good or bad as the case may be, he has to write a scene out of it. But otherwise it was none too profitable a piece of work. Mr. Stallings' talent is different from Mr. Hemingway's, wordier, for one thing. But this in itself is not necessarily a quality that is inferior compared to the elimination practiced by Mr. Hemingway. At their very worst, one quality may become excessive, ineffective and surfeiting, where the other becomes specious, barren, elusive and flattering; in neither case, at low level, is there anything to brag about. On the whole I found the play, despite the drag of much of the last act, interesting all through. The scene where the hero and the English nurse—she in a hysterical trance after her fiance's death and because of the strain of the life around her—meet for the first time, and fall into each other's arms, came off quite as convincingly, thanks partly to the acting, and gave us that same quality as in the novel, a sense of incredibility and at the same time of profound, elemental truth—Ernest Hemingway at his best. In the scene that closes the first act, the dressing of the hero's wound, the excellence of what would be a defect, if the Hemingway scarcity of words is to be preserved, appears in its brightest light. In this scene—almost wholly the dramatist's creation—the stream of words, the jumble of emotions and vocabulary, the themes of pain, love, affection, the claims for the honor of having got the man drunk because they loved him and he was in pain, the talk about the decoration, the lies proposed to get it with, the denials, the raucous lyricism, the high half-pathetic and half-comic energy and abundance, all this lies within Mr. Stallings' theater talent. It is what can give one of the things most needed in our theater: texture. Texture, fertility, richness, something of that incoherent exactitude of what is alive, a theater gift so well known to the Elizabethans, so scarce in the mere journalism, infecund realism and child-mindedness that for the most part make up our stage. A wonderful thing to see the curtain descend on such high abundance and poetic gusto!

Mr. Mamoulian's directing of A Farewell to Arms had some remarkable moments, now and again a group, or a piece of business: for one instance, the way in which Catherine, when her lover is gone, runs up on to the bed and buries her head in a burst of grief instead of the usual falling sidewise on the bed. Too often, however, Mr. Mamoulian's work was bad; too monotonously and joylessly speeded up, too many hard, sudden lights and shadows, too much repetition in the stresses of the speech, and obvious monotony in the rhythm of the English spoken by all the Italians. It is the kind of assertive directing that arrives at the point of astonishing expediency and then gets no final just subordination and essence.

As to Mr. Glenn Anders' portrayal of the hero, the way to start is to ask who could have done it any better. The faults are those occurring in the more sententious places, that talk on the bed, for instance, which is pretty bad acting and pretty bad Hemingway. Mr. Anders doubtless has to struggle against the portrait of the hero that is in most people's minds: that of the novelist himself, whose open-throated pictures are now well known, and whose abstention from any upkeep of his celebrity by a circulation around New York has added to the somewhat romantic impression of him that has got about. The hero of the novel has a warm fatalism where Mr. Anders gives us rather a certain sensitive impulsiveness. But there is a great section of the character that he understands as few others would, for its basic poetry and a kind of animal delicacy of perception, a cleansing brutalism, a certain intensity that is strangely nourished at the same time by the earth and the spirit, and blown darkly and lustily about the heart of life.

The part of Catherine Barkley, made credible in the novel only by stripping everything down to that single rich stream, human and mad, that the time and place allowed, is now entirely and wonderfully satisfying when transferred to the stage by Miss Elissa Landi, an English actress new to us. What she could do with another role remains to be seen. Except for that moment at the window, while the rain fell outside and she nerves herself to tell her lover that she is going to have a child—a dubious passage at best and much too writhingly directed—she is always right in her performance, and fortunately cast.

The smaller characters were, as plays go, better cast than usual; Mr. Mortimer Weldon, as the engaging doctor, a fat part, carried off the honors; Mr. Armand Cortez, as his asinine substitute, gave, after the two principal players, the best performance of the evening. Mr. Wood's provision for the settings was skimped and poor, and serves to show how easily one may be mawkish in the theater without being munificent.

CRITICISM

◆

The Mountain and the Plain

Carlos Baker

Goethe called his autobiography "Dichtung und Wahrheit," Poetry and Truth. The reverse of Goethe's title would admirably fit the collected works of Ernest Hemingway. For he is dedicated as a writer to the rendering of *Wahrheit*, the precise naturalistic representation of things as they are and were. Yet under all his brilliant surfaces lies the controlling *Dichtung*, the symbolic underpainting which gives so remarkable a sense of depth and vitality to what might otherwise be mere flat two-dimensional portraiture.

The literary histories commonly credit Hemingway with being the "archpriest of naturalists." This by now rather tiresome designation, if it is allowed to stand alone, is a little like calling St. Francis of Assisi the father of the S. P. C. A. and ignoring the good saint's activities and achievements in the more profound areas of human experience. That Hemingway the technician gets effects impossible to his naturalistic forebears or imitators has sometimes been noticed. The cause behind a majority of these effects, the deep inner *Dichtung* which runs through all his work, has never been fully recognized, let alone systematically explored.

Although one could work with almost any of the novels or short stories (including, by the way, the much-maligned "Across the River and Into the Trees"), "A Farewell to Arms" is a convenient and timely example. It is convenient because the general outlines of the story of Catherine Barkley and Lt. Frederick Henry are perhaps as widely known as any of the work of Hemingway. It is timely because, in the fall of 1950, this novel passed its twenty-first birthday without the slightest sign of diminution in the power it has always exerted on its readers. Infant mortality runs higher with novels than it does with human beings. When a novel survives undamaged the period of its nonage, and even comes to stand head and shoulders above the majority of contemporary writings, it is time not only for a celebration but also for an inquiry into the causes of its strength.

The *Dichtung* in "A Farewell to Arms" begins to operate on the first page. The justly famous opening is a genetically rendered landscape with thousands of moving figures. It does much more than start the book. It

From the *Virginia Quarterly Review* 27 (Summer 1951), 410–18. Reprinted by permission of *Virginia Quarterly Review*.

establishes the dominant mood (which is one of doom), plants a series of important images for future symbolic cultivation, and subtly compels the reader into the position of detached observer.

> In the late summer of that year we lived in a house in a village that looked across the river and the plain to the mountains. In the bed of the river there were pebbles and boulders, dry and white in the sun, and the water was clear and swiftly moving and blue in the channels. Troops went by the house and down the road and the dust they raised powdered the leaves of the trees. The trunks of the trees too were dusty and the leaves fell early that year and we saw the troops marching along the road and the dust rising and leaves, stirred by the breeze, falling and the soldiers marching and afterwards the road bare and white except for the leaves.

The opening sentence establishes the reader in a house in the village where he has a long view across the river and the plain to the distant mountains. Although he does not realize it yet, the plain and the mountains (not to mention the river and the trees, the dust and the leaves) have a fundamental value as symbols. The autumnal tone of the language is important in establishing mood. The landscape itself has the further importance of serving as the general setting for the whole first part of the novel. But under these values, and of fundamental structural importance, are the elemental images which compose this introductory setting.

The second sentence, which draws attention from the mountainous background to the bed of the river in the middle distance, produces a sense of clearness, dryness, whiteness, and sunniness which is to grow very subtly under the artist's hands until it merges with one of the novel's two dominant symbols, the mountain image. The other major symbol is the plain. Throughout the substructure of the book it is opposed to the mountain image. Down this plain the river flows. Across it, on the dusty road among the trees, pass the men-at-war, faceless and voiceless and unidentified against the background of the spreading plain.

In the third and fourth sentences of this remarkable paragraph the march-past of the troops and vehicles begins. From the reader's elevated vantage-point, looking down on the plain, the river, and the road, the continuously parading men are reduced in size and scale—made to seem smaller and more pitiful, more like wraiths blown down the wind, than would be true if the reader were brought close enough to overhear their conversation or see them as individualized personalities.

Between the first and fourth sentences, moreover, Hemingway accomplishes the transition from late summer to autumn—an inexorability of seasonal change which prepares the way for the study in doom on which he is embarked. Here again the natural elements take on a symbolic function. In the late summer we have the dust; in the early autumn, the dust and the leaves falling; and through them both, the marching troops impersonally seen. The reminder, through the dust, of the words of the funeral service in the prayer-book is fortified by the second natural symbol, the falling leaves. They dry out, fall, decay, and become part of the dust. Into the dust is where the troops are going—some of them soon, all of them eventually.

The short first chapter closes with winter, and the establishment of rain as a symbol of disaster. "At the start of the winter came the permanent rain and with the rain came the cholera. But it was checked and in the end only seven thousand died of it in the army." Already, now in the winter, seven thousand of the wraiths have vanished. The permanent rain washes away the dust and rots the leaves as if they had never existed. There is no excellent beauty, even in the country around Gorizia, that has not some sadness to it. And there is hardly a natural beauty in the whole first chapter of "A Farewell to Arms" which has not some symbolic function in Hemingway's first study in doom.

II

Despite the insistent, denotative matter-of-factness at the surface of the presentation, the subsurface activity of "A Farewell to Arms" is organized connotatively around two poles. By a process of accrual and coagulation, the images tend to build round the opposed concepts of Home and Not-home. Neither is truly conceptualistic; each is a kind of poetic intuition, charged with emotional values and woven, like a cable, of many strands. The Home-concept, for example, is associated with the mountains; with dry, cold weather; with peace and quiet; with love, dignity, health, happiness, and the good life; and with worship, or at least the consciousness of God. The Not-home concept is associated with low-lying plains; with rain and fog; with obscenity, indignity, suffering, nervousness, war, and death; and of course with irreligion.

The motto of William Bird's Three Mountains Press in Paris, which printed Hemingway's "in our time," was "Levavi oculos meos in montes." The line might also serve as an epigraph for "A Farewell to Arms." Merely introduced in the first sentence of the first chapter, the mountain image begins to develop important associations as early as Chapter Two. Learning that Frederick Henry is to go on leave, the young priest urges him to visit Capracotta in the Abruzzi. "There," he says, "is good hunting. You would like the people and though it is cold it is clear and dry. You could stay with my family. My father is a famous hunter." But the lowlander infantry captain interrupts: "Come on," he says in pidgin Italian to Frederick Henry. "We go whore-house before it shuts."

After Henry's return from the leave, during which he has been almost everywhere else on the Italian peninsula *except* Abruzzi, the mountain image gets further backing from another lowland contrast. "I had wanted," says he, "to go to Abruzzi. I had gone to no place where the roads were frozen and hard as iron, where it was clear cold and dry and the snow was dry and powdery and hare-tracks in the snow and the peasants took off their hats and called you Lord and there was good hunting. I had gone to no such place but to the smoke of cafés and nights when the room whirled and you needed to look at the wall to make it stop, nights in bed, drunk, when you knew that that was all there was. . . ."

Throughout Book I, Hemingway quietly consolidates the mountain image. On the way up towards the Isonzo from Gorizia, Frederick looks across the plain towards the Julian and Carnic Alps. "I looked to the north at the two ranges of mountains, green and dark to the snow-line and then white and lovely in the sun. Then, as the road mounted along the ridge, I saw a third range of mountains, higher snow mountains, that looked chalky white and furrowed, with strange planes, and then there were mountains far off beyond all these, that you could hardly tell if you really saw." Like Pope in the celebrated "Alps on Alps arise" passage, Hemingway is using the mountains symbolically. Years later, in "The Snows of Kilimanjaro," he would use the mighty peak of Africa as a natural image of immortality, as in "The Green Hills of Africa" he would build his narrative in part upon a contrast between the M'Bula Hills and the Serengetti Plain. When Frederick Henry lowers his eyes from the far-off ranges, he sees the plain and the river, the war-making equipment, and "the broken houses of the little town" which is to be occupied in the coming attack. Already now, a few dozen pages into the book, the mountain image has developed associations: with the man of God and his homeland, clear dry cold and snow, polite and kindly people, hospitality and natural beauty. Already it has its oppositions: the lowland obscenities of the priest-baiting captain, cheap cafés, one-night prostitutes, drunkenness, destruction, and the war.

When the trench-mortar explosion nearly kills Henry, the priest comes to visit him in the field hospital, and the Abruzzi homeland acquires a religious association. "There in my country," says the priest, "it is understood that a man may love God. It is not a dirty joke." By the close of Book I, largely through the agency of the priest, a complex connection has come clear between the idea of Home and high ground, cold weather, love, and the love of God. Throughout, Hemingway has worked by suggestion, implication, and quiet repetition, putting the reader into potential awareness for what is to come.

The next step is to bring Catherine Barkley by degrees into the center of the image. Her love affair with Henry begins as a "rotten game" of wartime seduction, with Catherine—still emotionally unstable from her fiancé's death—as a comparatively easy conquest. In the American hospital at Milan, following Henry's ordeal by fire at the front near Fossalta di Piave, the casual affair becomes an honorable, though unpriested, marriage. Because she can make a home of any room she occupies—and Henry several times alludes to this power of hers—Catherine naturally moves into association with ideas of home and love and happiness. But she does not reach the center of the mountain image until, on the heels of Frederick's harrowing lowland experiences during the retreat from Caporetto, the lovers move to Switzerland. Soon they are settled into a supremely happy life in the winterland on the mountainside above Montreux. Catherine's death occurs at Lausanne, after the March rains and the approaching need for a good lying-in hospital have driven the young couple down from their magic mountain—the closest approach to the priest's fair homeland in the Abruzzi that they are ever to know.

The total structure of the novel is developed, in fact, around the series of contrasting situations already outlined. To Gorizia, the not-home of war, succeeds the home which Catherine and Frederick make together in the Milan hospital. The not-home of the retreat from the Isonzo is followed by the quiet and happy retreat which the lovers share above Montreux. Home ends for Frederick Henry when he leaves Catherine dead in the Lausanne Hospital.

III

The use of rain as a background accompaniment in "A Farewell to Arms" has been widely and properly admired. Less apparent to the cursory reader of the novel is the way in which the whole idea of climate is related to the natural-mythological structure. (Hemingway's clusters of associated images produce emotional "climates" also, but they must be experienced rather than described.) The rains begin in Italy during October, just before Henry's return to Gorizia after his recovery from his wounds. The rains continue, at first steadily, then intermittently, throughout the disastrous retreat, Henry's flight to Stresa, and the time of his reunion with Catherine. When they awaken the morning after their reunion night, the rain has stopped, light floods the window, and Henry, looking out, can see Lake Maggiore in the sun "with the mountains beyond." Towards those mountains the lovers now depart.

Not until they are settled in idyllic hibernation in their chalet above Montreux are they really out of the rain. As if to emphasize climatically their "confused alarms of struggle and flight," the rain has swept over them during their escape up the lake in an open boat. But in the mountains, they are out of the lowlands, out of danger, out of the huge, tired débâcle of the war. Above Montreux, as in the priest's homeland of Abruzzi, the ridges are "iron-hard with the frost." The deep snow isolates them, and gives them the feeling of domestic safety and invulnerability.

For several months the idyll continues. "We lived through the months of January and February and the winter was very fine and we were very happy. There had been short thaws when the wind blew warm and the snow softened and the air felt like Spring, but always the clear hard cold had come again and the winter had returned. In March came the first break in the winter. In the night it started raining."

The reader has been prepared to recognize some kind of disaster-symbol in the arrival of the March rains. Much as in "Romeo and Juliet," which Hemingway once mentioned in connection with this novel, several earlier premonitions have been inserted at intervals. "I'm afraid of the rain," says Catherine in the Milan hospital one summer night, "because sometimes I see me dead in it." In the fall, just before Henry returns to the front, they are in a Milan hotel. During a break in the conversation the sound of falling rain comes in. A motor car klaxons and Henry quotes Marvell: "At my back I always hear Time's wingèd chariot hurrying near." He must soon take a cab to catch the train that will project him, though he does not know it yet, into the disaster of the great retreat. Months later, in Lausanne, the Marvell lines echo hollowly. "We knew the baby was very close now and it gave us both a feeling as though something were hurrying us and we could not lose any time together." And the sound of rain continues in background accompaniment until, with Catherine dead in the hospital room (not unlike the one where their child was conceived), Henry walks back to the hotel in the rain.

One further reinforcement of the central symbolic structure is provided by the contrast between the priest and the doctor, the man of God and the man without God. The Milan hospital and later the hotel have become home-symbols for Frederick Henry; on his return to Gorizia it does not "feel like a homecoming." A kind of damprot afflicts morale. In the war things are bad. Dr. Rinaldi is in the same case. Scientifically speaking, he has operated on so many casualties that he has become "a lovely surgeon." But he is not the old Rinaldi. He believes that he has syphilis, is treating himself for it, and is beginning to entertain some delusions of persecution. Except for the work, and the temporary opiates of women and drink, Rinaldi, the man without God, is a man without resources.

With the priest, things are not so bad. He is modestly surer of himself than before. The baiting does not touch him now. Out of the evils of the past summer, the priest has salvaged a kind of hope. He thinks he sees a "gentling down" among the soldiery. His own strength comes from the strength of his belief. He has resources which Dr. Rinaldi, the man without God, does not possess.

The priest-doctor contrast is borne out in the sacred-versus-profane course of the love affair, which has been launched at a low level through the agency of Rinaldi. In Book I, the doctor takes a jocularly profane view of the early infatuation, doubting that it can ever be anything else. But the underlying imagery suggests strongly that the Swiss idyll is carried on under the spiritual aegis of the priest. For it is to the Abruzzi-like Montreux that the lovers turn when they leave the war. Neither Rinaldi nor the priest appears, of course, in the latter part of the novel. But when, driven to the lowlands by the rains of spring, Catherine enters the hospital, it is naturally enough a doctor who takes over. Though he does what he can to save her life, she dies.

Projected in actualistic terms and a matter-of-fact tone, telling the Truth about the effect of war in human life, "A Farewell to Arms" is entirely acceptable as *Wahrheit*, a naturalistic narrative of what happened. To read it only as such, however, is to miss the controlling *Dichtung*: the deep central antithesis between the image of life and home (the mountain) and the image of war and death (the plain). This symbolic structure, essentially poetic in conception and execution, achieved without obvious insistence, enables Hemingway's first study in doom to succeed magnificently as something far more, and far more effective, than an exercise in romantic naturalism.

Death and Transfiguration

PHILIP YOUNG

A Farewell to Arms (1929), which borrows its title from a poem of that name by George Peele,[1] reverts to the war and supplies background for *The Sun Also Rises*. For the germs of both of its plots, a war plot and a love plot, it reaches back to *In Our Time*. An outline of the human arms in the novel is to be found among these early stories in a piece called "A Very Short Story." This sketch, less than two pages long, dealt quickly, as the novel does extensively, with the drinking and love-making in an Italian hospital of an American soldier, wounded in the leg, and a nurse, and had told of their love and their wish to get married. But where the book ends powerfully with the death in childbirth of the woman, the story dribbled off in irony. The lovers parted, the soldier leaving for home to get a job so that he could send for his sweetheart. Before long, however, the nurse wrote that she had a new lover who was going to marry her, though he never did; and then, shortly after receiving the letter, the soldier "contracted gonorrhea from a sales girl in a loop department store while riding in a taxicab through Lincoln Park."[2]

The war plot of *A Farewell to Arms*, on the other hand, is a greatly expanded version of that Chapter VI sketch in which Nick was wounded and made his separate peace—with Rinaldi, who also appears in the longer work. This wound, which got Nick in the spine, and "I" in the knee, and emasculated Jake, has returned to the knee, which is where Hemingway was most badly hit. Then the same story is rehearsed again in lengthened form. Recuperated enough to return to action after another convalescence in Milan, Lt. Frederic Henry becomes bitter about the society responsible for the war and, caught up in the Italian retreat from Caporetto, he breaks utterly with the army in which he is an officer. And this is again the old protagonist, who cannot sleep at night for thinking—who must not use his head to think with, and will absolutely have to stop it. He is also the man who, when he does sleep, has nightmares, and wakes from them in sweat and fright, and goes back to sleep in an effort to stay outside his dreams.

Unlike Jake Barnes, however, Frederic Henry participates fully in the

From *Ernest Hemingway: A Reconsideration* (University Park and London: The Pennsylvania State University Press, 1966). Copyright © 1966 by the Pennsylvania State University Press. Reprinted by permission of the publisher.

book's action, and as a person is wholly real. But he is also a little more than that, for just as the response of Americans of the period to the aimless and disillusioned hedonism of Jake and his friends indicated that some subtle chord in them had been struck, so something in the evolution of Frederic Henry from complicity in the war to bitterness and escape has made him seem, though always himself, a little larger than that, too. Complicity, bitterness, escape—a whole country could read its experience, Wilson to Harding, in his, and it began to become clear that in Hemingway as elsewhere "hero" meant not simply "protagonist" but a man who stands for many men. Thus it is that when historians of various kinds epitomize the temper of the American Twenties and a reason for it the adventures of that lieutenant come almost invariably to mind. And also, since these things could hardly be said better, his words: "I was always embarrassed by the words sacred, glorious, and sacrifice and the expression in vain. We had heard them, sometimes standing in the rain almost out of earshot, so that only the shouted words came through . . . now for a long time, and I had seen nothing sacred, and the things that were glorious had no glory and the sacrifices were like the stockyards at Chicago if nothing was done with the meat except to bury it. . . . Abstract words such as glory, honor, courage, or hallow were obscene. . . ." It is on the implications of these sentiments, and in order to escape a certain death which he has not deserved, that Henry finally acts. He jumps in a river and deserts: the hell with it. It was an unforgettable plunge.

Memorable too, in her devotion and her ordeal—though much less memorable, and much less real—is Henry's English mistress. Idealized past the fondest belief of most people, and even the more realistic wishes of some, compliant, and bearing unmistakable indications of the troubles to come when she will appear as mistress of heroes to come, Catherine Barkley has at least some character in her own right, and is both the first true "Hemingway heroine," and the most convincing one. Completely real, once again and at once, are the minor characters—especially Rinaldi, the ebullient Italian doctor, and the priest, and Count Greffi, the ancient billiard player, and the enlisted ambulance drivers.

Chiefly, again, it is their speech which brings these people to life and keeps them living. The rest of the book, however, is less conversational in tone than before, and in other ways the writing is changed a little. The sentences are now longer, even lyrical, on occasion, and, once in a while, experimental, as Hemingway, not content to rest in the style that had made him already famous, tries for new effects, and does not always succeed. Taken as a whole, however, his prose has never been finer or more finished than in this novel. Never have those awesome, noncommittal understatements, which say more than could ever be written out, been more impressive. The book has passages which rate with the hardest, cleanest and most moving in contemporary literature.

The novel has one stylistic innovation that is important to it. This is the use of an object, rain, in a way that cannot be called symbolic so much as portentous. Hemingway had used water as a metaphoric purge of past experience before, and so Henry's emergence from the river into a new life, as from a total immersion, was not new. What is new in *A Farewell to Arms* is the consistent use of rain as a signal of disaster. Henry, in his practical realism, professes a disbelief in signs, and tells himself that Catherine's vision of herself dead in the rain is meaningless. But she dies in it and actually, glancing back at the end, one sees that a short, introductory scene at the very start of the book had presented an ominous conjunction of images— rain, pregnancy and death—which set the mood for all that was to follow, prefigured it and bound all the ends of the novel into a perfect and permanent knot.

This is really the old "pathetic fallacy" put to new use, and—since there is no need to take it scientifically or philosophically, but simply as a subtle and unobtrusive device for unity—quite an acceptable one, too. Good and bad weather go along with good and bad moods and events. It is not just that, like everyone, the characters respond emotionally to conditions of atmosphere, light and so on, but that there is a correspondence between these things and their fate. They win when it's sunny, and lose in the rain.

Thus, then, the weather, which as both omen and descriptive background (made once again to count for something) is a matter of style, cannot be extricated from the book's plot, or structure. This is of course built on the two themes involved in the ambiguity of "arms," which are developed and intensified together, with alternating emphasis, until at the extremity of one the hero escapes society, and the heroine everything. Despite the frequency with which they appear in the same books, the themes of love and war are really an unlikely pair, if not indeed—to judge from the frequency with which writers fail to wed them—quite incompatible. But in Hemingway's novel their courses run straight and exactly, though subtly, parallel, and he has managed to fuse them. In his affair with the war Henry goes from desultory participation to serious action and a wound, and then through his recuperation in Milan to a retreat which leads to his desertion. His relationship with Catherine Barkley undergoes six precisely corresponding stages—from a trifling sexual affair to actual love and her conception, and then through her confinement in the Alps to a trip to the hospital which leads to her death. By the end of Hemingway's novel, when the last farewell is taken, the two stories are as one, in the point that is made very clear, lest there be any sentimental doubt about it, that life, both social and personal, is a struggle in which the Loser Takes Nothing, either.

This ideology, which is the novel's, has two related aspects which are implicit in the united elements of the plot. In the end, a man is trapped. He is trapped biologically—in this case by the "natural" process that costs him his future wife in the harrowing scenes at the hospital and is trapped by society—at the end of a retreat, where you take off or get shot. Either way it can only end badly, and there are no other ways. How you will get it, though, depends on the kind of person you are: "If people bring so much courage to this world the world has to kill them to break them, so of course it kills them. The world breaks everyone and afterward many are strong at the broken places. But those that will not break it kills. It kills the very good and the very gentle and the very brave impartially. If you are none of these you can be sure that it will kill you too but there will be no special hurry."

It does not really matter very much that there is something a little romantic about this passage, perhaps the finest in all of Hemingway, or that the novel is a romantic one as a whole. It must be just about the most romantic piece of realistic fiction, or the most realistic romance, in our literature. Henry's love affair, which blossoms glamorously from the mud of the war, is but the most striking of several factors which go together to make his war a remarkably pleasant one, as wars go, and much more attractive than wars actually are. The lieutenant has a somewhat special time of it, with orderlies and porters and little or no trouble with superiors, and good wine and good food and a lot of free time in which to enjoy them. But it is not important that these aspects of his army experience are highly untypical. Nor does it matter on the other hand that women usually survive childbirth, and many men are discharged from armies in good shape, and then life goes on much as before. What matters instead is that this time Hemingway has made his story, and the attitudes it enacts, persuasive and compelling within the covers of his book. And after we have closed the covers there is no inclination to complain that this was, after all, no literal transcription of reality which exaggerated neither the bitter nor the sweet. It was rather an intensification of life. Willingly or not, disbelief is suspended before a vision that overrides objections, withers preconceptions and even memory and imposes itself in their place.

This novel has the last word, always. Catherine Barkley, as it happened, was very good, very gentle, very brave. Unlike the hero, who broke and survived to become eventually quite strong, she would not break and so she was killed. It was very likely in rebuttal to the people who rejected the pessimism of this denouement that Hemingway pointed out three years later, in *Death in the Afternoon*, that love stories do not end happily in life, either: "There is no lonelier man in death, except the suicide, than that man who has lived many years with a good wife and then outlived her. If two people love each other there can be no happy end to it."

Notes

1.   As in the case of many of Hemingway's titles the allusion to the poem is slightly ironic, for Peele mourned the fact that he could no longer fight.

2. Except for the venereal element (which according to a paperback biographer was thus contracted by a *friend* of the author), it appears that this sketch tells how it actually was, the novel-to-be how it might have been. In life Catherine Barkley, the heroine of the novel, was Agnes H. von Kurowski, the Bellevue-trained daughter of a German-American father; Hemingway intended to bring her home from Italy and marry her. (Leicester's biography prints an excellent photograph of her; Marcelline's biography prints a picture Ernest sent home from Italy of a "nice-looking bearded older man . . . Count Greppie"—possibly the model for Count Greffi in the novel.)

Hemingway's Other Style

CHARLES R. ANDERSON

On the surface Hemingway's prose is hard and bare, secular and insistently non-literary. This observation is such a commonplace it would be inexcusable to repeat it at this late date except as a sounding board for observations of a very different order. Its purpose here is to serve as a starting point for examining passages written in an opposing style—warmly human, richly allusive, and at least suggestive of spiritual values. They are indeed rare, but they are usually crucial. And much of their effectiveness comes from contextual contrast with the prevailing mode in which Hemingway's fictions are written—the "purified," stripped, athletic prose for which he has long been famous. Undue admiration for this, as if simplicity were somehow superior to complexity in literature, has tended to make critics neglect his other style. Further, these lyric passages are so submerged beneath the tough exterior that many readers have overlooked them altogether.

A close look at one example, the brief dream sequence during the retreat from Caporetto in *A Farewell to Arms,*[1] will illustrate both the technique and the function of such passages. It comes in Chapter 28 at the main turning point in the narrative. For what began as an orderly retreat quickly degenerates into a rout, and by the end of Chapter 30, in the chaos at the Tagliamento River crossing, Lieutenant Henry has deserted from the Italian army. War, the first theme of the book, drops out from this point on and the second theme, love, emerges as the dominant one. This has been amply prepared for in the chapters just prior to the dream sequence, and they must now be combed for the threads that are woven by sleep into such a richly symbolic fabric.

In Chapter 23 during the hero's convalescence from battle wounds, at the base hospital in Milan, his love for Catherine Barkley had first matured and ripened. It reached a climax on his last evening before returning to the front, when the lovers found their only available rendezvous in a cheap hotel opposite the railroad station. For the first few minutes, depressed by the tawdry surroundings, her spirits sank: "I never felt like a whore before," she said (158). But refreshed by a dinner of woodcock and wine, and renewed

From *Modern Language Notes* 76 (May 1961), 434–42. Reprinted by permission of the Johns Hopkins University Press.

by love's feast, she decided that the red plush and mirrors were just right. He summed it up: "We felt very happy and in a little time the room felt like our own home. My room at the hospital had been our own home . . . in the same way" (159). With a tenderness just concealed under the clipped surface, their talk turned to her pregnancy and the serious problem of bearing their child in a world dislocated by war. Her only lament was that they were never settled in their "home" very long, but she concluded characteristically with chin up: "I'll have a fine home for you when you come back" (162). War not only disrupts peace and the chances of domestic happiness, but makes more urgent the note of transiency as a threat to love. What really lifts the whole scene up is the very brief literary allusion, made by Lieutenant Henry in the midst of their talk: "But at my back I always hear / Time's wingèd chariot hurrying near" (161). This quotation from Marvel, enriching enough in itself, is made more complex by being strained through the ironic discords of its echo in Eliot's *Wasteland,* as has been recently pointed out.[2] At this high point the tryst is broken abruptly by the arrival of the midnight train and the lovers are separated, in the rain.

Time is running out with the Italian defenses at the Austrian frontier too. On rejoining his corps, Henry finds the morale in a state of collapse, profanity and obscenity increasing with the general spread of war weariness. Though it is still autumn the winter rains have already set in, torrential and unending. Rain, a pervasive symbol throughout the novel for the depression and destruction of war, now becomes a deluge that washes away the resistance of the Italian army as it had previously eroded all the values of civilization. Less than a week after his return the combined German and Austrian forces launch a major offensive, the front gives way, and the long retreat begins. Since this is not a historical novel, the focus narrows to the three hospital cars under command of Lieutenant Henry. Their withdrawal is orderly at first, and the only two events that break the routine are seemingly trivial ones but pertinent to the present analysis: the comic evacuation of the soldiers' whorehouse at Gorizia on the first day (195), and the episode of the two young girls that occurs late that night (202), when the retreating column is stalled in the mud on the road to Udine. The driver of one of the hospital cars has given the adolescent sisters a ride and is playfully making passes at them. As they sob in terror he asks if they are virgins, and both nod their heads vigorously, "'Don't worry,' he said, 'No danger of ——,' using the vulgar word. 'No place for ——.' . . . Both the girls seemed cheered" (203). After witnessing this and deciding that all is well, Henry returns to his car and falls asleep.

This full rehearsal of the context in which the dream sequence takes place—bringing back to the reader's mind all he would be aware of when he had reached this point—has been necessary in order to show the dream's intricate relation to the main themes of the novel. Now for the passage itself:

It was still raining hard . . . Those were a couple of fine girls with Barto. A retreat was no place for two virgins. Real virgins. Probably very religious. If there were no war we would probably all be in bed. In bed I lay me down my head. Bed and board. Stiff as a board in bed. Catherine was in bed now between two sheets, over her and under her. Which side did she sleep on? Maybe she wasn't asleep. Maybe she was lying thinking about me. Blow, blow, ye western wind. Well, it blew and it wasn't the small rain but big rain down that rained. It rained all night. You knew it rained down that rained. Look at it. Christ, that my love were in my arms and I in my bed again. That my love Catherine. That my sweet love Catherine down might rain. Blow her again to me. Well, we were in it. Every one was caught in it and the small rain would not quiet it. "Good-night, Catherine," I said out loud. "I hope you sleep well. If it's too uncomfortable, darling, lie on the other side," I said "I'll get you some cold water. In a little while it will be morning and then it won't be so bad. I'm sorry he makes you so uncomfortable. Try and go to sleep, sweet." (204)

The dream device here adopted offers several advantages. Substantively, it affords the hero an escape from the horrors of war and reunion with his beloved, at least in spirit. Stylistically, it frees him from the requisite soldier talk, whether of bravura or nihilism, and permits a change of pace into tender, allusive, and lyrical language. Structurally, with the sprung syntax and free association of ideas characteristic of dreams, it justifies the author in abandoning the logic of prose for the indirection and symbolism of poetry. Hemingway takes full advantage of all these possibilities.

The key sentence in this passage, though written as prose, he undoubtedly expected the attentive reader to recognize as a direct quotation from an anonymous sixteenth-century lyric, "The Lover in Winter Plaineth for the Spring":

> O Western wind, when wilt thou blow
> That the small rain down can rain?
> *Christ, that my love were in my arms*
> *And I in my bed again!*[3]

With this clue, which has passed unnoticed by previous critics, the complex significance of the paragraph begins to unfold. It opens with the pouring rain that has turned late October into the winter of discontent, for the despairing Italians in retreat and for the hero separated from his love by a war that has become meaningless. (Only a dozen pages before, p. 191, had come the well-known rejection of his earlier idealism: "I had seen nothing sacred, and the things that were glorious had no glory and the sacrifices were like the stockyards at Chicago if nothing was done with the meat except to bury it.") In contrast to this, the last image before his eyes as he drops off to sleep suggests two different kinds of love: the sexual desire of men stranded in the loneliness of war (Barto's comic threat of seducing the two little girls), and the love of God ("Real virgins. Probably very religious"). Even the former is difficult of fulfillment during a disastrous military retreat, so that the soldier's twofold obsession—to sleep, and to sleep with a woman—is reduced for the moment to the former ("If there were no war we would all probably be in bed"). And in such a time and place the latter, sacred love, is simply unthinkable, unless one's thoughts revert to childhood's prayer in the sanctity of the home, which is exactly what they do in the next sentence: "In bed I lay me down my head." By the inverted word order of what would otherwise seem like a gratuitously incongruous element in this dream, unobtrusively but surely he invokes the familiar

> Now I lay me down to sleep,
> I pray the Lord my soul to keep;
> If I should die before I wake,
> I pray the Lord my soul to take.

"If I should die" is certainly applicable to a soldier surrounded on all sides by death; in terms of the whole novel it applies to Catherine too, looking forward to his reiterated cry "What if she should die?" as she lay actually dying in childbirth at the end (331). But in the context of the dream itself it recalls the little girls praying God to keep them pure.

This surprise reappearance of the young virgins Barto had made a proposal to, "using the vulgar word," leads to more elaborate word play: "Bed and board. Stiff as a board in bed." The first of these, in spite of its triteness, has a double significance; it is the minimum that a husband is required by custom to provide for his family, and negatively it is the legal term defining the first stage of divorce (*a mensa et thoro*, "from bed and board")—which exactly describes Henry's present involuntary separation from Catherine. The second phrase is a prurient pun; the board, by an ingenious scrambling of the first phrase, becomes stiffened into a phallic symbol of his longing for her. Readers conditioned by Freud have probably never failed to catch this, but too much taken with Hemingway's sexual frankness they may have been thrown off the trail of what follows. For it is when the hero's thoughts turn to his true love ("Catherine was in bed now") that his dream opens out into its full significance, which goes far beyond mere eroticism.

The crescendo begins with "Blow, blow, ye western wind," ushering in the complaint of the lover in winter, though the phrases from the old lyric are fragmentary and garbled at first. "Well, it blew and it wasn't the small rain but the big rain down that rained. It rained all night." When he was last with Catherine it had been raining too, but only a gentle rain that lent an air of privacy to their rendezvous, and though at night also a very different kind of night from the present disastrous one. In view of the whole novel's weather symbolism these were ominous symptoms, it is true, for a similar light rain will be falling on the spring night at Lausanne when Catherine dies (335–343). Indeed, there are only two memorable scenes in the book when it is *not* raining, and these are the two most vividly associated with a life of peace and love: first, near the beginning, the chaplain-priest's account of his home in the bright cool air of the Abruzzi mountains, where "a man may love God" without feeling foolish and where "the spring . . . was the most beautiful in Italy" (74–76); second, near the conclusion, at the chalet in the Swiss Alps where Catherine and Henry have their only real life together, their love soaring into an idyll in the clear winter sunshine for a few months before it goes down to its tragic end (299–327). But midway in the novel there is still a great distinction in his mind between the "big rain" symbolizing the general destruction of war and the "small rain" that merely plagued their love without dampening it. For the soldier in Italy as well as the poet in England, both winter-bound, it is the western wind that will bring the light spring rains and the end of separation. Caught in the deluge brought by the north wind *(tramonto)*, Lieutenant Henry quite naturally invokes through the old lyric the western wind that will bring the renewal of life and love, unaware of the tragic irony that for the doomed lovers it will be only a "false Spring" (321).

In his present war-dream he can only look back to the Milan episode, when in spite of the small rain it was not "winter" for them in either inner or outer climate, as a dream of love to be repeated. So his yearning (perhaps his foreboding too) wrings a cry of anguish from him: "Christ, that my love were in my arms and I in my bed again." This certainly strikes the note of physical passion, as it rightly should, since *A Farewell to Arms* is one of the great love stories of the century. But there are other meanings not too far submerged beneath the surface of the dream language. Even the exclamation "Christ," when uttered by sensitive souls under high emotional tension, hovers halfway between prayer and profanity. "Time's wingèd chariot," quoted earlier and echoed later, is what gives urgency to this soldier's plea for one more night with his beloved. And when the love of man for woman reaches the point of demanding expression in poetry, this in itself is a token of aspiration above the flesh. For all his worldly pose he has been concerned for some time with this dual aspect of his affair.

Early in the book, in that same conversation with the priest mentioned above, they were discussing sacred and profane love. Lieutenant Henry's mind was preoccupied with his changing attitude toward Catherine, which had begun on the level of sexual desire, differing only in behavioral pattern from that which the other soldiers satisfied through prostitutes. That kind of thing is only passion and lust, the priest said, remembering the ribald talk at mess. It is utterly different from the love of God: "When you love you wish to do things for. You wish to sacrifice for. You wish to serve."

When Henry asked, "If I really loved some woman would it be like that?" (75), the celibate would not venture an answer. But the development of his love for Catherine in the ensuing months has been clearly in this direction and its progress is actually recorded in the dream, from the symbol of carnal desire at the beginning to his solicitude for her and the child at the end. Even in the lyric he quoted there are overtones of a spiritual sort. The old poet surely knew of the traditional medieval symbol of Christ as the gentle rain, falling on the earth in spring to make it green and fertile again. So there is in these lines at least a suggestion of heavenly love cast in earthly terms, though the poem is secular in mode. And if Hemingway were not aware of this, how else explain the cryptic line, "That my sweet love Catherine down might rain"? As a man who confesses he does not know how to love God, she is the one he worships, her grace what he implores. Only her love raining down on him can make the earth green again with spring, and the downward flow of her delivery in childbirth will bring the renewal of life in the fruitfulness of love.

With the free association of ideas expected in dreams, this sequence is followed out by the next sentence, "Blow her again to me," since it suggests the whole context of a cradlesong in *The Princess,* from which it is lifted:

> Sweet and low, sweet and low,
>   Wind of the Western sea,
> Low, low, breathe and blow,
>   Wind of the western sea!
> Over the rolling waters go,
> Come from the dying moon, and blow,
>   Blow him again to me;
> While my little one, while my pretty one, sleeps. . . .

For those who think of Hemingway as exclusively a spokesman for the hardboiled this must come as a shock, a lullaby from Tennyson! But there it is inescapably in the text, and it actually measures the final motion of the dream, from the most basic sexual desire to the highest sentiments of home and married love. By changing one pronoun he makes the quotation his own, shifting the scene from a mother waiting for the return of a sailor-father to his "babe in the nest," and fitting it to the exigencies of a novel where the soldier yearning for his beloved simply prays that the same western wind will turn winter into spring and "Blow *her* again to me." In terms of Tennyson's lullaby the reunion will take place "Under the silver moon"; in terms of the novel it will come after the torrential rains of the dark night of war are over ("In a little while it will be morning"). Meanwhile they can merely wait and dream. Catherine and Henry's child, still in the womb and not yet part of their life, is referred to only indirectly ("I'm sorry he makes you so uncomfortable"), but his coming accounts at least in part for the new tenderness of the lover, now directed solely to the pregnant mother. "Try and go to sleep, sweet," he ends his lullaby. The reader, from memory, can fill in all the rest—from "Sweet and low" to "sleep, my pretty one, sleep."

The protective device of the dream, which insulates him from the need to be hard, is enhanced by the fact that though he was talking out loud in his sleep it was in English, incomprehensible to his Italian companions. On waking, Lieutenant Henry is plunged back into the deluge of war, engulfed in death and disaster, profanity and obscenity and all the rest. So the lyrical interlude, cut off as abruptly as it began, stands in sharp contrast to the tough style which immediately takes over again, beginning with a four letter expletive from his driver: " '————' " Piani said. " 'They've started again' " (205). This continues, with increasing disintegration of all values, to the end of the retreat two chapters later. But the dream is not lost, merely locked in the hero's heart, and its major affirmations reappear twice in muted form. Once, while escaping from the enemy, as his men fall away from him one by one crying "Peace" and "Home," Henry asks the remaining loyal one why he did not run with the others. " 'I should think a married man would want to get back to his wife,' I said. 'I would be glad to talk about wives' " (229). Again, while escaping from his own battle police, who would have shot him if he had not broken from them and dived into the river. Now lying on the floor of a freight car, temporarily safe but half-dazed, he falls into a kind of daydream: "I could remember Catherine but I knew I would get crazy if I thought about her . . . so I would not think about her, only about her a little . . . lying with Catherine on the floor of the car. Hard as the floor of the car . . . and lonesome inside and alone with wet clothing and hard floor for a wife" (240). Home and married love! Throughout, such words have come to represent all that men dream of as not-war, just as war is the desolate world of not-home, where love can only take its chances. And these same words, strangely enough, have been more often on his lips than on hers—the sentiment of the hardened soldier even more than of the expectant mother. After the loss of his idealism for a cause, they become the measure of all his conduct to the end of the book. But the alert reader of the dream passage already knows the high place these terms hold on Lieutenant Henry's index of values. Flesh or spirit? Flesh *and* spirit.

It would be imprudent to draw sweeping conclusions from the interpretation of a single passage in one novel, but it might be provocative of further close readings to suggest them. When Hemingway dispensed with the lyrical mode altogether, it may be ventured, he could be guilty of abject parody of his own athletic style, as in *Across the River and Into the Trees*. When he allowed it to become too dominant the result could be spongy, as in the Hispanic rhetoric and soft ideology of *For Whom the Bell Tolls*. Most recently, it could be suggested of *The Old Man and the Sea*, he achieved a real measure of success by going all the way into romantic fable, and this may indeed be the beginning of a new direction yet to be coped with. But the Hemingway

still mostly admired and argued over is the author of the early fictions—
The Sun Also Rises, A Farewell to Arms, and half-a-dozen of the best short
stories. If their impudent manner and their surface nihilism had been all
they had to offer, they would have dropped from the lists long ago. Perhaps
their staying power derives not from their tough exterior alone but also from
their tender spots of sensibility carefully nurtured in a dehumanized world—
those passages of muted lyricism that provide both a measure and a meaning
for the protective toughness. Rare and brief as they are, they achieve a special
resonance by being sounded against the hard polished surface of his typical
prose. It was by laying one style against the other that Hemingway became
a modern writer for our century, rather than merely the spokesman for a
lost generation.

Notes

1.   For convenience the edition in Scribner's "Modern Standard Authors" series is used.
Page references are given in parentheses in the text, following each quotation or citation.
2.   Donna Gerstenberger, "The *Waste Land* in *A Farewell to Arms,*" *MLN,* LXXVI
(1961), 24–25. It should be added, to complete the record, that Hemingway also echoes
these lines at the end of the novel, just before Catherine's sudden death: "We knew the baby
was very close now and it gave us both a feeling as though something were hurrying us and
we could not lose any time together" (321).
3.   *The Oxford Book of English Verse* (Oxford, 1925), p. 53, marked "16th C.?" (Italics
mine.)

Hemingway's "Resentful Cryptogram"

Judith Fetterley

Perhaps others were struck, as I was, when I first read Erich Segal's *Love Story* by the similarity between it and Ernest Hemingway's *A Farewell to Arms*. Both stories are characterized by a disparity between what is overtly stated and what is covertly expressed. Both ask the reader to believe in the perfection of a love whose substance seems woefully inadequate and whose signature is death. "What can you say about a twenty-five-year-old girl who died," asks Oliver Barrett IV on the opening page of *Love Story*. The answer is, as the question implies, not very much. Because the investment of this love story, like so many others, is not in the life of the beloved but in her death and in the emotional kick-back which the hero gets from that death— Oliver Barrett weeping in the arms of his long-estranged but now-reconciled father. What one can't, or won't, say is precisely that which alone would be worth saying—namely, that you loved her because she died or, conversely, that because you loved her she died. While *A Farewell to Arms* is an infinitely more complex book than *Love Story*, nevertheless its emotional dynamics and its form are similar. In reading it one is continually struck by the disparity between its overt fabric of idealized romance and its underlying vision of the radical limitations of love, between its surface idyll and its sub-surface critique. And one is equally struck by its heavy use of the metaphor and motif of disguise.[1] When Sheridan Baker describes *A Farewell to Arms* as a "resentful cryptogram," he is essentially extending this metaphor to the form of the novel itself.[2] That deviousness and indirection are often the companions of hostility is no new observation and feminists have always known that idealization is a basic strategy for disguising and marketing hatred. If we explore the attitude toward women which is behind *A Farewell to Arms*, we will discover that, despite such ringing phrases as "idyllic union," "their Swiss idyll," "growth to a genuine commitment," it is one of immense hostility, whose full measure can be taken from the fact that Catherine dies and dies because she is a woman.

Let us begin by examining the attitude of the culture which surrounds Frederic and Catherine and which provides the background for their love.

From the *Journal of Popular Culture*, 10 (Summer 1976): 203–214. Reprinted by permission of *Journal of Popular Culture*.

In the male world of the Italian front women are seen solely in sexual terms and relegated to a solely sexual role. This attitude is made quite clear through the way in which the Italian doctors treat the British nurses they encounter: "What a lovely girl . . . Does she understand that? She will make you a fine boy. A fine blonde like she is . . . What a lovely girl" (p. 99—all references are to the Scribner paperback edition). Of doctors one asks if they are any good at diagnosis and surgery, will they make you a fine leg; of nurses one asks if they are sexually adequate, are they pretty, will they make you a fine boy. Rinaldi's response to Catherine is equally couched in sexual terms. His one question about Catherine when Frederic returns to the front after his hospitalization in Milan is, "I mean is she good to you practically speaking," i.e. does she go down on you, i.e. is she a good whore (p. 169). Rinaldi's inability to see women in other than sexual terms emerges quite clearly from a remark he makes to Frederic before the latter leaves for Milan: "Your lovely cool goddess. English goddess. My God what would a man do with a woman like that except worship her? What else is an Englishwoman good for? . . . I tell you something about your good women. Your goddesses. There is only one difference between taking a girl who has always been good and a woman. With a girl it is painful . . . And you never know if the girl will really like it" (p. 66). The implications behind this pronouncement are clear: if a woman is good only for worship, then she really isn't any good at all because women only exist for one thing and the real definition of a good woman is she who knows what she exists for and does it and lets you know that she likes it. Any woman who wishes to think of herself in other than sexual terms is denying her humanness and trying to be a superhuman, a goddess, for humanness in women is synonymous with being sexual.

The contempt and hostility for women which saturate Rinaldi's paradigm are equally clear in scenes like the one in which the soldiers watch their whores being loaded into a truck for the retreat. "I'd like to be there when some of those tough babies climb in and try and hop them . . . I'd like to have a crack at them for nothing. They charge too much at that house anyway. The government gyps us" (p. 189). Herded like animals, they are seen by the men as so many pieces of meat whose price on the market is too damn high for what you get. And the result? Syphilis and gonorrhea. This attitude toward women has its obvious correlative in an attitude toward sexuality in general. Coarse, gross, the subject matter *par excellence* for jokes whose hostility is hardly worth disguising, sex is seen as the antithesis of sensitivity, tenderness, idealism, and ultimately of knowledge. The priest who comes from the cold, white, pure mountainous world of the Abruzzi, where women are safely distanced and men relate to each other, knows something that Frederic Henry who is down there on the plain among the whores, who "had gone to no such place but to the smoke of cafes and nights when the room whirled and you needed to look at the wall to make it stop," does not know yet and who, when he learns it, can not hold on to, and that is that sex is a dangerous and wasteful commodity and that the best world indeed is that of men without women. The priest alone is able to carry out the implications of his culture's attitude toward sex.

The difference between what men deserve in the world which produces these doctors and soldiers and priests and what women deserve can be seen in the disparity between the treatment of Catherine's death and the treatment of the deaths of men at war. "'You will not do any such foolishness,' the doctor said. 'You would not die and leave your husband'"; "'You are not going to die. You must not be silly'" (pp. 319, 331). The tone here is one appropriate to a parent addressing a recalcitrant child and the remarks are at once a reprimand and an implicit command which at some level assumes that Catherine is in control of whether she lives or dies. Indeed, Catherine herself has internalized the attitude of her doctor. She presents that *reductio ad absurdum* of the female experience: she feels guilty for dying and apologizes to the doctor for taking up his valuable time with her death—"I'm sorry I go on so long." Though the two major attendants upon her death are male, no shadow of blame or responsibility falls on them. Catherine never questions Henry's responsibility for her situation, for she seems to operate on the tacit assumption that conception, like contraception, is her doing. And while Frederic is quick to smell incompetence when it comes to his leg, no doubts are raised about the doctor who performs the caesarian on Catherine, though usually the need for such an operation is spotted before the child has strangled to death. Rather the responsibility for both her death and the child's is placed on Catherine. In contrast, the soldier who, analogously, hemorrhages to death in the ambulance sling above Frederic Henry does not see himself as stupid, bad, irresponsible. Even more incongruous is the idea of a doctor referring to a dying soldier in such terms. Indeed, when Miss Van Campen tries it on Frederic and accuses him of irresponsibility of self-induced jaundice, the results are quite different from those of the comparable scene between Catherine and her doctor. A soldier's primary responsibility is to himself but a woman is responsible even in the moment of her death to men. As long as there is a man around who needs her, she *ought* not to die. Thus Catherine's death is finally seen as a childish and irresponsible act of abandonment. If we weep during the book at the death of soldiers, we are weeping for the tragic and senseless waste of their lives, we are weeping for them. If we weep at the end of the book, however, it is not for Catherine but for Frederic Henry abandoned in a cold, wet, hostile world. All our tears are ultimately for men because in the world of *A Farewell to Arms* male life is what counts. On first consideration, Frederic Henry seems quite different from the culture of the World War I Italian front. He is sensitive and tender, capable of a personal relationship with a woman that lasts more than fifteen minutes, and of an idealization of love which appears to be the secular analogue of the priest's asexual spirituality. Catherine is a "sacred subject" and Frederic resists Rinaldi's attempt to sexualize everything and to reduce his feeling for Catherine to the genitals. At one point when Catherine is teasing him, she refers to Frederic as "Othello with his occupation gone" (p. 257). One is struck by the allusion because it seems to point out so clearly just how different Frederic is from the culture in which he finds himself. One can not imagine him strangling Catherine in a fit of jealous rage. But when one considers what in fact happens in the book, one is tempted to feel that the difference between Frederic and Othello is essentially superficial and rests only in the degree to which each is able to face his immense egocentrism and the fear and hatred of women which are its correlatives. If one is struck by the violence of the novel's ending, one is also struck by the way in which that violence is distanced to the biological trap of Catherine's womb and to the mythic "they" who break the brave and beautiful. Yet the image of strangulation persists and nags us with the thought that Frederic Henry sees himself in the fetus which emerges from Catherine's womb and that her death is the fulfillment of his own unconscious wish.[3]

Frederic Henry's hostility to women is in some ways quite clear. In the course of the novel, he has a series of encounters with older women in positions of authority. In all of these encounters there is an underlying sense of hostility and while overt expression of this hostility is rare—e.g. the end of the novel when he shoves the two nurses out of the room in order to make his peace with the dead Catherine—it is implicit in the fact that in his mind these women appear as smug, self-righteous, critical, anti-sexual, and sadistic. Consider, for instance, Frederic's interchange with the head nurse at the hospital where Catherine works. In response to his request for Catherine, he is informed that she is on duty and is told, "there's a war on, you know" (p. 22). By implication Frederic is defined as an egocentric, insensitive non-combatant who expects to get his pleasure while other men are dying. This woman speaks from a position of moral superiority which in effect operates to put Frederic Henry down. The hostility between Frederic and this kind of woman, adumbrated in this early encounter, comes out in full force in his relation to Miss Van Campen, the head of the hospital in Milan where he is taken after his injury. Their dislike for each other is immediate and instinctual, as if each realizes in the other a natural enemy. The war metaphor would seem to be as neatly extended to the area of male/female relationship as that of a power struggle when she describes Frederic as "domineering and rude," i.e. not the least bit interested in her authority or her rules. And, in fact, Frederic isn't interested because he thoroughly discredits her authority and pays no attention to her rules. Like the earlier nurse, Miss Van Campen conceives of herself as morally superior to Frederic and is critical of him, implying that he is a selfish egotist, as insensitive to the concerns of others as he is to the larger issue of the war. But we discount Miss Van Campen's criticism because she is presented so unsympathetically and because Frederic suggests that the basis of her hostility towards him is his sexual relation with Catherine. Presumably Miss Van Campen knows that Catherine and Frederic are lovers and is just waiting for a chance to get Frederic for it. She fits the stereotyped category, so comfortable to the male ego, of the frustrated old maid who, because she has never had sex, is jealous of those who do and persecutes them. Her hostility results from powerlessness while his is the product of power; she is hostile because of rejection and he is hostile out of a contempt whose ultimate measure can be taken by the fact that he sees rejection and powerlessness as the source of her hostility.

In the final phase of their struggle, Frederic employs the archetypal method by which men have sought to deny women who refuse to comply with the "feminine mystique" any possibility of power, authority, or credibility. He denies her ability to know anything by calling into question her sexuality and her status as a woman. All he need do to rout her utterly is remind her by implication that she is not a full woman, that she has had no sexual experience, that she knows nothing of the pain of the scrotum or the agonies of the womb. So insecure as a person because she has failed to be a woman, the merest mention of the sacred genitalia is enough to vanquish her. In true male fashion, Frederic uses his penis as the ultimate weapon and the ultimate court of appeal.

If the Van Campens of this world get to Frederic because of their pretensions to authority, other women get to him because of their incompetence. For instance, Mrs. Walker. Doing night duty in a just-opened and empty hospital, she is a awakened from her sleep to deal with an unexpected patient and proves to be totally unable to handle the situation: "I don't know," "I couldn't put you in just any room," "I can't put on sheets," "I can't read Italian," "I can't do anything without the doctor's orders" (pp. 82, 83). Frederic ultimately deals with her incompetence by ignoring her and communicating with the men involved who, in spite of their position as mere porters, are able to get him to a bed. Mrs. Walker is one of a number of weepy women in the novel who appear to have no way of dealing with difficulty other than crying. The attitude towards them is one in which contempt is mingled with patronizing pity. Poor Mrs. Walker, poor Fergy, poor whores, poor virgins. Here, of course, is a classic instance of the double bind: women are pathetic in their inability to handle difficulty but if they presume to positions of authority and, even worse, to execute the authority of these positions, they become unbearably self-righteous and superior. Damned if you do and damned if you don't. But ultimately less damned if you don't, because at least Walker is a Mrs.—no shadow here of not being a real woman—while it is Van Campen who bears the stigma of Miss. For Frederic Henry is finally more comfortable with women who do not threaten his ego by pretending to authority over him. This is part of his attraction to whores: "'Does she [the whore] say she loves him?' . . . 'Yes. If *he* wants her to.' 'Does he say he loves her?' . . . 'He does if *he* wants to'" (p. 105—italics mine).

While Frederic Henry is willing to evaluate his nurses in terms of skill, one can be quite sure that Frederic would never have fallen in love with

Catherine if she were not beautiful. The idyllic quality of such love rests firmly on the precondition that the female partner be a "looker." And Catherine is, she most certainly is beautiful and so she is eminently lovable. While Catherine's beauty is presented as a sufficient cause of Frederic's love, we are, of course, justified in taking a longer look at the basis of his emotion. Although one can explain his sudden falling in love on the basis of the trap metaphor which the novel develops so elaborately—things happen to you and all of a sudden you are in it and there is nothing you can do about it— it hardly seems fortuitous that the experience occurs when he is most in need of the loving service which Nurse Barkley appears so amply able to provide. Frederic has, after all, had several weeks of lying flat on his back with a blown-up leg and little else to think about except the absurdity of his position in relation to the war, his isolation, and the essential fragility of life. Such thoughts might make one prone to accept affection and service even if it requires the word "love" to get it. And Frederic, trapped as he is in a cast, in a bed, in a hospital, in a stupid war, seems only too willing to avail himself of Catherine's service. Frederic greatly likes her because she will work at night since it means she is available for his needs not only during the day but during darkness as well. While Frederic sleeps during the day, however, Catherine goes right on working. He is conveniently unaware of her exhaustion in the face of the double duty induced by his continual invitations to "play." It is Catherine's friend, Ferguson, who finally points it out to him and insists that he get her to rest.

The egotistic basis of Frederic's feeling for Catherine is clear from other vantage points as well. For instance, one can consider those few scenes in which Catherine would appear to be making demands on Frederic. During their second meeting, Frederic tries to put the make on Catherine. Because she feels that he is insincere, his gesture simply part of the routine which soldiers go through when they get a nurse on her evening off, she says no, and when that has no effect, she slaps him. Frederic responds to her initial refusal by ignoring it. Then when she slaps him, he gets angry and uses his anger in combination with her guilt to get what he wanted in the first place. Jackson J. Benson describes the situation beautifully:

> In his early encounters with the British nurse Catherine Barkley, Henry is the casual, uniformed boy on the make, but down deep inside he is really a decent sort. In other words, what makes Henry so sinister is his All-American-Boy lack of guile. He demonstrates an attitude and pattern of behavior that any Rotarian would privately endorse. He fully intends (he spells it out quite clearly) to take a girl, who is described in terms of a helpless, trembling Henry James bird, and crush her in his hands very casually as part of the game that every young, virile lad must play. It is a backhanded tribute to Hemingway's irony here that most readers don't seem to even blanch at the prospect.[4]

But if irony is so mistakeable, one may be justified in questioning whether or not it is intended. And why should Hemingway in this instance be separated from the cultural norm of "any Rotarian" so brilliantly embodied in Frederic and Catherine's views of the affair? In both their eyes Frederic's anger is justifiable, the legitimate response of a male thwarted in his rightful desires by a maiden unduly coy (*vide* Catherine's reference to Marvell's "To His Coy Mistress": "it's about a girl who wouldn't live with a man"), whose posture of trembling helplessness is simply a way of disguising what she really wants or at least ought to want.

Richard B. Hovey's analysis of the scene in which Catherine announces her pregnancy is excellent for our purposes:

> From any common-sense and manly point of view, Frederic is failing Catherine in this crisis. When she makes her big announcement and then confesses that she tried to induce a miscarriage, he makes practically no response. The lover-hero at this point reveals a startling lack of awareness, an unpleasing absorption in himself. Thereupon Catherine takes on herself all the blame for "making trouble"—and he allows her to do exactly that! . . . So it is Catherine, the one who must go through childbirth, who does the comforting. A depth of pathos—or of downright absurdity—is reached toward the end of the scene when both lovers concern themselves with whether the pregnancy makes *Frederic* feel trapped.[5]

Later in the novel, in the hotel room which they have taken to spend a last few hours together before Frederic leaves for the front, Catherine has a sudden attack of depression. The idea of taking a room not for the night but for two or three hours, the quality of the hotel, the decor of the room all combine to make her feel like a whore. At the moment when Catherine is experiencing this feeling of alienation, Frederic is standing by the windows whose red plush curtains he has just closed, in a gesture which signals their possession of the room as another "home" and encloses the two of them in an inner world which reflects his sense of their closeness. They are at this moment poles apart in their feelings. Then Frederic catches sight of Catherine in the mirrors which surround the room and discovers that she is unhappy. He is surprised—for how could they be reacting so differently when they two are one and that one is he—and disappointed for this will upset his plans for their last evening together. "You're not a whore," he says, as if simple assertion were sufficient to cancel the complex sources of her sense of degradation. He then proceeds to register his own feelings of disappointment, anger and frustration in unmistakeable terms: he re-opens the curtains and looks out, suggesting thereby that she has shattered their rapport and broken up their home. Quite literally, Frederic turns his back on Catherine. His meaning is clear; Catherine's unhappiness is something he can respond to only in terms of how it affects him; beyond that, it is her problem and when she gets herself together and is ready to be his "good girl" again, then he will come back. And if she doesn't? "Oh, Hell, I thought, do we have to argue now?" (p. 252). In other words, either she does what he wants or he gets angry. Hostility and love seem very close indeed here and the bulwark which separates them would appear to be Catherine's ability to fulfill the demands of Frederic's ego. Catherine acts as if she knows quite well where Frederic's love is coming from. She is hypersensitive to his ego; she is forever asking him, "What would you like me to do now?"; and she continually responds to their situation in terms of his needs: I'll get rid of Ferguson so that we can go to bed, you must go play with Count Greffi, don't you want a weekend with the boys, I know I'm not much fun now that I'm big.

But there are other aspects of Frederic Henry's character that Catherine seems to respond to, that her character takes its shape from and that form the basis of his love for her. Wyndham Lewis has amply commented on the essential passivity of Hemingway's protagonist and others have concurred with his observations. Among "the multitudinous ranks of *those to whom things happen*," Frederic Henry lacks "executive will," a sense of responsibility and the capacity to make a commitment.[6] In contrast to Frederic's passivity, one is struck by Catherine's aggressiveness. How, after all, can a heroine be allowed so much activity and still keep her status as an idealized love object? On closer analysis, however, one notices that Catherine's aggressiveness achieves legitimacy because it is always exercised in the service of Frederic's passivity. Whenever Catherine acts she does so in order to save him from responsibility and commitment. It is Catherine who creates the involvement between herself and Frederic; it is she who constructs their initial encounter in such a way as to place them in a "relationship" almost immediately; it is she who shows up at the hospital in Milan so that he can fall in love with her. In addition, Catherine takes full responsibility for their pregnancy and for figuring out where and how she will have their baby and then, when she dies, she takes, in conjunction with certain ill-defined cosmic forces, the responsibility for this, too. It is possible for Frederic to love Catherine because she provides him with the only kind of relationship that he is capable of accepting, one in which he does not have to act, in which he does not have to think about things because she does it for him ("You see, darling, if I marry you I'll be an American and any time we're married under American law the child is legitimate"), and one in which he does not have to assume responsibility and to which he does not have to make a final commitment because both her facile logic to the effect that they are already married and her ultimate death give him a convenient out.

But Catherine relates to Frederic's need to avoid responsibility in an even deeper way. Frederic gets bogged down in the midst of the Italian retreat, thousands of people on a single road not moving, going nowhere and if you try to take a side road your cars get stuck in the mud and you get shot as a deserter. The imagery of the retreat is a perfect analogue for the form of Frederic's thought which turns back upon itself to leave him locked between two impossibilities. He is cut off from the past; he can not get to the Abruzzi, that idealized world of the past where God is not a dirty joke and where social relationships are exquisitely simple. He can not go back because it is clear that the aristocratic and chauvinistic world of the Abruzzi is responsible for the horror of this war, a war of kings and dukes which the peasants disavow and in so doing call into question the whole archaic structure which the Abruzzi represents. But he can not go forward either. His question is not, if you never got back to Milan what happened, but rather, if you *got* back what happened? His mind recoils in fear at the thought of the future. Indeed, he is able to relate to Catherine precisely because and as long as their relationship has neither past (don't worry, you won't have to meet my father), nor future; as long as, like the Italian retreat, it goes nowhere. When it threatens to go forward, it conveniently ends by Catherine's death in childbirth, that "cloud," as John Killinger puts it, "spread by the author as a disguise for pulling off a *deus ex machina* to save his hero from the existential hell of a complicated life."[7] Through Catherine's death, then, Frederic Henry avoids having to face the responsibilities incumbent upon a husband and father. Her death reflects his desire to remain uncommitted and it gives him a marketable explanation for so doing.

To say, however, that Catherine fulfills Frederic's need to avoid responsibility and to remain uncommitted is certainly at some level to say she has failed him. This is the burden of Robert Lewis' commentary on *A Farewell to Arms*. His sense of Catherine's failure is clearly carried in the following remark: "Her death carries the hope with it of the destruction of her destructive love that excludes the world, that in its very denial of self possesses selfishly, that leads nowhere beyond the bed and the dream of a mystical transport of ordinary men and women to a divine state of love through foolish suffering."[8] As the tenor of this sentence suggests, it would seem that Catherine's very adaptability to Frederic's need "to reduce life to its lowest denominator, to make it simple, to make it thoughtless, to destroy consciousness and responsibility in a romantic, orgiastic dream" is in itself a source of hostility toward her.[9] But one can give the emotional screw of the novel one final turn. If Catherine finally fails Frederic, it may be that in so doing she is fulfilling his ultimate need, which is to feel betrayed. Frederic's mentality is saturated with the vision of betrayal. At one point, he jokingly refers to himself as Christ. Like all good jokes, this one reveals as much as it hides. And what it reveals in part is Frederic's instinctive affiliation of himself with one who was betrayed. This metaphor of betrayal also governs Frederic's war experience, for the only killings we ever see are those of Italians by Italians. The metaphor is driven home by the irony of the fact that when Frederic makes his break for the river, he is about to be shot as a traitor. It is the imagery of betrayal which equally governs his view of Catherine's experience, for she is finally betrayed by her own body, whose physical construction is in direct opposition to its biological function and which, in internecine strife, strangles to death her own life within her. It is this concept which permeates Frederic's view of nature (*n.b.* the larks who are tricked by mirrors into being shot) and which produces his view of the universe in which a "we" who are good and brave and beautiful are opposed by a "they" who wish to break us precisely because we are good and brave and beautiful, so that once again we are betrayed by the nature of life whose ultimate treachery lies in the fact that it makes our selves the agents of our destruction.

Catherine relates to Frederic Henry's vision of betrayal because she too betrays him. She gets him involved with her by offering him a relationship in which there will be no drawbacks, no demands, pressures or responsibilities, only benefits, and then she presents him with the ultimate responsibility of her pregnancy: "I know I've made trouble now" (p. 138). Further, after making him emotionally dependent on her, she abandons him; she dies happily ever after and leaves him alone to face a cold, wet, hostile world. At one point early in the novel when Frederic is going off to see Catherine, he asks Rinaldi to come with him. Rinaldi answers "No . . . I like the simpler pleasures" (p. 41). In Rinaldi's eyes Catherine is clearly a complication and what she has to offer can in no way compensate for the complications that come along with her. Frederic seems to echo Rinaldi's view of love when he says, "God knows I had not wanted to fall in love with her. I had not wanted to fall in love with anyone" (p. 93). And while at this moment he claims that, in spite of his not having wanted this complication in his life, he feels "wonderful," at other times he appears to feel differently. "You always feel trapped biologically," he says to Catherine and the announcement of her pregnancy is followed not only by the rain but by his waking in the night nauseated and jaundiced. The conjunction hardly seems accidental. If in Rinaldi's eyes, women give one syphilis, Catherine, it would seem, makes Frederic sick. Finally, at the end of the novel, we get the sense that Frederic sees himself as abandoned. Frederic feels he is alone in an empty world which no longer has in it for him any source of nourishment or sustenance. And the agency of this betrayal is Catherine, who cuts him off from life as effectively as she strangles her own son inside her. Frederic's attitude, then, is finally not much different from the doctor who reprimands Catherine on her deathbed for being so selfish as to think of dying and leaving her husband.

Let us recapitulate a moment. On the simplest level, Catherine allows Frederic to avoid responsibility and commitment. But in so far as this allows him to avoid growing up, she has failed him and is thus subject to hostility on this account. She is equally subject to hostility for having complicated his life and come so close to thrusting responsibility on him. Like all women who, in the last analysis, let you down, Catherine has betrayed Frederic. We know that Frederic wants to feel betrayed, needs to feel betrayed because the sense of betrayal is his emotional engine and the structure which supports his ego. It allows him at once the indulgencē of his egotism in the posture of self-pity and an excuse to avoid future commitments. If Catherine is just one more piece of evidence to validate his sentimental and egocentric philosophy that the world exists for the single purpose of breaking him, then she has once again failed him. *Da capo. Ad nauseam.* The point is that whatever way you look at it, Catherine is bad news. Thus we might finally see her death as the unconscious expression of the cumulative hostilities which Frederic feels towards her. Essentially, she gets what is coming to her.

The use of spatial imagery in *A Farewell to Arms* is, as Carlos Baker has observed, complex.[10] Part of its complexity is relevant to our understanding of the relationship between Frederic and Catherine. Very early in the novel a contrast is established between what I shall call, adapting the terms of Erik Erikson, outer and inner space. Frederic is trying to explain to the priest why he never got to the Abruzzi "where the roads were frozen and hard as iron, where it was clear cold and dry and the snow was dry and powdery and hare-tracks in the snow," but rather had gone to smoke-filled cafes and dark rooms in the night (p. 13). The tension between these two kinds of space is central to Frederic's imagination. He essentially shies away from images of outer space, investing them with loneliness and fear, and he embraces images of inner space, investing them with an aura of security. The tension is further heightened by the fact that the images of inner space are developed against the background of a cold, dark, wet, hostile outer world. Again, we get some sense of this contrast early in the novel when Frederic moves back and forth between the mountains where the fighting is and where the forest is gone and there are only "stumps and the broken trunks and the ground torn up" and where the remnants of the trees project, isolated against a background of snow; and the town with "trees around the square and the long avenue of trees that led to the square" where he sits looking out the window, drinking and watching the snow falling (p. 6). This image of Frederic Henry inside, warm, dry, and secure, watching the world outside, isolated by light, struggle against the cold and wet, is endlessly recurrent in the novel. It is this vision of inner space which he seeks equally in Catherine, loving as he does to let her hair fall over him like a tent and focussing incessantly on every room they inhabit and how they make it a "home." When Frederic arrives at the hospital in Milan, it is, significantly, empty. There is nobody in it, no patients, seemingly no staff, no sheets on the bed for anybody to be in, and no room of one's own. By the time he leaves, the hospital has become a home from which he is ejected into the outer world of the war. The height of the creation of inner space with Catherine is, of course, their rooms in the house in the Swiss mountains with the big stove in the corner and the feather bed for the lovely dark nights and the air crisp and cold to define for them the security of being inside, snuggled and warm.

While this archetypal image evokes feelings of warmth and security, it equally evokes feelings of immense vulnerability for the inner space so carefully and elaborately created is continually threatened by intrusions from the hostile, infinitely larger, outer world; it is but a momentary stay against the confusion of crowded troop trains where you spend the night on the floor with people walking over you and of stalled retreats where, like a sitting duck, you wait to be picked off by planes coming in from Austria; it can at any moment be changed in a moment to simply an analogue for the outside world. The immense vulnerability of inner space is poignantly captured when Frederic and Catherine, on their way to the station for his departure to the front, encounter a soldier and his girl standing, in the mist and cold, tight up against a wet stone buttress, his cape pulled around them both. It is a posture which they consciously or unconsciously imitate a few moments later in sympathetic appreciation of their equal vulnerability. It is pathetic or ironic, or both, that Catherine, driven away in a carriage, her face lighted up in the window, motions Frederic to get back in under the archway and out of the rain.

The threat to inner space comes not only from outside but equally from inside, from its very nature. When Frederic is retreating from retreat and trying to get back to Milan, he hops a train and dives in under the canvas of a flat car where he is out of sight, secure, warm, and dry. In the process he hits his head against something and discovers, on feeling about, that what is sharing this world with him is a gun. This connection of the inner world with death is fully developed through Catherine. Her womb, carrying an embryo secure, warm and nourished, is an obvious analogue for the world which Frederic creates with her. But at the end of the novel we discover that Catherine's womb is, in fact, a chamber of horrors filled with blood and death. In an ironic reversal of expectations, the real danger to Frederic Henry turns out not to be the world of war, the outer world which seems so obviously threatening, but the world of love, the inner world which seems overtly so secure.

The connection of sex and death is incessant in Hemingway's writing. In *A Farewell to Arms* the association is made by the second page of the book: "their rifles were wet and under their capes the two leather cartridge-boxes on the front of the belts, gray leather boxes heavy with the packs of clips of thin, long 6.5 mm. cartridges, bulged forward under the capes so that the men passing on the road, marched as though they were six months gone with child." The idea that pregnancy is death and the womb an agent of destruction could hardly be stated more clearly. Thus the real source of betrayal in the biological trap is not simply biology; it is, specifically, female biology. Women, who promise life, are in reality death and their world of inner space is finally nightmare. Conversely, the outer world of men which seems overtly to be given over to death, is finally the reservoir of hope and possibility. In the handling of these metaphors of space, then, we once again encounter the immense hostility toward women which underlies *A Farewell to Arms*. Perhaps the "they" of Frederic's philosophy can indeed be located in time and space. And perhaps that is why Frederic Henry is afraid of the numbers above two when, in a scene charged with unstated emotion, he stands over Catherine controlling the gas which could so easily, under the guise of easing her pain, kill her. So true to the end is this novel to the forms of disguise, a resentful cryptogram indeed.

Notes

1. See, in particular, the documentation of Robert W. Lewis, Jr. in "The Tough Romance," in *Twentieth Century Interpretations of "A Farewell To Arms,"* ed. Jay Gellens (Englewood Cliffs: Prentice-Hall, 1970), pp. 42–43.

2. *Ernest Hemingway: An Introduction and Interpretation* (New York: Holt, Rinehart and Winston, 1967), p. 73.

3. It is interesting in this connection to read Wyndham Lewis' essay on *A Farewell To Arms*, reprinted in *Twentieth Century Interpretations* (pp. 72–90) as "The Dumb Ox in Love and War." While he describes, and ultimately decries, the paralysis of the will which characterizes the Hemingway protagonist, he picks as his point of comparison and his representative of "passionate personal energy" Prosper Merimee's Don José who dealt in a truly Othello-like way with his particular Desdemona, Carmen. In part, then, what Lewis' essay seems to be is a lament for the good old days when men's hostility for women could be openly expressed and socially justified. Indeed, the politics of this change are, as Lewis implies, immense.

4. *Hemingway: The Writer's Art of Self-Defense* (Minneapolis: University of Minnesota Press, 1969), pp. 82–83.

5. *Hemingway: The Inward Terrain* (Seattle: University of Washington Press, 1968), pp. 78–79.

6. Wyndham Lewis, pp. 73, 90.

7. *Hemingway and the Dead Gods* (Lexington: University of Kentucky Press, 1960), p. 47.

8. Robert W. Lewis, Jr., p. 53.

9. *Ibid.*, p. 52.

10. *Hemingway: The Writer as Artist* (Princeton: Princeton University Press, 3rd. ed., 1963), pp. 94–109.

A Hospitalized World

GERRY BRENNER

Like *The Scarlet Letter*'s scaffold, *Anna Karenina*'s railroad tracks, *Bleak House*'s court of chancery, *A Passage to India*'s caves, *As I Lay Dying*'s coffin, *Confidence Man*'s riverboat, *Huckleberry Finn*'s raft, and *The Old Man and the Sea*'s skiff, *A Farewell to Arms*' hospitals are central to many of its events. And whether in an ambulance, aid station, or hospital, Hemingway's hero and heroine are never far from the flag that waves above their actions—the Red Cross. Admittedly Hemingway's World War I experiences partly determine hospitals as the novel's chief stage property. But were the novel truly dictated by personal experience, then Frederic Henry would not have been wounded as an officer of an ambulance unit but rather as Hemingway had been, as a *cantinier*, doling out sweets, tobacco, and postcards to Italian troops.[1]

Esthetic considerations must have been among Hemingway's reasons for altering the facts of his own experiences. The medical duties of an ambulance officer and a nurse lend greater plausibility to Frederic's love story than had Frederic been a *cantinier*. And his medical status makes inconspicuous the hospitals, which unify the plot's action: Frederic and Catherine meet in the hospital in Gorizia, reunite and consummate their romance in the Milan hospital, and separate in the Lausanne hospital. And the alteration from *cantinier* to ambulance officer allows the ubiquitous image of the Red Cross to unify the novel's settings and to urge the inevitability of its conclusion: from Frederic's compatriot's hernia to Catherine's fatal hemorrhage the novel's steady tattoo of injury and ailment prepares for calamity. That Red Cross banner even invites the ironic view that Frederic and Catherine's Swiss idyll is less pastoral romance than medical reciprocity. That is, since the Swiss flag inverts the colors of the Red Cross flag, it could be argued that as Catherine nursed Frederic through his convalescence in Milan, he inverted their relationship in Switzerland, nursing her through pregnancy—almost.

As a stage property, hospitals generate more than esthetic felicities.

They indicate that Hemingway's principal subject is not war and love but wounds. Whether caused by war, family, or accident, and whether physical, emotional, spiritual, or psychological, wounds define the world of this novel: injury ridden. The traditional "physician" for such wounds, the priest, can poorly administer to the needs of such a world. Yet equally ineffective are the surgeons, medics, and nurses who work in the novel's hospitals and care for injured bodies. Their anesthetics, operations, dressings, and therapy cannot prevent that most normal of human functions—the cycle of reproduction—from going terribly awry. Neither can they cure the wounds that accompany Frederic when he walks away from the hospital at the novel's end. Symbol of the clean, well-lighted place to which modern man turns in the hope of being made whole, Hemingway's hospitals seem small improvement over the institutions they historically replace, churches.

Unlike Sinclair Lewis's hospitals, which expose the abuses of the medical profession in *Arrowsmith*, or Thomas Mann's sanatorium, which completes the education of his hero in *Magic Mountain*, Hemingway's hospitals cannot heal the deeper injuries common to the human condition. But their failure is symptomatic of the failure of any system that offers or allows the illusion that it can give humankind health, order, meaning, or significance. In short, the thesis of *A Farewell to Arms* is that no institution, belief, system, value, or commitment can arm one against life's utter irrationality.[2] Recognizing this thesis clarifies the novel's structure, my first concern. It also explains why and when Frederic narrates his story, the characters of both Frederic and Catherine, and the aptness of their fantasy-driven romance, my second set of concerns. And it explains some reasons why Hemingway wrote the novel, one of the concerns of my afterword.

The sequence of Frederic Henry's major decisions reveals both his awareness of life's irrationality and the novel's underlying structure. His decision that family and country offered him no meaningful value is borne out by his disparaging references to the former and by his expatriation from the latter. His decision to stop studying architecture in Italy indicates that it obviously failed to satisfy his needs too. But that pursuit, however brief it may have been, also indicates that initially he decided to study a profession concerned with design, formal order, and tangible structures. Frederic is offhanded about his joining the Italian army and getting assigned to an ambulance unit. Yet except for medicine, no profession theoretically requires more discipline, regimentation, and obedience to orders than the military. That fact may underlie Frederic's decision to enlist, for it shows his continued search for order.

The opening chapters of the novel indicate that Frederic has served for more than a year, so he has been in the army long enough to know the gap between the military's theoretical order and reality. Futility, then, not irony, propels his remark that medicine stops the cholera epidemic only after seven thousand men die. And Catherine sees that the Italians occupy a "'silly front'" (20), dismantling any elevated notion of military rationality. Frederic notes early how ridiculous it was to carry a pistol that so sharply jumped upon firing that one could hit nothing (29). During the retreat later he sarcastically thinks that it is only as disorderly as an advance (188). Although Frederic falls in love with Catherine during his Milan convalescence, it is not until his next major decision, to desert the army at the Tagliamento, that he also decides to commit himself to her, seeking order and meaning now in their intimate relationship. Her death, of course, insists that nothing can immunize her against irrational forces. Neither science and Rinaldi's medical skill, nor faith and the priest's prayers, nor love and Frederic's care—none of these can keep her alive. Hemingway's borrowing the novel's title from that of George Peele's poem, then, is ironic, for he rejects the poem's conviction that "duty, faith, love are roots, and ever green"—that they offer meaningful value.[3]

While deciding at the Tagliamento to commit himself to Catherine, Frederic makes two other decisions: to eschew thought and the processes of reasoning, and to seek order through his senses and the processes of nature. He tells himself that he was made not to think but to eat, to drink, and to sleep with Catherine (233).

Frederic's justification for the former decision rests upon more than the travesty of rationality he hears the battle police at the bridge declaim. After all, the military landscape abounds in irrationality. Pleasure palaces on the front lines? An offensive campaign in the mountains? Gas masks that fail to work? An ambulance unit of anarchists? Bridges not blown to slow the German offensive? Medals of honor for victims of accidents? No less irrational is the social landscape Frederic portrays. Were it not for the pain in his legs, his arrival at the Milan hospital would be Chaplinesque: an unkempt nurse, unprepared rooms, unmade beds, unanswered bellcords, and an absent doctor. Puzzled and angry he asks how there can be a hospital with no doctor (87). Just as the fixed horse races violate one activity over which chance and unpredictability should rule, so too do Frederic and Catherine violate the idea of a hospital: their romance transforms a ward for physical suffering into a haven of sensual gratification. The "comic opera" of their interrogation by the Swiss police at Locarno further justifies Frederic's derision of reason, aped as reason is by absurd civil formalities. His refrain throughout the last third of the novel, then, that he does not want to think, does not reflect a wish to escape or delay responsibility. It expresses his belief that thinking is a poor remedy for human problems.

Frederic's decision to embrace sensory experience and nature's processes is just as poor a remedy. Nature is no more orderly, controllable, or predictable than reason. Frederic's shrapnel-filled legs fail to raise his temperature. But Miss Gage patronizingly tells him that foreign bodies in his legs would inflame and give him a fever (85). Contrary to Miss Van Campen's belief, he cannot keep from contracting jaundice. Neither can Catherine prevent conception, assuring Frederic that she did everything she could, but that nothing she took made any difference (138). More to the point, Catherine's narrow hips thwart nature's reproductive cycle. And the umbilical cord, rather than nourishing fetal life, becomes a hangman's noose. At the novel's end neither spring nor rain will bring their normal regeneration.

The British major at the club in Milan tells Frederic how to respond to their world: "He said we were all cooked but we were all right as long as we did not know it. We were all cooked. The thing was not to recognize it" (133–34). Stripped as Frederic has been of virtually everything that would give him reason to continue living, when Catherine dies he cannot avoid seeing that he too is "cooked." And that prompts his next-to-last decision, to tell his story.

Frederic's motive for telling his story is elusive. If his motive is altruism, then as an ex-ambulance officer he may believe that to cure such a "cooked" world first requires diagnosing its condition and that telling his story will do that. If his motive is vindictiveness, then he may sadistically want to force others to see that they too are "cooked." If it is self-pity, then he may hope that telling his story will console himself and justify his apparent callousness. If his motive is self-aggrandizement, then he may feel that telling it will gain our admiration. If it is objectivity, then he may simply be telling it "the way it was." His motive, however, is revealed by his narrative manner, which leads me to three conclusions that I take up in reverse order. His manner reveals that he is disoriented by what has happened to him and so is an untrustworthy narrator; that he tells his story soon after Catherine's death; and that if he can discover in his story meanings that will nurture a desire to continue living, then his motive has been therapeutic. If not, then his motive has been testamentary: his story will explain his last decision—to commit suicide.

Farewell presumably conforms to the tradition of the *Bildungsroman*. Charting Frederic's development, the novel teaches that he grows by learning something: neither to "say 'farewell to arms' " nor to "sign a separate peace" but to "live with life," to "tolerate it"; "to become eventually quite strong" by being broken; to become "humanely alive" by caring for Catherine and saying "farewell to 'not-caring-ness' "; to reject eros for agape; to value life by discovering death and the "step-by-step reduction of the objects" he had found meaningful.[4] These statements about Frederic's "growth" assume that at the time he writes his story Frederic-the-narrator understands the significance of what has happened to him. Moreover, they assume that he has been chastened by experience and so will be a better person morally than he was at the beginning of his story. Most importantly, they assume that Frederic goes on living after he has told his story. And so they imply that Frederic's motive has been therapeutic.

Slightly modifying the end of Frederic's most anguished internal monologue, I ask, "'But what if he should die? Hey, what about that? What if he should die?' " (321). The well-known "original" ending to the novel finds Frederic alive "and going on with the rest of my life—which has gone on and seems likely to go on for a long time."[5] But that staccato of negatives— nos, nothings, and nots—in Hemingway's splendid revision courts a differ- ent conclusion. Frederic's decisions have shown him turning to—but finding no life-sustaining meaning in—family, country, profession, religion, duty, reason, nature, or love. Having found only life's irrationality, Frederic would more likely decide now to commit suicide than to go on living an utterly hollow life. He is likely to tell himself the same thing he tells the dog sniffing the garbage cans, that there is nothing (315).

Whether Frederic goes on living or commits suicide is, of course, unknowable. But that fact cautions against predicting moral conduct from him now that Catherine is dead. Indeed, to confirm any of the statements about what Frederic learns and how he will now behave requires knowing what he does after he returned in the rain to the hotel (332). Clearly, he tells his story. But what does he do after he has told it? No Marlow, David Copperfield, Nick Carraway, or Jack Burden, Frederic gives no epilogue and scarcely any glimmer of where or to whom he tells his story. But Frederic does indicate when he tells it. He tells it shortly after Catherine's death.

We have long been schooled to conclude the opposite: as narrator, Frederic "speaks from a position several years remote from the occurrence of the action he describes"; and "the entire warm and loving story that consti- tutes the novel [is] a story told years after its occurrence."[6] To be sure, Frederic gives the impression that some years have elapsed by referring to "the late summer of that year" or by remarking, "We had a lovely time that summer." And his essayettes, like those on abstract words or on how the world breaks everyone, reveal an eye steadied by time. Even his recall of Catherine seems to indicate narrative distance when, in a two-paragraph sequence, he recounts how he took down her hair as she sat quietly on his bed, dipping down suddenly to kiss him as he took out each hairpin and lay it on the sheet, dropping her head to let her hair cascade over him when he removed the last two pins, then, later, twisting it up and letting the light from the doorway draw out its shining luster (114). The second paragraph of this representative and lyrical reminiscence has the summarizing quality of a memory recounted several years after the events of the novel. But the first paragraph's detailed immediacy is not a summary, does not generalize, is not brief. So recently had Frederic and Catherine gone through this ritual that he can reconstruct it, hairpin at a time. The paragraph's evocative recall has the quality of wish to it: to conjure the scene fully may dispel the reality of Catherine's death. And to savor the erotic pleasure he found in taking down her hair confesses the pain of no longer being able to repeat it, a pain that time would have lessened.

And Frederic's essayettes: do they reveal an eye steadied by time, "slacken somewhat the objective tautness, the firm gaze upon outward reality, which is so characteristic of [*The Sun Also-Rises*]?"[7] That is not their effect on me. They obtrusively, but fittingly, break the "illusion of continuous action" because Frederic is unable to reflect calmly or maturely upon his experiences. His essayettes self-pityingly complain against the world that breaks everyone (249) and the "they" who throw one into a game, tell the rules and then kill the first time they catch one off base (327). But the essayettes are justifiable. Having just suffered physical, emotional, and psychological injuries, Frederic lacks the composure to control or suppress his feelings with the objective tautness or firmness of Jake Barnes, whose injury considerably antedates his story.

Let us briefly compare Frederic with the first-person narrator of "Now I Lay Me," allegedly Nick Adams, to see better that Frederic narrates his story shortly after it happens. Nick does two things that measure the distance between himself as he tells his story and himself as he was when an insomniac. First, he carefully differentiates between then and now, gives a time frame. The opening paragraph says, "So while *now* I am fairly sure that [my soul] would not really have gone out [of my body], yet *then, that summer*, I was unwilling to make the experiment" (*Stories*, 363; italics added). The last paragraph also acknowledges that "he [John, my orderly] came to the hospital in Milan to see me *several months after* and was very disappointed that I had not yet married; and I know he would feel very badly if he knew that, *so far, I have* never married" (371; italics added). Second, Nick records, outline-fashion, the "different ways of occupying myself while I lay awake" (363). He refishes streams, recites prayers "for all the people I had ever known," and remembers "everything that had ever happened to me" (365) or "all the animals in the world by name" (367). Or he just listens. Both the time frame and the outline that shape Nick's recitation of the sequence of his nocturnal ritual are absent in Frederic's story. But rightly so, for until time gives Frederic some perspective upon his experiences, his narrative will tend to lose its thread, as it does in this sentence:

> That night in the mess after the spaghetti course, which every one ate very quickly and seriously, lifting the spaghetti on the fork until the loose strands hung clear then lowering it into the mouth, or else using a continuous lift and sucking into the mouth, helping ourselves to wine from the grass-covered gallon flask; it swung in a metal cradle and you pulled the neck of the flask down with the forefinger and the wine, clear red, tannic and lovely, poured out into the glass held with the same hand; after this course, the captain commenced picking on the priest. [6–7]

The more orderly narrators of "Now I Lay Me" or "In Another Country"— both of whom resemble Frederic—would not digress as Frederic does. They would delete the irrelevancies of how everyone ate and drank, and attend instead to the point: "That night in the mess the captain commenced picking on the priest." They might allow the phrase "after the spaghetti course," or at most the clause "which everyone ate very quickly and seriously," but no more.[8]

I exercise this issue of when Frederic tells his story because the novel hangs together best when heard on the heels of Catherine's death. To believe that considerable time has elapsed before he tells it invites the corollary conclusion: that the style of Frederic's story is "tough." Hemingway may be "a hard man who has been around in a violent world, and who partially conceals his strong feelings behind a curt manner."[9] But can the same be accurately said of Frederic? Does he refuse, as Walker Gibson argues, to be concrete about such details as *the* year, *the* river, *the* plain, and *the* mountain in his opening sentence to insinuate an intimacy between himself and his reader? Does he imply that we, fellow insiders, know what he speaks of without requiring him to elaborate upon it? Does he fail to subordinate his ideas and to define causal relationships because he knows that we know that he knows that we know? Does he, for example, say, "There was fighting in the mountains and at night we could see the flashes from the artillery" (3), confident that we know that what he means to say is, "We knew there was fighting in the mountains, for at night we could see the flashes from the artillery"?[10] To support my nays to these questions the terms of one of *Farewell*'s most spirited detractors are excellent—although I adopt them for altogether opposite reasons. According to John Edward Hardy, in Frederic's "anonymous and crippled sensibility . . . Hemingway produces what seems to me a radically maimed prose, a style that does not simply reflect but is the victim of the spiritual malady that afflicts his characters."[11]

Both the "tough" and "maimed" labels judge Frederic's style upon the basis of the perennial illusion that Hemingway, a crippled tough, a sentimentalist masquerading behind he-man brusqueness, wants his reader to endorse Frederic's values, to emulate his conduct, and to imitate his style. Setting this issue aside for now, I turn instead to the descriptive accuracy of the label "maimed." It is because Frederic is maimed, defensive, and still feeling vulnerable—not because he is hardened—that he tells his story in a "curt," "laconic," "close-lipped" style: the secure can afford to be expansive. It is because Frederic is crippled that he tries to retaliate with ironic indignation, not sophistication, with understated emotion, not wit, as when he tells that the only result of his contracting jaundice was that he was denied his leave (145). It is because Frederic's recent experiences make him skeptical of reason and causality that he avoids subordinating his ideas. And it is because he is preoccupied with his feelings and experience, rather than with our understanding, that Frederic is an inconsiderate, and ultimately an untrustworthy, narrator.

Frederic is inconsiderate of the audience who hears his story because he is mentally disoriented, so preoccupied with his recent injuries that he is unaware that his listener is unfamiliar with the details of his life. Frederic

ignores the amenities of formally introducing himself—"Call me Ishmael"—
not to presume quickly upon the reader as insider, but because when he
begins his story he is unsure of who he is. When his fictional predecessor,
Jake Barnes, began his story, he already knew who his scapegoat was; even
the deleted first chapters of his novel had similarly announced, "This is a
novel about a lady."[12] But Frederic cannot begin by focusing on the person
most important in his story. Sorely wounded, he avoids touching directly
its most tender spot, Catherine. He keeps her offstage until his narrative is
into its fourth chapter, enough time for its anesthetic, as it were, to take
effect. Guilt, severe emotional stress, and paranoid tendencies also explain
Frederic's reluctance to identify himself. Ferguson and Catherine call him
"Mr. Henry" once each in chapters 5 and 6. But whether Henry is his
surname or his Christian name is unclear. Nor is it clarified when his name
gets joked about during the second mess scene, whether his name is Frederico
Enrico or Enrico Frederico (40). Rinaldi only once calls him Frederico (76),
on the eve of his departure to Milan. Not until Miss Gage asks him in book
2 what his name is does he divulge it: " 'Henry. Frederic Henry' " (84).

Many things demonstrate that Frederic is a disoriented and, ultimately,
untrustworthy narrator. For all of its poetry, the much-praised opening
paragraph to *Farewell* is confusing—as any reader new to Hemingway and
the novel will affirm.[13] The first sentence alone generates no fewer than seven
unanswered questions. And the following paragraphs fail to answer the
questions of who the narrator is, where he is, why and what he is doing
there, and when these events are taking place. So ambiguous is Frederic's
narration that we can even mistakenly think that he sees his friend the priest
while sitting with a fellow officer rather than with a whore.[14] The mess table
riddles, allusions, jokes, and shadow games certainly convey the impression
that this must have been the way it really was. And they advance the
novel's irrationality. But they also convey Frederic's trouble with selecting,
organizing, and discriminating between significant and insignificant details.
So do his occasionally lengthy recordings of, say, the inebriated dialogue of
Rinaldi and the major from the mess in the last chapter of book 1. More
revealing of his disordered sensibility are soberly written sentences that need
considerable rereading before sense emerges. Telling of Gorizia, for example,
Frederic drones on in a 164-word sentence about its brothels, railway bridge,
the destroyed tunnel, trees around the town square, tree-lined avenues, house
interiors, street rubble, and visits by the small, long-necked, gray-bearded
king in his automobile (5–6).

Most persuasive of Frederic's disoriented sensibility in his confession
that he cannot analyze or define his experience. In his only unequivocal
reference to the time he is writing his story, he admits, "I tried to tell [the
priest] about the night and the difference between the night and the day
and how the night was better unless the day was very clean and cold and I
could not tell it; *as I cannot tell it now*" (13; italics added). During revision

Hemingway struck from the manuscript one of Frederic's monologues with the same confessional thrust. As the third paragraph of chapter 12, Frederic comments,

> I do not like to remember the trip back to Milan. If you have never travelled in a hospital train there is no use making a picture of it. This is not a picture of war, nor really about war. It is only a story. That is why, sometimes, it may seem that there are not many people in it, nor enough noises, nor enough smells. There were always people and noises unless it was quiet and always smells but *in trying to tell the story I cannot get them all in always but have a hard time keeping to the story* alone and sometimes it seems as though it were all quiet. But it wasn't quiet. If you try and put in everything you would never get a single day done. *Also when you are wounded or a little out of your head or in love with someone* the surroundings are sometimes removed and they only come in at certain times. But I will try to keep the places in and tell what happened. It does not seem to have gotten anywhere and it is not much of a love story so far but it has to go the way it was although I skip everything I can.[15]

Given his theory of omission, it seems reasonable that Hemingway deleted this confession because he was confident that Frederic's narrative manner had already exposed his psychologically crippled sensibility, that the explicit confession of his condition was inartistic.[16]

Admittedly Frederic has long stretches of narrative—like the retreat—that exhibit little, if any, disorientation. But I do not contend that he is totally disoriented. After all, once he gets into his narrative its chronology coheres, his characters gather consistency, and even his use of details loses ambiguity, as a comparison of the first chapters of books 1 and 3 shows. No "diary of a madman," Frederic's story holds firmly enough to external reality to compel empathy. He is "one of us," not a clinical case. His disorientation, his being "a little out of his head," then, waxes and wanes, just as his regard for the priest seesaws against his affection for Rinaldi.

Not to see Frederic disoriented at all mandates the conclusion that Hemingway lacks esthetic distance from his narrator: Frederic's self-pity is Hemingway's. This view ignores Hemingway's early exposure to, and the influence of, writers who calculatedly created untrustworthy narrators to achieve esthetic distance. To discount the facts that Hemingway worked with and read writers like Ford, Stein, and Joyce and that one of his favorites was Conrad is to imply that Hemingway was an authorial naif. To deny his detachment from his characters also ignores Hemingway's early achievements in characterization. Surely one of his earliest discoveries was the importance of limited characters in fiction, characters perceptive enough about their experiences to engage readers emotionally, but just imperceptive enough to detach them simultaneously. Hemingway's justly acclaimed Nick Adams stories astutely maintain that tension between a youth's discerning intelligence and his obtuseness. Just think of "Three-Day Blow." Hemingway undercuts Nick's adolescent swagger and savvy by having him naively think he can resume his relationship with Marge and that it will be the same as before. To Nick's confident, "There was not anything that was irrevocable" (*Stories*, 124), I hear the retort, " 'Isn't it pretty to think so?' "

It is Hemingway's variation on this tension that makes Frederic an untrustworthy narrator. Perceptive enough to recount the decisions and events that have led him into a cul-de-sac, he is too disoriented, because he is emotionally unstrung, to confront and answer the many questions he generates. What was it, Frederic, that the priest had always known that you did not know and that, when you learned it, you were always able to forget (14)? And what happened, Frederic, between you and your family that caused your rift? And what are you going to do, Frederic, after you've finished telling your story? And most of all, Frederic, was Catherine crazy? Or was she sane?

To see that Frederic is a "little out of his head" gives us a better view of both Catherine and the nature of their love. She is a poorly characterized heroine, as readers have long complained. More accurately, she is poorly characterized only if Hemingway's intent was to create a "round," richly complex human being. But I find little to support the idea that such an intent was among Hemingway's considerations. [17] Some readers may wish to elevate Catherine to sainthood. [18] But her fragile grasp of reality persuades me that Frederic loves a marginally neurotic woman who is more than a little out of her head. [19]

I find it impossible to gainsay Catherine's addiction to fantasy. Her romantic dream of marrying her childhood sweetheart was interrupted by the war. But still she envisioned him arriving at the hospital at which she was stationed, cut by a sabre and sporting a head bandage or else shot in the shoulder: " 'Something picturesque' " (20). By calling this a " 'silly idea,' " she implies that when she found out that he had been blown to bits, her schoolgirl fantasies also disintegrated. Yet her responses to Frederic's romantic advances border on neurosis. During their second meeting she one moment scolds him for talking nonsense (26) and the next pleads that he be good to her, telling him that their life together will be strange (27). And their third meeting flips from " 'Oh darling, you have come back, haven't you' " (30) to " 'You don't have to pretend you love me. That's over for the evening' " (31).

By the time Frederic sees Catherine in Milan he realizes, "I was crazy about her" (92). And so it is understandable that he resists the truth of his initial conclusion—that "she was probably a little crazy" (30)—by not contesting her later assertion that she is no longer crazy: " 'When I met you I was nearly crazy. Perhaps I was crazy' " (116). Yet her desire to dwell amid fantasies does not abate. When he denies having slept with other women, she ironically tells him to keep lying to her, that she wants him to lie to her (105). But her avowals to obey his wishes, lacking that irony, are fantasy-driven, declaring that she will say and do and want what he wishes her to say and do and want, for "'there isn't any me any more'" (105–6). Frederic admits that they pretended that they were married, and when he presses the issue and tells her that he wants to marry her for her sake, the urgency with which she must cling to fantasy is unmistakable in her insistent—if not imperious—reproach: "'There isn't any me. I'm you. Don't make up a separate me'" (115).

Symptoms of her flight from reality are strewn throughout the novel. She conceals her pregnancy and denies that it worried her; but her insistence that Frederic not worry edges toward hysteria, confirming his impression that "she seemed upset and taut" (137). Possessive, she gets "furious" if anyone else touches Frederic. And she wants to be completely alone with him, rejoicing that they know only one person in Montreux, that they see nobody (303). Her wish to merge her identity with his, telling him that she desires him so much that she even wants to be him, exhibits psychological dependency, not selflessness. Paranoid, she initiates the two-against-the-others view that Frederic adopts later in the novel; when he assures her they won't fight between themselves, she insists that they must not, for if anything were to come between them, then they would have no chance against the rest of the world (133). Her indefatigable cheerfulness is admirable. But it too signals a defensive reaction. When Frederic wants to discuss problems, she blithely disregards them just as she blithely tells her hairdresser in Montreux that she is pregnant with her fifth child or her obstetrician that she has been married for four years. Her final words are poignant. But they are completely in character, one last bit of fantasy, promising that she will come to spend the nights with him (331).

Frederic cannot ignore the fact that he loves a psychologically maimed woman. To her irrational fear of the rain he asks her to stop, adding that he does not want her to be "'Scotch and crazy tonight'" (126). His last word here, "tonight," rejects her wish to believe that she no longer has "crazy" moments. During the farewell scene in the Milan hotel before Frederic returns to the front, he records this exchange: "'I'm a very simple girl,' Catherine said. 'I didn't think so at first. I thought you were a crazy girl.' 'I was a little crazy. But I wasn't crazy in any complicated manner. I didn't confuse you did I, darling?' 'Wine is a grand thing,' I said. 'It makes you forget all the bad'" (154). Frederic's failure to answer her question, denying her what she wants to hear, recurs during their Switzerland "idyll." He wakes one moonlit night to find Catherine also awake. She asks if he remembers how she was "nearly crazy" when they first met. He comforts her by admitting that she was "'just a little crazy.'" She then asserts that she is no longer that way, that she is "'not crazy now'" (300). Frederic's response, "'Go on to sleep,'" can be tender, loving. But it does refuse to confirm her assertion, allowing us to conclude that perhaps she protesteth too much. And after she falls asleep, Frederic notes that he lay awake for a long time, thinking things over and watching the moonlight on Catherine's sleeping face (301). This suggests to me that it is a strain on Frederic to maintain the illusion of her sanity. Yet again, in response to Catherine's cheery jabber about cutting her hair and getting thin again and being "a new and different girl" and going together to get it cut or going alone and surprising him, Frederic registers that he "did not say anything" (304). Rather than implying masculine superiority to such concerns, his silence again implies weariness at having to support continuously Catherine's need for their "grand" romance.

Reluctant though Frederic is at times to nurse Catherine's delusion of sanity, he fears her mental relapse and tries to shield her. Just as he gives her the gas she needs during labor, he faithfuly administers the medicine she needs to keep from cracking up. In one overdose of ardor he assures her that she is his " 'good girl,' " a " 'lovely girl,' " a " 'grand girl!' " a " 'fine simple girl,' " and a " 'lovely girl' " (153–54). And the banality of their love talk in Switzerland seems partly calculated by Frederic to give Catherine the narcotic she needs, the assurance that his love is unflagging, that he is content to be alone with only her, that their togetherness does not bore him, that " 'we're the same one' " (299).

Though Frederic shoulders the psychological burden that Catherine's fragile mental condition imposes upon him, he should not get uncritical applause. After all, he too is psychologically dependent, needs her as much as she needs him. He tells her that he has a " 'fine life' " (298). And he tells us that they had a "fine life" and were "very happy" (306), that not once did they have a "bad time" (311). But what prompts these statements is Frederic's need to convince himself of his happiness, just as his assurances to Catherine had been calculated to make her feel secure in his love. Hemingway deleted from the novel other passages of Frederic stepping out of his self-mesmerizing account of the sequence of events to reflect upon the nature of his relationship with Catherine.[20] But he does keep one of Frederic's reflections: "Often a man wishes to be alone and a girl wishes to be alone too and if they love each other they are jealous of that in each other, but *I can truly say* we never felt that" (249; italics added). Jake Barnes's sarcastic " 'Isn't it pretty to think so' " again tempts me. But that would miss the point of Frederic's boast. Crediting it as fact and not wish, I think it measures the extent to which a crippled couple has retreated from even the reality of their own psychic individuality. Indeed their isolationism, their illusion of self-sufficiency, and their wish to make the convulsions of their erotic love the center of everything add up to a regressive withdrawal from reality. Frederic does not hide this fact, admitting that when reunited at Stresa they felt that they had returned home to be together and to waken in the night and find one another there, not absent: *"all other things were unreal"* (249; italics added). Summed up in Frederic's " 'Let's get back to bed. I feel fine in bed' " (251), their escapist fantasy amply proves that the object of their romantic love is to fend off reality, replete as it is with suffering and irrationality. "The weak side of this technique of living," as Freud so cogently and poignantly noted, "is that we are never so defenseless against suffering as when we love [because we make ourselves dependent upon one other person], never so helplessly unhappy as when we have lost our loved object or its love."[21] The unhappy survivor of this defense against reality, a man neither innately strong nor confident nor supported by any traditional values, Frederic would have little reason to continue living once he has told his story, written his testament.

Notes

1. Carlos Baker, *Ernest Hemingway: A Life Story* (New York: Scribners, 1969), p. 44; Michael S. Reynolds's *Hemingway's First War: The Making of "A Farewell to Arms"* (Princeton: Princeton University Press, 1976) definitively refutes the notion that personal experience dictated the specifics of the novel.

2. The motif of irrationality has been variously dealt with, nowhere more succinctly than in Frederick H. Marcus, "*A Farewell to Arms*: The Impact of Irony and the Irrational," *English Journal* 51 (1962): 527–35. The basic difference between our views of the thesis is that he believes that Frederic can escape irrational forces by retreating to the world of appetite—sex, drinking, and eating. I do not.

3. For discussions of the relationship between Peele's poem and Hemingway's novel, see Jerome L. Mazzaro, "George Peele and *A Farewell to Arms*: A Thematic Tie," *Modern Language Notes* 75 (1960): 118–19; Clinton Keeler, "*A Farewell to Arms*: Hemingway and Peele," *Modern Language Notes* 76 (1961): 622–25; and Bernard Oldsey, "Of Hemingway's *Arms* and the Man," *College Literature* 1 (1974): 174–89.

4. Respectively, Ray B. West, Jr., "*A Farewell to Arms*," in *The Art of Modern Fiction*, ed. Ray B. West, Jr., and Robert W. Stallman (New York: Holt, Rinehart & Winston, 1949), p. 633; Philip Young, *Ernest Hemingway: A Reconsideration* (University Park: Pennsylvania State University Press, 1966), p. 94; Earl Rovit, *Ernest Hemingway* (New York: Twayne Publishers, 1963), pp. 105–6; Robert W. Lewis, Jr., *Hemingway on Love* (Austin: University of Texas Press, 1965), pp. 49–52; and Dewey Ganzel, "*A Farewell to Arms*: The Danger of Imagination," *Sewanee Review* 79 (1971): 576–97. The first four of these are reprinted in Jay Gellens, ed., *Twentieth Century Interpretations of "A Farewell to Arms": A Collection of Critical Essays* (Englewood Cliffs, NJ: Prentice-Hall, 1970), pp. 27, 32, 39–40, and 48–51, respectively.

5. Carlos Baker reprints "The Original Conclusion to *A Farewell to Arms*" in *Ernest Hemingway: Critiques of Four Major Novels* (New York: Scribners, 1962), p. 75 (hereafter cited as *Critiques*). But see Bernard Oldsey, *Hemingway's Hidden Craft: The Writing of A Farewell to Arms* (University Park: Pennsylvania State University Press, 1979). He not only explains why the version Baker reprinted should more precisely be referred to as "The Original *Scribner's Magazine* Conclusion" (pp. 71–72) but also analyzes the forty-one variants of Hemingway's conclusions to the novel. Among them, only variant 41, in his listing among "Miscellaneous Endings," expressly "entertains possibility of suicide" (p. 107). That will prove to many readers that Hemingway saw Frederic's suicide as less probable than the other kinds of endings that Oldsey groups under eight headings. And I am taken with Oldsey's idea that Hemingway's final ending subsumes, iceberg-fashion, those other kinds of endings: the *Nada*, Fitzgerald, Religious, Live-Baby, Morning-After, Funeral, and Combination (i.e., epilogue) endings. Yet not only is the final ending nihilistic, like the *Nada* endings. But even Oldsey concludes that it was "conceived ... in the spirit of rejection" and is "a compressed exemplification of the process of rejection and negation" (p. 82). What action would better express that "spirit" and "process" than suicide? Moreover, though Hemingway was uncertain about

how to end his novel, the variant endings show that his final version flatly rejected the affirmative variants. Most important to note, Hemingway also discovered that his final ending was so congruent with the novel's character, thesis, and atmosphere that the rest of his text did not require serious modification, extensive revision. Readers who must salvage something positive from the novel, who nurse the illusion that the novel affirms selfless love, will, of course, opt for Frederic's growth or "initiation" and the theraputic motive behind his storytelling. Like any great novel, this one bears both that reading and mine.

6. Grebstein, *Hemingway's Craft*, p. 73; and Oldsey, *Hemingway's Hidden Craft*, p. 91. My following three sentences present, I hope fairly, the proofs upon which Professor Grebstein bases his conclusion, pp. 73–76. Oldsey, in contrast, offers no support for his assertion, one that he makes in several places.

7. E. M. Halliday, "Hemingway's Narrative Perspective," *Sewanee Review* 60 (1952); 210; rpt. in Baker, *Critiques*, p. 178.

8. Julian Smith, in "Hemingway and the Thing Left Out," *Journal of Modern Literature* 1 (1970–71): 163–82, offers a different but interesting reading of the narrators of both stories.

9. Walker Gibson, "Tough Talk: The Rhetoric of Frederic Henry," in his *Tough, Sweet, and Stuff: An Essay on Modern Prose Styles* (Bloomington: Indiana University Press, 1966), p. 40. The following questions I raise in the text are based upon Gibson's conclusions about Frederic, pp. 34–41. In fairness to him, he achnowledges that he bases them upon a small sample, the novel's first two paragraphs. But that neither subdues his dogmatism nor causes him to consider the inadequacy of his tidy, triadic format. If, for instance, the speaker of Marvell's "Coy Mistress," a speech by Winston Churchill, and the story told by Frederic Henry all employ "tough" styles, then wherein lies the value of classification that groups together a lover, a patriot, and a disoriented storyteller? Gibson's case for defining Frederic as "tough" is one of the more explicit discussions of the "Hemingway style." But also see Walter J. Ong, S.J., "The Writer's Audience Is Always a Fiction," *PMLA* 90 (1976): 9–21, who follows Gibson to conclude that Hemingway's style serves the purpose of casting the reader "in the role of a close companion of the writer" (p. 13). Ong, too, fails to consider that disoriented and neurotic people use language, particularly demonstrative pronouns, "that," and definite articles, in much the same way as Frederic does.

10. Gibson, "Tough Talk," pp. 36–37.

11. John Edward Hardy, "*A Farewell to Arms*: The Death of Tragedy," in his *Man in the Modern Novel* (Seattle: University of Washington Press, 1964), p. 136.

12. Philip Young and Charles W. Mann, *The Hemingway Manuscripts: An Inventory* (University Park: Pennsylvania State University Press, 1969), item 18. See also Philip Young and Charles W. Mann, "Fitzgerald's *Sun Also Rises*: Notes and Comments," *Fitzgerald/Hemingway Annual 1970*, pp. 1–9.

13. Recent scholarship should disabuse me of this view. Professors Reynolds (*Hemingway's First War*, p. 56), Oldsey (*Hemingway's Hidden Craft*, p. 64), and Wirt Williams (*The Tragic Art of Ernest Hemingway* [Baton Rouge: Louisiana State University Press, 1981], pp. 71, 72–74) remark on the poetic quality of the opening. The first two arrange it as a piece of free verse, overlooking the fact that the cadences of a disoriented narrator, an emotionally disturbed person, even a normal person under emotional stress, form rhythmic patterns that could be similarly scanned. Indeed, Oldsey argues that the opening is a poetic and evocative overture to the novel (pp. 62–68). Interesting through this idea is, it reads like an exercise in New Criticism, one that has no basis in the manuscripts that presumably underpin his study.

14. Sheridan Baker, *Ernest Hemingway: An Introduction and Interpretation* (New York: Holt, Rinehart & Winston, 1967), p. 67. I cite Baker not to pillory him for his misreading here but to note that he too recognizes a "strange confusion" in a narrative voice of the opening chapters; his conclusions, however, differ considerably from mine.

15. Grebstein, *Hemingway's Craft*, p. 212; italics added.

16. I wonder if Hemingway ever ruefully felt about *A Farewell to Arms* what he wryly acknowledged about "Out of Season": that he omitted the end of the story, the old man's hanging himself, basing the omission on his theory "that you could omit anything if you knew that you omitted and the omitted part would strengthen the story and make people feel something more than they understood. Well, I thought, now I have them so they do not understand them. There cannot be much doubt about that" (*Feast*, 75).

17. Daniel J. Schneider, in "Hemingway's *A Farewell to Arms*: The Novel as Pure Poetry," *Modern Fiction Studies* 14 (1968): 283–92, also argues that Hemingway did not intend to create a rich, complex character in Catherine; his argument, however, rests on the idea that Hemingway uses her, as he uses action, only to reflect the lyric consciousness of a narrator concerned with conveying image clusters that reveal his mood of bitterness, despair, and so on. Williams, in *The Tragic Art*, argues a similar reading, pp. 66–67, 70–85.

18. See, for example, Chaman Nahal, *The Narrative Pattern in Ernest Hemingway's Fiction* (Rutherford, NJ: Fairleigh Dickinson University Press, 1971), p. 62; and Wylder, *Hemingway's Heroes*, p. 86.

19. For a different reading of Catherine's "craziness," see George Dekker and Joseph Harris, "Supernaturalism and the Vernacular Style," *PMLA* 94 (1979): 311–18.

20. See Grebstein, *Hemingway's Craft*, pp. 212–15.

21. Sigmund Freud, *Civilization and Its Discontents*, trans. and ed. James Strachey (New York: Norton, 1962), p. 29.

Pseudoautobiography and Personal Metaphor

Millicent Bell

Autobiographic novels are, of course, fictions, constructs of the imagination, even when they seem to incorporate authenticating bits and pieces of personal history. But all fiction is autobiography, no matter how remote from the author's experience the tale seems to be; he leaves his mark, expresses his being, his life, in *any* tale. *A Farewell to Arms* can illustrate both of these statements.

Ernest Hemingway's novel is not the autobiography some readers have thought it. It was not memory but printed source material that supplied the precise details of its descriptions of historic battle scenes on the Italian front in World War I.[1] The novel's love story is no closer to Hemingway's personal reality. He did go to Italy and see action, but not the action he describes; he did fall in love with a nurse, but she was no Catherine Barkley. A large amount of the book fulfills the principle expressed in the deleted coda to "Big Two-Hearted River": "The only writing that was any good was what you made up, what you imagined."[2] Still, there is much that must represent authentic recall in the book. Innumerable small details and a sense of general conditions in battle, the character of the Italian landscape, the Italian soldier, the ambulance corps—all impressed themselves upon Hemingway in 1918 in the Dolomite foothills near Schio as surely as they might have further east around the Tagliamento a year earlier. And there are fetishes of autobiography, trophies of the personal, chief among these the famous wounding at Fossalta, which Hemingway often recalled.[3]

Why is this last episode reproduced so exactly as it happened—the shell fragments in the legs, the sensation of dying and coming to life, the surgical sequel? In the coda, Nick—who is Hemingway—had "never seen a jockey killed" when he wrote "My Old Man"; "he'd never seen an Indian woman having a baby" like his namesake in "Indian Camp." But Hemingway had been wounded just as Frederic is. The answer may be that it was a trauma obsessively recurring to mind, irrepressibly present in his writing because of its crucial, transforming effect upon his life.[4] Still, in the novel the wounding is not at all transforming, does not provide the occasion for

From *Ernest Hemingway: The Writer in Context*, ed. James Nagel (Madison: University of Wisconsin Press, 1984), 107–28. Reprinted by permission of the author and the publisher.

the "separate peace" declared by Nick at a similar moment in chapter 6 of *In Our Time*, often incorrectly thought to be the novel's germ. It does not even cause the novel's hero to suffer from sleeplessness afterward, the consequence of a similar wounding for the narrator of "Now I Lay Me," written only two years before *A Farewell to Arms*. Perhaps in life as in the novel the wounding was simply a very striking experience, the young man's first brush with death. But as an authentic, indelible memory it was deliberate evidence, in any case, that the fiction was *not* all made up. Perhaps, then, the authentic wounding is chiefly a sign, a signature of the author's autobiographic contract with himself.

Hemingway's style, his realist pose, suggests, guilefully, that much more has been borrowed directly from experience than is actually the case. Perhaps the testimonial incorporation of the real, which guarantees autobiographic realism, may also be mimicked. When the "real" is made up to become the "realistic," when the seemingly accidental detail appears to have been stuck into the narrative for no other reason than that it happened, than that it was there, the writer has deliberately made it look as though he is yielding to memory and resisting the tendency of literature to subdue everything to a system of connected significance. In *A Farewell to Arms,* as elsewhere in his writing, Hemingway made the discovery of this secret of realist effect, and his art, which nevertheless presses toward poetic unity by a powerful if covert formalist intent, yet seems continually open to irrelevance also. The result is a peculiar tension requiring the strictest control. Only a manner which conceals implication as severely as Hemingway's can nevertheless suggest those coherences, those rhythmic collocations of mere things, in the manner of imagist poetry, pretend notation of what the witnessing eye might simply have chanced to see. And this restraint is reinforced by deliberate avoidance of the kind of comment that might impose significance or interpretation. It is even further strengthened by the often-noted qualities of Hemingwayan syntax, the simple or compound declarative lacking subordination, and the vocabulary high in nouns and verbs and low in qualifiers. The frequency of the impersonal passive voice that presents events simply as conditions, as in the many sentences that begin with "There were," suppresses not only the sense of agency but the evaluating presence of the observer. If, despite these effects, there is often poetic meaningfulness it is also true that the poetic is sometimes renounced altogether and the realistic detail maintains its irrelevance, refusing any signification in order to affirm the presence of the actual, whether or not truly remembered, reported, historical.[5]

But this stylistic contest only reflects the struggle of the writer between the impulses to tell it "as it was" and to shape and pattern a story; it is not that struggle itself. The "realistic" style is, in fact, most conspicuous and most successful in the most "invented" parts of the book, the war scenes. It is not so evident in those other scenes where Hemingway draws upon memory—the Milan and Switzerland sections. Hemingway had been a patient in the Red Cross hospital in Milan and had spent convalescent weeks in the city; and he had taken vacation tours in the Alpine lake region. But the action situated in those places in the novel has no authenticity to match that of the great Caporetto chapter in which Frederic participates in events Hemingway had not. Still, it is the war scenes, probably—to turn our paradox about once more—that express Hemingway's deepest feelings by way of metaphor, his sense of the war as an objective correlative of his state of mind. The love affair located in familiar, remembered scenes fails of authenticity though it takes something from the writer's experiences with his nurse, Agnes von Kurowsky, and something from his love for Hadley Richardson, and even Pauline Pfeiffer's caesarian operation; it succeeds less well than the invented war scenes in achieving either the effect of realism or the deeper autobiography of metaphor. It is as the latter that it can, however, be explained.

Any first-person story must imitate the autobiographic situation, but there is particular evidence that Hemingway gave his narrator his own sense of the difficulty of reconciling *Wahrheit* and *Dichtung*. The novelist's struggles to achieve an appropriate ending to his book are visible in the manuscript drafts at the John F. Kennedy Library.[6] They show that his chief problem was that he felt both that a novel needed formal closure and also that life was not "like that." He rejected, in the end, the attempt to pick up dropped threads and bring Rinaldi and the priest back into the narrative from which they had been absent since the end of chapter 26, a little beyond the novel's midpoint. It may be argued that these two *companions de la guerre* are felt even in their absence, that there are no dropped threads, the priest in particular being absorbed into the transformed conception of love which the American lieutenant and the English nurse discover in the later portions of the book. But there is really no such absorption; Frederic and Catherine remain very much what they were at the beginning, this mentor and the skeptical doctor both being left behind. Of the "three people of any importance in this story" to whom Hemingway referred in the rejected opening for chapter 10, only Catherine persists.[7] Hemingway must have decided this made an ending—the tightening isolation of his hero requires the loss of the larger human world—but in one of the discarded drafts he permits Frederic to express the misgivings of his creator. "I could tell how Rinaldi was cured of the syphilis . . . I could tell how the priest in our mess lived to be a priest in Italy under Fascism," the pseudoautobiographic narrator observes. But he knows that a story must end somewhere. That he realizes that his closure cannot be complete is due to his awareness that life does not have endings. "Things happen all the time. Everything blunts and the world keeps on. You get most of your life back like goods recovered from a fire. It all keeps on and then it keeps on. It never stops for you. Sometimes it stops when you are still alive. You can stop a story anytime. Where you stop is the end of that story. The rest goes on and you go on with it. On the other hand you have to stop a story. You have to stop at the end of whatever it was you were writing about."[8] The rejected passage can be read not merely as a device to excuse the odd shape of the novel but as a reflection of Hemingway's personal dilemma, his desire to respect the claim of art and also to get back his own past like "goods recovered from a fire."

Getting back his life by writing fiction was not, in this case, a matter of endings, of plot. The indeterminacy of remembered experiences does not matter, because the coherence of events is not so important as the unity of the mind which is the container for them. If Hemingway was to fulfill the autobiographic expectation, the promise made by authentic transcriptions like the Fossalta wounding, it would not be by trying to tell, literally, "the story" of his past. The novelist wrote about himself, and perhaps never so truly as in A Farewell to Arms, but he did so by projecting, lyrically, an inner condition. Mood and tone, not events, provide unity, and these were more intensely the concomitants of the present life of the writer than of his younger self. The novel is about neither love nor war; it is about a state of mind, and that state of mind is the author's.

That plot is not dominant in A Farewell of Arms has not been properly recognized. Critics who have stressed the prevalence of poetic metaphors in the novel have failed, on the whole, to see that such patterns establish its "spatial" composition, minimize progressive effects.[9] In fact, an unvarying mood, established by the narrative voice, dominates everything it relates, bathes uniformly all the images and levels events which are seen always in one way only. That the principal descriptive elements—river, mountains, dust or mud, and above all, rain—are all present in the opening paragraphs suggest not so much that later scenes are being predicted as that the subsequent pages will disclose nothing that is not already evident in the consciousness that has begun its self-exhibition.

The famous wounding is no turning-point in the journey of that consciousness. But even the later "separate peace" in chapter 32 after Frederic's immersion in the Tagliamento is not really a change of direction, a peaking of the plot, though Hemingway's hero does say as he lies on the floor of the flatcar that takes him to Milan, "You were out of it now. You had no more obligation" (p. 232). In chapter 7, even before his wounding, it should be remembered, he has already said, "I would not be killed. Not in this war. It did not have anything to do with me" (p. 37). It is impossible to tell at what point this narrator has acquired his conviction of separateness amounting to alienation from the events which carry him along the stream of time.

By the time he turns away from the war at the Tagliamento in October 1917, Frederic will have had two years in which to acquire the apathy of war weariness. But this is not his malady. Already on the opening page, in 1915, the voice that speaks to us exhibits that attitude psychoanalysts call "blunting of affect," the dryness of soul which underlies its exquisite attentiveness. One has heard of the "relish of sensation" implied in this and other passages of descriptive writing by Hemingway. But "relish" is too positive a word for the studied emotional distance from the perceived world which is in effect here. For the view from Gorizia across the Isonzo, toward the passing troops and the changing weather, this narrator seems hardly to feel anything beyond a minimal "things went very badly." An alienated neutrality governs the reiterated passives, the simple declaratives. "There were big guns. . . . There was fighting. . . . There were mists over the river. . . . There were small gray motor cars" (p. 4). The next year (chapter 2) is the same. "There were many victories. . . . The fighting was in the next mountains. . . . The whole thing was going well. . . . The war was changed" (pp. 5–6). The different character of military events makes for no change in the tone. We are prepared for the personality who emerges into view as he describes his leave. He had not gone to Abruzzi but had spent drunken nights when "you knew that that was all there was," and he had known the "not knowing and not caring in the night, sure that this was all . . . suddenly to care very much" (p. 13), swinging from not caring to caring and back again, from affectlessness to affect and then again to its loss. If there is something that transcends this alternation, the ecstasy of either love or religion, it is so fugitive as to be almost unnameable: "If you have had it you know. . . . He, the priest, had always known what I did not know, what, when I learned it, I was always able to forget" (pp. 13–14).

"Always" is an important word here. There is no hint that Frederic has at any time had a beginning in illusion, that he ever started out like Stephen Crane's Henry Fleming in *The Red Badge of Courage* (something of a model for *A Farewell to Arms*) with a naive belief in exalted meanings. The well-known passage, "I was *always* embarrassed by the words sacred, glorious, and sacrifice, and the expression in vain" is not the culmination of a process by which these concepts have withered. His embarrassment goes as far back as he can remember. He has had it always, "Gino was a patriot," Frederic continues, "so he said things that separated us sometimes, but he was also a fine boy and I understand his being a patriot. He was born one" (pp. 184–85). And the opposite attitude, disbelief in such things, may also be inborn. Rinaldi has told Frederic that for him "there are only two things"—drink and sex—and his work. Frederic hopes that he will get other things but the doctor says, "No. We never get anything. We are born with all we have and we never learn" (p. 171). If Frederic may be conceived of as having been also born with all he has, this explains why he is described as having enlisted in the ambulance corps for no reason at all, unlike Hemingway who was swept into the wave of American enthusiasm to aid the Allies. Frederic just happened to be already in Italy when the war broke out. He had been studying architecture. He has never had any belief in the big words. "Why did you do it?" asks Catherine, referring to his enlistment. "I don't know. . . . There isn't always an explanation for everything," he answers.

And yet this sufferer from blunted affect can fall in love. It is one of the "givens" of the story, though it seems to demand a capacity which, like the emotion of patriotism, he was born without. "When I saw her I was in love with her," he says when Catherine appears again at the hospital. "I had not wanted to fall in love with anyone. But God knows I had" (pp. 91, 93). Catherine, as well, had experienced this hardly credible conversion. Although we never get so direct a view of her mental operations—this is Frederic's story, after all—she appears, in the earlier scenes, to be as incapacitated as Hemingway's other English nurse who has lost a fiancé in the war, Brett Ashley. There is more than a hint that she too suffers the dissociation of feeling from sensation that accounts for her unfocused sexuality when Frederic first makes love to her. But now she feels. The raptures of both lovers, however, are curiously suspect.

Frederic has only delusively attached himself to an otherness. Far from the war's inordinate demand upon his responses, he has been converted to feeling in the isolation of his hospital bed, where, like a baby in its bassinet, he is totally passive, tended and comforted by female caretakers, the nurses, and particularly by this one. The image is regressive, and the ministering of Catherine, who looks after all his needs, including sexual, while he lies passive, is more maternal than connubial. The relation that now becomes the center of the novel is, indeed, peculiar enough to make us question it as a representation of adult love. More often noted than Frederic's passivity is the passivity of Catherine in this love affair, a passivity which has irritated readers (particularly female readers) because it seems to be a projection of male fantasies of the ideally submissive partner. It results from her desire to please. She is a sort of inflated rubber woman available at will to the onanistic dreamer. There is, in fact, a masturbatory quality to the love of each. The union of these two is a flight from outer reality and eventually from selfhood, which depends upon a recognition of the other; the selfhood that fails to find its definition in impingement upon the world at large and the establishment of distinction from it eventually proves incapable of recognizing the alien in the beloved and therefore the independent in itself. The otherness that Frederic and Catherine provide for one another is not enough to preserve their integral selves, and while the sounds of exteriority become more and more muffled in the novel, their personalities melt into one another. It is for this reason that Hemingway's novel, far from being the *Romeo and Juliet* he once carelessly called it, is more comparable to *Anthony and Cleopatra,* a play which shows that the world is not well lost for love, though nothing, of course, can be further from the masterful images of Shakespeare's adult lovers than Hemingway's pitiful pair.

Affective failure, then, shows itself not merely in the war sections of the novel but in the parts where one would imagine it to have been transcended, the love story of Catherine and Frederic. Catherine constantly reminds her lover of her resolution not to offer him otherness but to collapse her own selfhood into his. She asks what a prostitute does, whether she says whatever the customer wants her to, even "I love you." She will outdo the prostitute: "But I will. I'll say just what you wish and I'll do what you wish and then you will never want any other girls, will you . . . I want what you want. There isn't any me any more. Just what you want" (pp. 105, 106). The idyll of their Milan summer is spent in such games as this: "We tried putting thoughts in the other one's head while we were in different rooms. It seemed to work sometimes but that was probably because we were thinking the same thing anyway" (p. 114). She refuses his offer to marry her, and when he says "I wanted it for you" replies, "there isn't any me. I'm you. Don't make up a separate me" (p. 115).

Their solitariness *à deux* is only emphasized by their occasional contacts with others who are outside the war, those met in the Milan cafés or at the racetrack who are not the true alienated but the self-serving and parasitic, and even by their encounter with the genuine war hero, Ettore, who is wounded in the foot, like Frederic, and has five medals, and whom they cannot stand. After she becomes pregnant, Catherine says, "There's only us two and in the world there's all the rest of them. If anything comes between us we're gone and then they have us." When the time comes for him to leave for the front, they walk past a couple embracing under a buttress of the cathedral, and she will not agree that they are like themselves. " 'Nobody is like us,' Catherine said. She did not mean it happily" (p. 147). Not surprisingly, they both are orphans of a sort. Catherine has a father but "he has gout," she says to Frederic; "You won't ever have to meet him." Frederic has only a stepfather, and, he tells her, "You won't have to meet him" (p. 154). When they are waiting for the birth of their baby in Switzerland, she asks him about his family: "Don't you care anything about them?" He replies, "I did, but we quarrelled so much it wore itself out" (p. 304).

Book 3, the justly praised Caporetto section, returns Frederic to Gorizia where others have spent a different sort of summer. Rinaldi, depressed, overworked, perhaps syphilitic, says, "This is a terrible war, baby," drinks too much, and is impatient of Frederic's acquisition of a "sacred subject." The priest tells him how the terrible summer has made the major gentle. No one any longer believes in victory. But Frederic confesses that he himself believes in neither victory nor defeat. He believes, he says, "in sleep." It is more than a joke, even though in a moment he apologizes that "I said that about sleep meaning nothing" (p. 179). The regressive process, the withdrawal from reality, the surrender of complex personal being, the limitation of relationship to that with an other who is really only a mirror of self approaches more and more the dreamless sleep of apathy, the extremity of ennui. There is a suggestion of the pathologic in the "I was deadly sleepy" with which the chapter ends (p. 180).

The retreat is reported by a sensibility already asleep, by an emotional apparatus already itself in retreat from the responsibilities of response. "The houses were badly smashed but things were very well organized and there were signboards everywhere" (p. 181). However much this sounds like irony to us, irony is not intended by the speaker, who does not mean more by saying less. His downward adjustment of feeling is the one often made by soldiers—or by concentration camp victims, or long-term prisoners—by which emotions are reduced to the most rudimentary since the others have become insupportable. His battle-weary companions express their own reduction by a preoccupation with food. The entire retreat is a massed legitimization of apathy and a symbol of it.

Frederic's affectlessness is climaxed by his "cold-blooded" shooting of one of the Italian sergeants who has refused to obey his order to move the stalled ambulance. "I shot three times and dropped one," he observes, as though describing the pursuit of game, and Bonello then takes the pistol and "finishes him," as a hunting companion might finish off an animal still quivering where it has fallen (p. 204). One may say that this is simply war—Sherman's war—and feeling has no place in it. But this does not make it less shocking that the perceiving hero is so matter-of-fact. Even Bonello expresses a motive: he is a socialist, and all his life he has wanted to kill a sergeant, he tells Frederic, who expresses no personal motive at all, and who has never felt that it was his war. Yet for giving up his part in it he has also no special motive. His case is not like that of the demoralized soldiers who are flinging down their arms and shouting that they want to go home. He cannot go home. And now a profoundly significant flash of memory comes to him as he rests in the hay of a barn: "The hay smelled good and lying in a barn in the hay took away all the years between. We had lain in the hay and talked and shot sparrows with an air-rifle when they perched in the triangle cut high in the wall of the barn. The barn was gone now and one year they had cut the hemlock woods and there were only stumps, dried tree-tops, branches and fireweed where the woods had been. You could not go back" (p. 216).

The "separate peace" was made long ago. Again we must note the reference to a congenital disengagement when he says with what only looks like a newly acquired minimalism, "I was not *made* to think, I was *made* to eat. My God, yes. Eat and drink and sleep with Catherine" (p. 233). Removing his uniform after his escape, he strips himself of the last vestige of social self. He no longer can interest himself in the war news, as he had in the earlier Milan section, and does not give us summaries of military events. "I had a paper but I did not read it because I did not want to read about the war. I was going to forget the war," he says at the beginning of chapter 34. It is now that he says, "I had made a separate peace." "Don't talk about the war," he tells the barman at the hotel. And he reflects, "The war was a long way away. Maybe there wasn't any war. There was no war here. Then I realized it was over for me" (pp. 243, 255). But how committed to this war has he ever been?

The rest is a "fugue" in the technical psychiatric sense of a period during which the patient, often suffering loss of memory, begins another life from which all his past has been drained. Thus, the "all for love" that remains for Frederic and Catherine is qualified by the lovers' knowledge that the whole empire of normal being has been surrendered. "Let's not think of anything," says Catherine (p. 252). The lover boasts that he has no wish to be separate from his beloved: "All other things were unreal." He tells her, "My life used to be full of everything. Now if you aren't with me I haven't a thing in the world" (p. 257). Their universe of two is reducing itself further, and their games continue to suggest this constriction. He might let his hair grow longer, she suggests, and she might cut hers short so that even their sexual difference may be lessened. "Then we'd both be alike. Oh, darling, I want you so much I want to be you too." He says, "We're the same one," and she, "I want us to be all mixed up. . . . I don't live at all when I'm not with you." He replies, "I'm no good when you're not there. I haven't any life at all any more" (pp. 299–300).

These scenes are a drift toward death, which is why the novel must end in death, Catherine's and the baby's, though Hemingway considered allowing the child to survive. Such a survival would have contradicted all that has gone before by introducing a new otherness when its parents are losing the otherness of each other. The two lovers already live on the margin of life. Count Greffi is an even more mythological figure than Mippipopolous in *The Sun Also Rises*, whom he resembles. The very old man, so close to death, is a fit sentinel upon that border they are about to cross before they pass, by a symbolic boat voyage, out of Italy. Their Switzerland is not on the map, notwithstanding the fact that it resembles the Switzerland of Hemingway's vacation tours. In their chalet, wrapped in the cottony blanket of the winter snow, cared for by their good-natured landlord and his wife, whose lives have a reality with which they make no connection, and in contact with no one else, they are united as before in his hospital bed. Their destiny is out of their own hands as they become, quite literally, patients awaiting surgery, playing bed games. Perhaps Frederic will pass the time by growing a beard. Their loss of connection with human modes of being produces fantasies of an animal identity, like that of the fox they see in the snow who sleeps with his brush wrapped about his face, curled in the regressive fetal position. What would they do if they had tails like the fox? They would have special clothes made, or "live in a country where it wouldn't make any difference" to have a fox's tail. Catherine says, truly, "We live in a country where nothing makes any difference. Isn't it grand how we never see anyone?" (p. 303). The country is, of course, the country of the dead, toward which she is bound.

If indeed "all fiction is autobiography," no special demonstration is required to support the idea that *A Farewell to Arms* expresses the author's inner being, his secret life. Yet there is particular reason to suppose this in the case of this novel which is the presentation of a state of mind, a mood and condition of being. These, it may be arguable, belonged to the writer himself at the time of writing. As a war novel, it is curiously late. In 1929, American society was preoccupied with other things than its memories of the battles of the First World War. Hemingway, already the author of a novel dealing with a later period and married for the second time, had come a long way from the naïve nineteen-year-old of 1918. Any such analysis is speculative, but there is reason to suppose that for the writer as for Frederic Henry the barn was gone where he had lain in the hay as a boy: "You could not go back." This realization must have been particularly acute when this novel was being written. Since 1925 his life had been one of personal turmoil. He had found himself in love with Pauline Pfeiffer, forced to decide between her and the woman whom he still claimed also to love and who had been, he would declare, a faultless wife. In 1927, he had remarried and, in the following year, while Pauline was pregnant, he was struggling to make progress on this second novel, plagued by various accidental disasters—an eye injury, head cuts from a fallen skylight—such as he always seemed prone to. Pauline's baby was delivered by caesarian section after a labor of eighteen hours during a Kansas heat wave. The first draft of A Farewell to Arms was finished two months later, but before Hemingway began the task of revision, his father, Dr. Clarence Hemingway, who had been depressed for some time, committed suicide by shooting himself in the head.

Beyond the immediate strain and horror of such events must have been their power to intensify Hemingway's most buried anxieties. His remarriage, which he did not quite understand, created a keen sense of guilt in him along with the recognition that he contained compulsive forces he was powerless to restrain. Marriage, moreover, could be destructive not only because it had resulted in pain and divorce in his own case; as a child he had seen its effects in the secret contests of will between his parents. Pauline's dangerous, agonized parturition seemed to confirm his feeling that death as readily as life was the consequence of sexuality. He may well have felt what he had imagined the Indian father to feel before cutting his throat in "Indian Camp." That early story suggests that Hemingway had always seen something terrifying in the birth process. Now he incorporated a birth process fatal to both fictional mother and child in the conclusion of his novel.

His father's suicide must have awakened further all his most inadmissible emotions, above all his feelings of hostility and guilt toward his parents. Readers of Carlos Baker's biography do not need a review of Hemingway's childhood and youth with its history of rebellions and chastisements.[10] The spirited boy, adoring and striving to emulate his father, also incurred this father's disciplinarian severity, and young Ernest's resentment of his punishment was so intense that he would sometimes, when he was about eighteen, sit hidden in the doorway of a shed behind the house drawing a bead on his father's head with a gun while the doctor worked in his vegetable garden.[11] Yet it was this same father who had taught him to shoot, initiated him in the craft and passion of killing animals. His feelings toward his mother, whose musical-artistic inclinations might be thought to be the source of his own impulses toward the life of art, would, in the end, prove more bitterly hostile. As he grew to manhood he felt, it would seem, more betrayed by her attempts to control his behavior, especially after the war had proved him a man and even a hero. There is the well-known incident of youthful high-jinks in the woods, shortly after his twenty-first birthday, which resulted in his expulsion from the Hemingways' summer cottage at Walloon Lake. But more hurtful must have been his parents' moralistic censure of his writing. First *In Our Time* and then *The Sun Also Rises* received their uncomprehending disapproval, against which he politely pleaded.

Beneath the politeness there was sometimes a threat. After receiving her criticism of his first novel Hemingway wrote his mother with only half-concealed scorn, "I am sure that it [the novel] is not more unpleasant than the real inner lives of some of our best Oak Park families. You must remember that in such a book all the worst of the people's lives is displayed while at home there is a very lovely side for the public and the sort of which I have had some experience of observing behind closed doors."[12] Behind what doors but those closed upon the conflicts he had known between his parents themselves? Hemingway was prone to hint for years that he might write an Oak Park novel that would tell all: "I had a wonderful novel to write about Oak Park," he said in 1952, "and would never do it because I did not want to hurt living people."[13] After his father's death in 1928 he wrote his mother offering her some advice about how to handle his uncle George, whom he held responsible for his father's money worries, and he also added menacingly, "I have never written a novel about the [Hemingway] family because I have never wanted to hurt anyone's feelings but with the death of the ones I love a period has been put to a great part of it and I may have to undertake it."[14] It is a curious statement, with its slip into the plural "ones" when among his near relatives only his father had died. And was not his mother to be counted among the "ones I love"? There seems to be an unclear implication that she as much as his uncle—whom he had always disliked—might be exposed by his writing. The Oak Park novel was never written. Yet if he rejected the temptation to write about his family life—except in the hints given in such a story as "The Doctor and the Doctor's Wife"—he did not stop writing works that might convey his insight into the "unpleasant" and defy his mother's moralistic hypocrisy. And the covertly autobiographic impulse persisted.

From the time of his father's suicide, he must have felt himself to be just such an orphan, though with a living parent, as Catherine and Frederic describe themselves. "My father is the only one I cared about," he wrote Maxwell Perkins after the doctor's suicide.[15] He then may already have believed what he later stated to Charles Scribner, that his mother had destroyed her husband, and his bitter sense of having been unloved by her fused with his identification with his father: "I hate her guts and she hates mine. She forced my father to suicide."[16] But such liberations from filial love are never quite complete. Underneath must have been the longing for approval, for a lost infantile security. Hemingway's own sexual history, that ultimate personal expression, may have taken some shape from the mixture of need and anger which probably composed his emotions toward his mother. The need to reject as well as the need to be wanted again may explain the course of his love life, with its three marriages and, as his life advanced, its rather greater propensity of promiscuity. Promiscuity, of course, may also be based on the fear that one cannot feel at all. Beneath the intensely expressive, even violent personality of the visible Hemingway there may have been a self that was haunted by the demon of boredom. Apathy, which might seem the least likely affliction of this articulate and active man, may have been what he feared most, knowing his own inner indifference. If so, then *A Farewell to Arms* does have a special relation to the mind of the maker, is autobiographic in a metaphoric way.

Some confirmation of this view may be gained by study of Hemingway's text as the result of revision and excision in accordance with his well-known iceberg theory.[17] In looking for the submerged element that supports a style so economic, so dependent upon implication rather that explication, one is prompted to consider the nature of what has been pruned away. Obviously, the Hemingway esthetic promotes the elimination of the merely redundant, the detail that adds nothing, the explanation that can be supplied by the reader's own surmise, the additional episode which may thicken the reality of the story but also complicates its meaning too much. Some of this discard may well supply autobiographic clues to the intentional process by which the work was molded. Sometimes, one suspects, the rejected matter comes out of the too-exact transcript of memory.

Even before the manuscript of *A Farewell to Arms* had been studied, it was obvious that Hemingway might have planned his novel at some earlier stage to include other elements besides those finally selected. Julian Smith has argued that two stories written in 1926 just after the breakup of Hemingway's first marriage amplify the novel so precisely at certain points that they may have been conceived of as part of it at one time.[18] One of these is "In Another Country," whose title, with its reference to Marlowe's *Jew of Malta* ("Thou hast committed—/Fornication—but that was in another country; and besides, the wench is dead"), Hemingway once considered using for the novel.[19] The second story linked with the novel is "Now I Lay Me," entitled "In Another Country—Two" in a late draft.[20] Both short stories fulfill the title of the collection in which they were printed in 1927, *Men Without Women*, which attaches them in an interesting way to the novel begun soon after, the novel about the failure, in the end, of the sexual bridge over the gulf of solitude.

Both stories are really about marriage. In "In Another Country" the narrator, recovering from his wounds in a Milan hospital and receiving mechanical therapy—like Hemingway and Frederic Henry—is warned not to marry. An Italian major who has just lost his wife tells him that a man "cannot marry" because "if he is to lose everything, he should not place himself in a position to lose that." Had Hemingway chosen to include the story as an episode in *A Farewell to Arms* it might have served to predict Catherine's death as well as the conclusion that nothing, not even love, abides. In "Now I Lay Me" the hero has been wounded in the particular fashion and with the particular sensations Hemingway remembered from his own experience and attributed to Frederic. He does not sleep well—because of the sound of the silkworms and because he is afraid of dying—and passes restless nights thinking about two kinds of boyhood experience: trout fishing and the quarrels between his parents, with his mother's hen-pecking of his father. He is advised by his orderly *to* marry but does not, and does not intend to, unlike the narrator of the companion story, who tells the major that he hopes to be married.

There are any number of ways in which both stories can be related to Hemingway's personal experience, but it is clear that together they suggest a fear associated with marriage—either one will somehow kill it oneself, as he had done with his own first marriage, or it will kill you, or at least emasculate you, as his mother had emasculated his father. Despite the seemingly positive assurance of the orderly in the second story that marriage will "fix everything," the effect of both tales is to suggest that death and destruction arrive in the end. Love cannot heal the Hemingway hero who longs to return to some presexual condition in the untainted woods of boyhood.

The connection of the two stories with the novel written so soon after them is a matter of conjecture, but Hemingway's manuscript drafts of *A Farewell to Arms* may justifiably be searched for evidence of his compositional intentions and his autobiographic sources. The draft indicates that Hemingway had, for example, included a much more detailed version of the description of wounding already used in "Now I Lay Me" and also a more detailed and more emotional description of Frederic's sensations on waking up in the hospital in Milan. The final version screens out autobiographic irrelevance, for Frederic, in the draft, makes on Hemingway's behalf one of those representative comments that show him struggling against the flood of memory: "If you try and put in everything you would never get a single day done and then the one who made it might not feel it."[21] In the end the writer made these occasions consistent with the rest of the novel as a representation of the state of mind that is the grounding of his hero's being. In the first three books, as Reynolds has observed, the revisions nearly efface Frederic as a personality.[22] He becomes an almost completely apathetic sufferer. Though self-expression is allowed to emerge in the love affair, it does not really make for reversal of this condition, for in the place of the grand afflatus of love, the language of amorous avowal that these lovers speak is self-diminishing.

A complex revision of a crucial passage is the alteration of the conversation between Frederic and the priest in chapter 11. In the manuscript draft Frederic lists some of the things he loves, and adds at the end, "I found I loved god too, a little. I did not love anything too much."[23] In the revision there is no such list or remark, but there is, instead, the priest's statement: "When you love you wish to do things for. You wish to sacrifice for. You wish to serve" (p. 72). Hemingway may be thought to have promoted by this addition the hope of moral growth in his hero, who then asks, in the printed text, "How about loving a woman? If I really loved some woman would it be like that?" He cannot answer his own question nor does the priest answer it, and though, much later, Count Greffi calls love "a religious feeling," Frederic, still dubious, can respond only, "You think so?" (p. 263). Can we analogize the love of God and Frederic's love of Catherine, in fact? Does human love acquire the highest possible meaning for him? Not really. He cannot be said to attain the priest's ideal of service and sacrifice. Nor does the formula apply to Catherine herself. Her death is not redemptive, is not a true Imitation of Christ. It is not voluntarily offered and does not save Frederic from anything or give him faith. Only irony attends the sequel in which the surrender of self seems the consequence of weakness rather than the bounty of strong love. The revision removes the small assertion of faith that Frederic makes, "I found I loved god too, a little," and when the priest declares, "You should love Him," the answer is simply, "I don't love much," or, as the draft has it, "I did not love anything very much," which seems a statement of affective deficiency in general, a general inability to donate emotion.

Frederic's estrangement from feeling is not the consequence of any particular wounding or of war disgust, or of any experience of adulthood, but of deeply founded sense of loss. A passage Hemingway took out of the novel gives confirmation. It begins with the opening sentence of chapter 40, "We had a fine life" (p. 306), followed in the finished novel by a brief description of the way the couple spent their days during the last of their winter stay in the Swiss mountains. Hemingway decided not to use the long passage that originally followed this opening sentence in which Frederic reflects, anticipating the tragic conclusion, "wisdom and happiness do not go together," and declares his reductive certitude: "The only thing I know is that if you love anything enough they take it away from you." In this discarded passage, as in the rejected ending of the novel, Hemingway felt the need to refer once again to Rinaldi and the priest, those seemingly forgotten mentors of contrary wisdom, and it is plain that Frederic cannot accept the latter's faith, though he says, "I see the wisdom of the priest in our mess who has always loved God and so is happy and I am sure that nothing will ever take God away from him. But how much is wisdom and how much is luck to be born that way? And what if you are not built that way?" Earlier in the novel Gino is described as a patriot because he is "born that way" and Rinaldi is a skeptic for the same reason. But here, in the excised passage, Frederic speaks of himself: "But what if you were born loving nothing and the warm milk of your mother's breast was never heaven and the first thing you loved was the side of a hill and the last thing was a woman and they took her away and you did not want another but only to have her; and she was gone, then you are not so well placed."[24] For Hemingway, too, cannot it have been true that "the warm milk of [his] mother's breast was never heaven"? Is this the underwater knowledge of self which supports the poignancy of what remains in the final text of the novel?

Hemingway's difficulties with the ending can now be seen to have been caused by something besides his desire to be true to life's inconclusiveness. His hero's emotional or philosophic *nada* threatened the very process of making sense, achieving illumination. Hemingway decided to eschew any hint of apocalypse, rejecting even Fitzgerald's suggestion that he place at the end the passage in which Frederic describes how all are finished off impartially, though the good, the gentle, and the brave go first—as dark a revelation as one could imagine, but still a revelation of sorts. What would do best, he realized, would be simply the hero's numb survival without insight, his notation without catharsis.

Notes

1. The dependence of *A Farewell to Arms* on Hemingway's research rather than on direct observation is comprehensively demonstrated in Michael S. Reynolds's *Hemingway's First War: The Making of 'A Farewell to Arms'* (Princeton: Princeton University Press, 1976).

2. *The Nick Adams Stories*, ed. Philip Young (New York: Bantam, 1973), p. 217.

3. As related, for example, to Guy Hickok: "I felt my soul or something like it coming right out of my body, like you'd pull a silk handkerchief out of a pocket by one corner. It flew around and then it came back and went in again and I wasn't dead anymore." "A Portrait of Mister Papa," by Malcolm Cowley, *Life* (10 January 1949), repr. *Ernest Hemingway: The Man and his Work*, ed. John K. M. McCaffrey (New York: Cooper Square, 1969), p. 35.

4. It is Philip Young's influential thesis that "one fact about this recurrent protagonist (the Hemingway hero) as about the man who created him, is necessary to any real understanding of either figure, and that is the fact of the 'wound,' a severe injury suffered in World War I which left permanent scars, visible and otherwise." *Ernest Hemingway: A Reconsideration* (University Park: Pennsylvania State University Press, 1966), p. 6.

5. A typical example of such calculated irrelevance might be the sentences that conclude the opening paragraph of chapter 9 which describes the hero's pause, with his ambulance drivers, on the way to the battle location where he will be wounded: "I gave them each a package of cigarettes, Macedonias, loosely packed cigarettes that spilled tobacco

and needed to have the ends twisted before you smoked them. Manera lit his lighter and passed it around. The lighter was shaped like a Fiat radiator." *A Farewell to Arms* (New York: Scribner's, 1929), p. 47. All further references to the novel will be to this edition.

6. The variant manuscript endings are described by Reynolds (*Hemingway's First War*) and by Bernard Oldsey, *Hemingway's Hidden Craft: The Writing of 'A Farewell to Arms'* (University Park: Pennsylvania State University Press, 1979).

7. Reynolds, *Hemingway's First War*, p. 22.

8. Reynolds, *Hemingway's First War*, pp. 46–47.

9. The most influential description of the novel as a system of imagery has been Carlos Baker's in *Hemingway: The Writer as Artist*, rev. ed. (Princeton: Princeton University Press, 1963), pp. 94–96. But Baker's contrasted symbology of mountain and plain suggests a dynamics of psychological and moral movement correlated with physical description. In my own view there is no such movement.

10. Carlos Baker, *Ernest Hemingway: A Life Story* (New York: Scribner's, 1969).

11. Baker, *A Life Story*, p. 54.

12. *Ernest Hemingway: Selected Letters, 1917–1961*, ed. Carlos Baker (New York: Scribner's, 1981), letter to Grace Hall Hemingway, 5 February 1927, p. 243.

13. Charles Fenton, *The Apprenticeship of Ernest Hemingway* (New York: Farrar, Straus & Young, 1954), p. 1.

14. Hemingway, *Selected Letters*, letter to Grace Hall Hemingway, 11 March 1929, p. 296.

15. Hemingway, *Selected Letters*, letter to Maxwell Perkins, 16 December 1928, p. 291.

16. Hemingway, *Selected Letters*, letter to Charles Scribner, 27 August 1949, p. 670.

17. "If a writer of prose knows enough about what he is writing about, he may omit things that he knows and the reader, if the writer is writing truly enough, will have a feeling of those things as strongly as though the writer had stated them. The dignity of movement of an iceberg is due to only one-eighth of it being above water. A writer who omits things because he does not know them only makes hollow places in his writing." See *Death in the Afternoon* (New York: Scribner's, 1932), p. 192.

18. Julian Smith, "Hemingway and the Thing Left Out," *Ernest Hemingway: Five Decades of Criticism*, ed. Linda W. Wagner (Lansing: Michigan State University Press, 1974), pp. 188–200.

19. Reynolds, *Hemingway's First War*, pp. 295, 296.

20. Cf. Philip Young and Charles W. Mann, eds., *The Hemingway Manuscripts: An Inventory* (University Park: Pennsylvania State University Press, 1969), p. 44.

21. Reynolds, *Hemingway's First War*, p.33.

22. Reynolds, *Hemingway's First War*, p. 59.

23. Reynolds, *Hemingway's First War*, pp. 286–87.

24. Reynolds, *Hemingway's First War*, pp. 40–41.

Catherine Barkley and Retrospective Narration

JAMES NAGEL

Much of the recent scholarship on *A Farewell to Arms*, especially criticism that deals with the portrait of Catherine Barkley, proceeds on the assumption that the novel is a "realistic" construct and that the author and the characters presented can be "judged" in an objective sense for their behaviour and personalities.[1] This assumption has led some critics to complain that Catherine is too idealistic, too selflessly loving and giving to be believed as a character. The logical extreme of this contention, represented by the views of Judith Fetterley, is that such "idealization is a basic strategy for disguising and marketing hatred," that "Frederic wants and needs Catherine's death," and that through her death he "avoids having to face the responsibilities incumbent upon a husband and father. Her death reflects his desire to remain uncommitted and it gives him a marketable explanation for doing so."[2] These opinions, buttressed more by contemporary social and political views than by any viable reading of the novel, have nonetheless developed a currency in Hemingway scholarship that needs to be tempered by a fresh reading of the novel as a work of art, a novel told by a narrator with a definable point of view, at a certain time, and for a discoverable purpose. All of these matters affect and determine the content and tone of the story presented in the novel.

A Farewell to Arms is fundamentally *not* a realistic novel about World War I narrated by Ernest Hemingway; it is, rather, a retrospective narrative told by Frederic Henry a decade after the action has taken place for the purpose of coming to terms emotionally with the events. As is the case with all first-person retrospective novels, a popular form in American literature, the narrative has a dual time scheme: the time of the action set against the time of the telling. The time of the action is easily dated in that it relates to actual historical events, the most important of which is the retreat from Caporetto in October of 1917. This is the retreat during which the Italian troops fall into disorder, the soldiers desert their posts, and the army shoots its own men as they attempt to cross the bridge over the Tagliamento river.

From *Ernest Hemingway: Six Decades of Criticism*, ed. Linda W. Wagner (East Lansing: Michigan State University Press, 1987), 171-85. Reprinted by permission of the author and the publisher.

Frederic Henry is stopped at the bridge and would surely have been executed had he not escaped by plunging into the river. At this point he has been in the army for two years, 1915-1917. After the Caporetto episode, he and Catherine escape into Switzerland in the autumn of 1917, make their way to Montreux for the winter, and then proceed to Lausanne in the spring of 1918, where, in April, Catherine hemorrhages and dies during childbirth.

When the novel is told is more difficult to establish, but most likely the time of the narration is roughly synonymous with the period of composition in 1928. As he wrote the novel, a decade removed from his own war experiences in Italy, Ernest Hemingway imagined a protagonist telling his story at the same temporal distance from the events he relates. Although the precise date of the narration cannot be established, the fact that Frederic Henry at one point says that Babe Ruth was a pitcher *then*, at the time of the action, implies that he is not one *now*, at the time of the telling. Babe Ruth did his last pitching in 1919 while playing for the Boston Red Sox. He joined the New York Yankees in 1920 and became known primarily as a hitter. But he would not have been sufficiently notable to qualify as a time referent until after the season of 1927, when he hit 60 home runs to set a major league record that was to last over three decades. By March of the following year, when Hemingway began *A Farewell to Arms*, Ruth would have been one of the most popular figures in America, and it would make sense to have Frederic refer to him.[3]

Apart from the Babe Ruth references there are numerous time indicators that establish that the telling is a long period after the Catherine's death and that there is a continual disparity between the time of action and the time of telling. Frederic reflects at one point that the priest knew *then* some important things about the value of domestic life that he came to realize only *now* (p. 14). He says that he has forgotten some of the details of the events, as he naturally would over a period of years (p. 291). That the events recalled are at some temporal distance from the moment of narration is evident throughout Frederic's story. At one juncture he observes that Count Greffi was living to be 100 which, since he is 94 during the billiard game in Stresa, would be six years later than the time of action (pp. 142, 263). But more important than the precise moment of the telling is the awareness that many of the judgements expressed in the novel must be perceived as having derived not from insight contemporaneous with the action but from the older and painfully wiser perspective of Frederic Henry as narrator.

What an awareness of the dual time scheme of the novel reveals is that Catherine Barkley exists in the novel only in the memory of Frederic Henry, only in the reflections of a man who came to love her, who lost her, and who grieves and assesses his behaviour a decade after she has died. To expect him to present a fully realized portrait, an objective and realistic account of his lost love, is to be insensitive to the emotional context of the telling of the novel. What he renders is understandably less a realistic portrait than a "lyric evocation," the tragic but sweet image that lingers in the mind. Indeed, the pertinent standard for assessing the "realism" of the portrait of Catherine would be not whether she resembles actual persons in their complexity and imperfection but whether Frederic's memories of her seem plausible, whether they are the kinds of reflections a man would have about the woman he lost. As Sheldon Grebstein has said, "In the memory every attribute of the loved one becomes exalted and rendered more precious than in life."[4]

These evaluations from the time of the telling are often broad philosophical observations, summary judgments gleaned from the total impact of the experience, and only occasionally assessments of a single event. When Frederic reflects on the wisdom of the priest early in the novel, it is clear that his respect for the domestic values the priest espouses developed *after* he had lost Catherine and the child and not before, in the period in which his nightly visits to the Villa Rossa constituted a debasement of the values he would later endorse: "But I did not know that then, although I learned it later" (p. 14). His account of his first encounter with Catherine involves the idea of the loss of Catherine for Rinaldi, however superficial their relationship was; the nearly pathological grief of Catherine for the lover who was killed; and a corresponding bereavement for Frederic Henry at the rime he tells the story. Catherine's comments about her fear of the rain and how she sees herself dead in it would not have had nearly the emotional resonance at the moment she said it as it does when Frederic remembers it.

Henry recalls at one point that with Catherine he felt alone against the world in his close union with her, and he reflects, clearly from a later viewpoint, "it has only happened to me like that once" (p. 258). That comment, along with the attendant observation that the world breaks everyone and the courageous it has to kill in order to break, seem most distinctly the painful conclusions of a lover who has lost everything and is trying to find some meaning or consolation in what has happened. This passage is related to the one at the end of the novel in which Frederic, having learned that the baby is dead, realizes that Catherine too will die and that "the first time they caught you off base they killed you" (p. 338). At times there is a correlation between the feelings of the action and the feelings of the telling, as when he remembers the time he got drunk before he went to see her at the hospital and she refused to see him; it was his first feeling of loss for her, but not his last (p. 43). Indeed, the very scenes that Frederic chooses to present in his story suggest a principle of selection from memory along several lines of thought: his duplicity as opposed to her selflessness and nobility; his growing commitment to her as he moves from the hope of sexual exploitation to genuine love; his progression from an intense involvement in a group to his present status, at the time of narration, of loneliness and isolation.

His early role-playing in their relationship, in many ways a standard lover's ploy, is unusual only in Catherine's extreme vulnerability, her lover having been killed. When Frederic first hears of Catherine it is from Rinaldi, who has been seeing her and who is himself engaged in a modest deception, attempting to impress on her that he is a "man of sufficient wealth" (p. 12). Frederic remembers that at the same time Rinaldi went to call on her, Frederic was having a conversation with the priest, who had advised him to go to the Abruzzi region on leave, which Frederic failed to do. As he tries to explain his motivation to the priest, he says:

> I tried to tell about the night and the difference between the night and the day and how the night was better unless the day was very clean and cold and I could not tell it; as I cannot tell it now. . . . He had not had it but he understood that I had really wanted to go to the Abruzzi but had not gone and we were still friends, with many tastes alike, but with the difference between us. He had always known what I did not know and what, when I learned it, I was always able to forget. But I did not know that then, although I learned it later. (p. 14)

Later in the novel, the priest and Frederic discuss the nature of love, moving from spiritual to carnal, and the priest's observations are instructive: " 'When you love you wish to do things for. You wish to sacrifice for. You wish to serve.' 'I don't love.' 'You will. I know you will. Then you will be happy' " (p. 75). Significantly, Frederic associates his earliest memories of Catherine with his betrayal of the domestic values of the priest, in the first instance, and with his denial of love in the second. Before the novel is over, however, he will come to endorse the positions his friend had earlier taken.

In his first meeting with Catherine, he learns that she was engaged to a young man for eight years who was killed the year before in the Somme. Now, in reflection, she regrets not having had sexual relations with him: "I could have given him that anyway. But I thought it would be bad for him" (p. 19). Frederic's comments during this conversation are guarded and calculated, as he senses immediately the nature of her condition and the ways in which it might work to his advantage. He is restrained and charming, and it is clear that Catherine is taken with him, as Rinaldi acknowledges: " 'Miss Barkley prefers you to me. That is very clear. But the little Scotch one is very nice.' 'Very,' I said. I had not noticed her. 'You like her?' 'No,' said Rinaldi' " (p. 21).

In the early stages of the courtship, Frederic is insincere and calculating, confident of her attraction to him and of his eventual conquest. Even when Catherine slaps him when he tries to kiss her on their next encounter, he feels assured: "I was angry and yet certain, seeing it all ahead like the moves in a chess game" (p. 26). He seems emotionally uninvolved even when she does kiss him a moment later. " 'Oh, darling,' she said. 'You will be good to me, won't you?' What the hell, I thought. I stroked her hair and patted her shoulder. She was crying" (p. 27). When he returns to his room that evening, Rinaldi knows precisely what the situation is: "You have that pleasant air of a dog in heat," he says (p. 27). Through the telling of their memories of these encounters, Frederic reveals the cynicism of his early relationship with Catherine and develops an unflattering portrait of his motivation and character. The confessional edge of telling these painful memories must have a cathartic function for Frederic, for there can be little pleasure in recalling them.

That Frederic has dwelt on the nature of the early stages of his relationship with Catherine is also evident from the precision he brings to the relating of the events. Having thought it all through, he can even remember the number of days between meetings, even though it all happened many years earlier: "I was away for two days at the posts. When I got home it was too late and I did not see Miss Barkley until the next evening" (p. 29). The formality of their interaction is echoed by Catherine: as she is Miss Barkley to him, he is Mr. Henry to her (p. 38), at least at the beginning of the scene. The significance of the formal titles is that this encounter in Chapter VI forms a transition in their relationship from formal to personal, from flirtatious interest to direct expressions of affection: "She looked at me. 'And you do love me?' 'Yes.' 'You did say you loved me, didn't you?' 'Yes,' I lied. 'I love you.' I had not said it before" (p. 31). In this scene the emphasis is on the growing intensity of emotion between them, with love on her side and seductive expectation on his. At the time of telling the values are confessional, as Frederic reveals the painful truth to himself and his readers: "I thought she was probably a little crazy. . . . I knew I did not love Catherine Barkley nor had any idea of loving her" (p. 31). Frederic recalls that he regarded their interaction to be like a "game, like bridge, in which you said things instead of playing cards." He also remembers that Catherine, on a deeper level, was very much aware of his duplicity, despite her surface delusion: "This is a rotten game we play, isn't it?" she says to him (p. 32). As they part for the evening Frederic walks home past the Villa Rossa, the brothel he had previously frequented, but he rejects the temptation and goes home. This gesture suggests that his sexual desires have transferred to Catherine, about whom he now has erotic fantasies (p. 39). It also reveals a degree of commitment to Catherine that he had not yet formulated in language.

These implications are strengthened in the next chapter when Frederic returns from the front. While there he thought often about her, about how he would go see her, and they would make love in the night. When he returns, however, he becomes caught up in the fraternalism of the mess hall, drinks too much in a contest with Bassi (p. 41), goes drunk to see Catherine, and is informed that she will not see him that night. His feelings are a revelation to him: "I went out the door and suddenly I felt lonely and empty. I had treated seeing Catherine very lightly, had gotten somewhat drunk and had nearly forgotten to come but when I could not see her there I was feeling lonely and hollow" (p. 43). This is a poignant memory for Frederic to relate in 1928, when his feelings of loneliness and hollowness at the loss of Catherine would be inexorable and pervasive. This initial rejection was his first realization of his need for her and of the pain of her absence. The double function of the scene is that the pain of loss is a key issue in both of the time schemes of the novel. This passage is one of the best examples of the congruence of emotion on both temporal levels.

When Frederic finally does see her the next day, the encounter fulfills none of his fantasies, for he is on his way to the front and stops at the hospital for only a few moments. Both of them handle the incident of the night before with great delicacy. He accepts, strategically, the fiction of her illness: "I stopped to ask if you were better." He does not wish to force her to an accusation of his boorish behaviour of the night before, and she too wishes to pursue their relationship on the best of levels: "I'm quite well," she said, "I think the heat knocked me over yesterday" (p. 44). This is once again game playing, but it is a mutual acceptance of falsity for a benevolent purpose, since they can proceed in the relationship much more easily from this position than from one of accusation, and confession, apology, and forgiveness. She gives him a Saint Anthony medal to protect him at the front, and Frederic leaves wearing Saint Anthony. As he says, intruding into the flow of the action, "after I was wounded I never found him. Some one probably got it at one of the dressing stations" (p. 46).

Frederic does not see Catherine again until after he is wounded and is recovering in the hospital in Milan. The plot leaves the romance story to focus on the war until the two lovers are joined again through the coincidence of his wounding and her assignment to the American hospital. That his first sight of her prompts his feelings of affection had been foreshadowed by his growing involvement with her in her earlier scenes: "I looked toward the door. It was Catherine Barkley. She came in the room and over to the bed. 'Hello, darling,' she said. She looked fresh and young and very beautiful. I thought I had never seen anyone so beautiful. 'Hello,' I said. When I saw her I was in love with her. Everything turned over inside of me" (p. 95). At the time of the telling, of course, even these memories of love and happiness would have a poignant edge, a value quite distinct from those of the action. Frederic's relation of this part of their romance continues to record the most positive memories of Catherine coupled with some unflattering admissions on his part.

For example, he remembers that after they had made love for the first time, "the wildness was gone and I felt finer than I had ever felt" (p. 96). But this sweet memory is linked to the awareness that at the time he had not wanted to fall in love, not with her or with anyone (p. 97). In addition, he soon lies to her about his having had previous love affairs (although he later confesses that he has had gonorrhea [p. 309]) and, specifically, about having told prostitutes that he loved them (pp. 108–09). In contrast, Catherine was almost entirely selfless in her devotion: "I want what you want. There isn't any me any more," she says to him (p. 118). Later, when they discuss the complexities of getting married under Italian law, she says that she could not be more married as it is and that "there isn't any me. I'm you. Don't make up a separate me" (p. 119). Once again, Frederic's emotions at the time of the telling must be very different from those of the time of the events, when his success as lover would have given him great satisfaction. Now, in the telling, he focuses on his equivocation and duplicity to counterpoint her total absorption in their emotional bond. In this sense, entertaining and relating these events would be more a means of expiating guilt than one of enjoying the pleasure of the past.

The final episode of their relationship that Frederic narrates deals with Catherine's pregnancy and the consequences that follow from it. Early in the romance Nurse Ferguson had warned Frederic that she did not "want her [Catherine] with any of these war babies" (p. 113), just as she had suggested that they would never get married (p. 112). These observations are obviously more meaningful to Frederic as he tells the story than at the time of the action, for there is no indication in what they do or say to each other that they take any precautions against pregnancy or even give the consequences of their behaviour the slightest thought. So it is not remarkable that Catherine soon reveals she is pregnant, although it is notable that she seems to suggest that she made an attempt to abort the child: " 'I took everything but it didn't make any difference' " (p. 144). This remark would be significant at the time of the telling because if she had aborted the child Catherine would, in all likelihood, still be alive. Similarly poignant for Frederic to remember would be her concern for him contrasted to his admission to her that " 'you always feel trapped biologically' " (p. 145). When she objects to the word "always," with its suggestion that he may have impregnated another woman previously, he can only offer apologies without denials: " 'I could cut off my tongue,' I offered."

The further development of this plot line is once again interrupted by the concerns of the war, as Frederic returns to the front in time for the disastrous retreat from Caporetto. When he arrives in Gorizia he finds Rinaldi disillusioned with the war but sensitive as ever to his friend's condition. Rinaldi sees at once that Frederic has changed: " 'You act like a married man,' he said. 'What's the matter with you?' " (p. 173). Frederic will admit only that he is in love with Catherine. Later, as he records the rambling thoughts of his dreams, he once again affirms his love: "Christ, that my love were in my arms and I in my bed again. That my love Catherine. That my sweet love Catherine down might rain. Blow her again to me" (p. 204). It is important to be aware that these are sentiments Frederic expresses not only at the time of the action, when they occur as part of a dream reverie, but also at the time of the telling when, in a more rational context, the feelings are recalled and formulated by a narrator who also wishes to have his love back again.

As Frederic flees the front by riding on an armaments train, hiding under a canvas tarp, he reveals more of the depths of his emotional dependence on her: "I could remember Catherine but knew I would get crazy if I thought about her when I was not sure yet I would see her . . ." (p. 240). This is another passage with profound implications on both levels of the novel. At the time of the action it suggests a situational vulnerability: Frederic has not yet recovered emotionally from the trauma of having shot a man, of having nearly been shot himself in his attempt to cross the Tagliamento, and is still in the act of desertion. If he is discovered and captured, without papers or orders, he may yet be executed. He cannot be sure he will make it back to Milan, or that Catherine will be there, and he is realistic in thinking that there is much uncertainty in his circumstances. At the time of the telling, however, the emotions are somewhat more deep: his suggestion of going crazy if he is unable to be with her would suggest an almost irremediable sadness in the present. A decade is a long time for a sense of loss to persist, especially with the intensity with which Frederic tells his story.

When he arrives in Milan he learns that Catherine has been transferred to Stresa, a convenient location, he learns from his friend Simmons, since they can row across the lake to safety in Switzerland. At the time of the action the value of this observation is simply part of the strategy of escape; from the time of the telling, there is a bitter irony. In planning to escape the dangers of Italy, Frederic and Catherine hasten to her death in Lausanne. When Frederic finally sees her in Stresa, it is clear that she is deeply in love with him: "Catherine looked at me all the time, her eyes happy," he says (p. 255). Here, too, there is pleasure in the past and pain in the present, in the memory of her devotion. Frederic then relates how accusatory Ferguson was about the pregnancy, and how Catherine came to his defense. But the emphasis is on how they were reunited in Stresa and how wonderful it was to be together.

The process of telling this part of his story leads Frederic to a series of generalizations about love that come not from feelings contemporaneous with the action, when the only thoughts would have been about the strategy of escape or the pleasure of love, but from the later period of loneliness and retrospective assessment: "Often a man wishes to be alone and a girl wishes to be alone too and if they love each other they are jealous of that in each other, but I can truly say we never felt that. We could feel alone when we were together, alone against the others. It has only happened to me like that once" (p. 258). The last comment, that such love has come only once, also suggests that Frederic has not replaced Catherine emotionally in the intervening years.

Linked to these reflections are Frederic's observations about the nature of the world and the status of the individuals in it. These thoughts are clearly from a later perspective as well: "If people bring so much courage to this world the world has to kill them to break them, so of course it kills them. The world breaks every one and afterward many are strong at the broken places. But those that will not break it kills" (pp. 258-59). There would be no motivation for these sentiments prior to Catherine's death in Switzerland. As retrospective observations, they create the irony of two lovers fleeing joyfully toward their own disaster. Significantly, this passage is juxtaposed in Frederic's narrative to the billiard game with Count Greffi in which Frederic and the Count discuss death (p. 270). Count Greffi died six years after their conversation in Stresa, so Frederic's memories of the direction of their discussion have resonance for the Count as well as for Catherine.

But Frederic's recapitulation of the days immediately prior to the escape to Switzerland stresses his love for Catherine, the real subject of his narration. By going back over it all he can once again feel the emotions of that period at the same time he acknowledges what he has lost: " 'My life used to be full of everything,' I said. 'Now if you aren't with me I haven't a thing in the world' " (p. 266). It must be painfully evident to Frederic, as he tells his story, with Catherine long dead, that he has not "a thing in the world." This idea is reiterated a moment later when he says to her " 'I'm just so in love with you that there isn't anything else.' " As he remembers their love-making that afternoon, he recalls his emotions: " 'I felt faint with loving her so much' " (p. 268). He has come a long way from the cynical seducer who first met Catherine, who behaved only with calculation and brash assurance. Despite himself, he became a "lover" in every sense, one whose sense of being is engrossed in the beloved.

Frederic's telling of the escape across the lake that November night is largely an adventure story with relatively little reflection on the significance of the events or their later consequences. As always, however, there is resonance in the past for the present, as in the comment Catherine makes when he warns her to be careful not to allow the oar to hit her in the stomach when she takes her turn rowing: " 'If it did'—Catherine said between strokes—'life might be much simpler' " (p. 284). Once again Frederic remembers comments about causing an abortion which, from hindsight, could have saved her life.

The technicalities of entering Switzerland comprise a largely comic episode, despite the importance of the lovers' being admitted. But once that seems assured, what Frederic recalls is the regional rivalries among the guards and the extent to which Switzerland is a tourist business rather than a country. What is more important, however, is that as the story Frederic tells comes closer and closer to the ultimate tragedy, his interpretive comments diminish until at the end he is relating only events.

The fact that he does not intrude into the rendition of the action, however, does not mean that they do not have a deeply felt meaning for him. Frederic, as is the case with all narrators, must select material from memory to be told, and the events described may have a different meaning, or a deeper significance, for him as he tells them than as they happened. Throughout the early sections of Book Five, for example, Frederic describes the happiness he and Catherine had together the winter of 1918 in Montreux.

The joy of the events is tinged with a sense of loss and tragedy from the time of the telling, however. Frederic mentions the close marriage of his landlords, Mr. and Mrs. Guttingen, who were "very happy together too" (p. 300). At the time it happened Frederic would have looked to them optimistically as a model of a good marriage: at the time of the telling he portrays them as a reminder of what he has lost. The distance between the two times is evident in the difficulty Frederic has in remembering certain details, ones not directly associated with Catherine: "There were three villages: Chernex, Fontanivent, and the other I forget" (p. 301).

There are other subtle touches with the narrative point of view. Now that Frederic can no longer see Catherine at all, he recalls how he could see her image in three mirrors simultaneously at the hairdresser's (p. 303). When she expresses her deep love for him, there is also a reminder that she is narrow in the hips and that the baby must be kept small (p. 304). At the beginning of the novel, when his relationship with Catherine was not at a crucial stage, he tended to narrate broad sweeps of time, using seasons as indicators of passing periods. As he tells about these crucial months, however, he becomes increasingly precise, specifying months, then days, and, finally, in the hospital, hours and minutes. He indicates that the snow in Montreux came on December 22, for example, since the snow will isolate them in their romantic haven. They were so happy together, that winter, that they felt no desire for the companionship of other people, as they discuss on two occasions (pp. 308, 313). The weight here is on how close they have become, how they seem to be one entity. Frederic once again makes the assertion to her that " 'I'm no good when you're not there. I haven't any life at all any more' " (p. 310). These sentiments may convey not only how he felt in Switzerland but how he feels at the time of narration.

Their happiness continues into the middle of January (by which time Frederic has grown a beard), through February, and into early March, when the rains come and ruin the landscape. From the calculations of their plan to go to Lausanne to have the baby, it would seem most likely that Catherine dies in early April, the cruelest month, since she is eight months pregnant in early March (p. 316). Frederic remembers that they stayed in one hotel for three weeks in Lausanne (p. 320), during which time she bought baby clothes and he boxed in the local gymnasium. It is "one morning" sometime later that Catherine experiences labor pains and the episode in the hospital began.

It is significant that Frederic's rendition of the trauma of labor and the death of Catherine is almost entirely free of retrospective observations. His comments about Catherine's suffering being the "price you paid for sleeping together" are his representation of his thoughts at the time of the action, since he does not yet know that she will die later that day (pp. 330–31). Similarly, his expectation that "now Catherine would die" is also a projection of the working of his mind at the time of the events, not a later assessment

(p. 338). The famous "ants" passage, in which, in the past, Frederic observed ants coming out of a burning log and dropping off into the fire, most likely represents thinking at the time of the action when he would long for the ability to be a "messiah" and control death, thus saving Catherine. Frederic relates the events of this final episode without interpretation, suggesting that the facts speak for themselves and also, perhaps, that the recapitulation of the most painful episode of his life is almost too much for him, that his emotions can be controlled only in restraint. In this sense he is much less moved by his own physical wounding, about which he seems free to assess and evaluate without fear of the feelings involved; it is Catherine's death that he handles with emotional caution.

In his memory, it is Catherine who conducted herself bravely, and he retains only the most positive recollections of her fortitude and sensitivity. From the beginning of labor she regarded the worst pains as the best (pp. 323–24) and expressed concern not for herself but for him and any inconveniences that her problems might cause him. While she struggles through a prolonged labor, he goes for breakfast and then lunch and later dinner. He remembers the day, understandably, with great precision, giving the hours of key developments, the minutes between contractions (p. 327). There is irony, of course, in the reassurances he receives that Catherine is all right, that the baby is healthy, that he should not worry. His emotion of the time is told without apology: when he hears that she has begun to hemorrhage, he says that everything was gone inside of him. Rather than comment about his emotions, he captures his thinking in a stream of consciousness passage: "Dear God, don't let her die. Please, please, please don't let her die. God please make her not die. I'll do anything you say if you don't let her die. You took the baby but don't let her die. That was all right but don't let her die. Please, please, dear God, don't let her die" (p. 341). When he is finally admitted to her bedside, he leans over her and starts to cry. Catherine knows that she has very little time to live. Rather than descend into a false religiosity, as had Frederic earlier, Catherine does not want a priest and asks only to spend her last moments with him. Characteristically, she is concerned for him: she wants him to have the companionship of other women after she has died; she says she will come stay with him nights, since she knows he has insomnia and suffers from loneliness; she reassures him that she is not afraid of death and sees it only as a "dirty trick" (p. 342). In a passage Hemingway deleted from the manuscript, Frederick thinks: "And if it is the Lord that giveth and the Lord that taketh away, I do not admire him for taking Catherine away. . . ."[5] His rendition of the events after her death is abbreviated and unemotional: nothing after her death seems to matter, and the language is restrained because the emotion would be too much to bear, too painful for the telling.

But Frederic has told his story, and the honesty of his telling suggests that he is now ready to face the truth of the early stages of their relationship and implies that he has grown a great deal, emotionally and morally, in the years after her death. Frederic is not glossing over his behavior; the most he could hope for at the time of the narration is the therapeutic value of a full accounting, of an honest assessment of his feelings throughout their relationship. The contrasting pattern in what Frederic reveals of Catherine's attitudes is most acute: she, as he chooses to recall and relate, was selfless from the start, open in her feelings, willing to give far more than she received from him, and soon became totally fused with him. At the time of the telling it is these sentiments that Frederic would remember: a man who finds the memory of his lost love too precious to surrender, even after a decade, is not going to dwell on petty points; he would, of course, subordinate any deficiencies in her nature to concentrate on what is of moment to him now, the quality of his loss, the death of a love he has not replaced.

It is understandable that the story he tells is rendered in language that is controlled and understated, since the pain of the memories is almost too much to bear even after a decade. In another passage that Hemingway excised from the manuscript, Frederic reflects that "the position of the survivor of a great calamity is seldom admirable."[6] Especially acute must be the emotions of telling what he said to Catherine in Stresa: " 'My life used to be full of everything,' I said. 'Now if you aren't with me I haven't a thing in the world' " (p. 266). *A Farewell to Arms* is a novel told by a man who feels he has nothing left in the world, nothing but the memories of the most painful and yet meaningful episode of his life.

It is important, however, as it is for all first-person narratives, to attempt to assess the motivation for revealing such intimate details. One impulse might be the desire to come to terms at last with the true nature of the events: as Robert W. Lewis, Jr., has suggested, "Henry has undergone an initiatory and learning experience that he is now ready to interpret."[7] Another impulse might be for Frederic to change his condition at the time of the telling. Frederic's story is one of progressive isolation. He begins as a member of the Italian army, with a primary identification with his own unit, moves to a union with Catherine, secluded within their transient home in Switzerland, and ends without connection, alone in the rain.[8] But after a decade of reflection, his act of telling his story is fundamentally one of relating, of speaking to others about the intimate moments in his life, and this act implies the beginning of a movement into the world once again. Before doing so he seems to feel the need to evaluate his experiences and his younger self, however painful the process might be.[9] Although his observations stress the indifference of the universe, the perversity of fate, the vanity of human wishes, Frederic's comments also prepare him to move beyond his loss.[10]

What is clear is that although his motives and attitudes were not always noble in the early stages of his romance with Catherine, through his love for her he grew to be a better man, one who could love fully and assess himself truly.[11] There seems to be no justification for concluding, as Gerry

Brenner does, that having told his story Frederic has little reason to go on living and will soon commit suicide.[12] Rather, the suggestion is that he is now prepared to resume living once again, to seek new relationships and new commitments, and to end his fixation on loss and pain, a process that has taken him a decade.

Before he does so, however, he apparently feels the need to think it all through once again and to tell his story from the beginning. What he tells is more a eulogy that a realistic account, particularly with regards to the portrait of Catherine.[13] Indeed, it is clear from the nature of the telling of *A Farewell to Arms* that she cannot be judged apart from the recognition that she exists in the novel only in Frederic's memories, that she is a projection of his thinking a decade after she has died. Far from "wanting" or "needing" her to die, Frederic has clearly been unable to reconcile himself to her loss during the intervening years and only now, through the act of the telling, does he come to terms with his sense of emptiness through the story he tells. The story he tells about Catherine, despite the fact that she dies at the end of it, shows her moving from a condition of psychological desolation to one of balance and love.[14] He now needs to find his own way through that process. His reflections and philosophical speculations reveal a man who knows much about what he must live without and what he will always live with, with the memories of the war and the love and loss of Catherine Barkley.

Notes

1.   Ernest Hemingway, *A Farewell to Arms* (New York: Scribner's, 1957).

2.   See Judith Fetterley, "*A Farewell to Arms*: Ernest Hemingway's 'Resentful Cryptogram,'" *The Authority of Experience: Essays in Feminist Criticism*, ed. Arlyn Diamond and Lee R. Edwards (Amherst: University of Massachusetts Press, 1977), pp. 258, 270. [Reprinted in this volume.]

3.   For the information on the career of Babe Ruth and its role in dating the time of the narration of the novel, I am indebted to Dale Edwards, "When Does Frederic Henry Narrate *A Farewell to Arms*," *Notes on Modern American Literature*, 4 (1980), Item 14.

4.   Sheldon Norman Grebstein, *Hemingway's Craft* (Carbondale: Southern Illinois University Press, 1973), p. 76.

5.   Quoted in Scott Donaldson, "Frederic Henry's Escape and the Pose of Passivity," *Hemingway: A Revaluation*, ed. Donald Noble (Troy, NY: Whitson Publishing Co., 1983), p. 181.

6.   Quoted in Donaldson, p. 181.

7.   Robert W. Lewis, Jr., *Hemingway on Love* (Austin: University of Texas Press, 1965), p. 39.

8.   See Michael S. Reynolds, *Hemingway's First War: The Making of* A Farewell to Arms (Princeton: Princeton University Press, 1976), p. 271.

9.   See Arnold F. Davidson, "The Dantean Perspective in Hemingway's *A Farewell to Arms*," *Journal of Narrative Technique*, 3 (1973): 123, for a comment on Frederic's isolation.

10. See Davidson, pp. 123–24.

11. I am indebted to the insights of Arthur Waldhorn, *A Reader's Guide to Ernest Hemingway* (New York: Farrar, Straus and Giroux, 1972), p. 130.

12. See Gerry Brenner, *Concealments in Hemingway's Works* (Columbus: Ohio State University Press, 1983), p. 41. [Reprinted in part in this volume.]

13. Joyce Wexler, "E. R. A. for Hemingway: A Feminist Defense of *A Farewell to Arms*," *Georgia Review*, 35 (1981), 121, develops a similar logic.

14. I am indebted here to Roger Whitlow, *Cassandra's Daughters: The Women in Hemingway* (Westport: Greenwood Press, 1984), p. 22.

The Search for "Home"

PETER GRIFFIN

For his first six years, Ernest Hemingway and his sisters, his physician father Clarence, and his mother Grace, lived in a spacious, mid-Victorian house in Oak Park, Illinois, owned by Grace's father, Ernest Hall. To all appearances, it was a happy life, thoroughly documented in the "Memory Books" Grace kept and in the hundreds of photos Clarence loved to take. Yet something was very wrong in the Hall-Hemingway household, as it was called. Although Ernest Hall had little formal education, read mostly Walter Scott, had been discharged from military service for an accidental, self-inflicted wound, and had earned his money in the cutlery trade, his daughter, Grace, re-formed him as a war hero, an entrepreneur, and a man of high culture—all achieved, she said, through his powerful will. Grace made her father the family icon, a standard by which she weighed—and found wanting—her husband and, eventually, her son. Dr. Hemingway occupied less the role of father than that of older brother to Ernest—teaching him, mainly, to hunt and fish—and was called by both Grace and her father, "dear boy."[1]

Ernest Hemingway grew up hating his mother; he hated her until she died. He said so to his wives, his sons, and his friends.[2] But his hatred took a curious form. In a short story he never published and never even titled, Hemingway wrote a chapter of autobiography more revealing than anything he would commit to print.

The story begins: "He had known he wouldn't get up anymore. . . ."[3] The "He" is "Orpen," a "tired, fought-out" soldier involved in a rear guard action. Lying on his stomach behind some cover on a hill, Orpen keeps watch over a key bridge which should have been blown up, but hasn't been. Suddenly, out of the fog, comes a thrust of graycoats. Orpen and the men with him begin to fire. Orpen himself kills a cyclist. "You pressed a trigger, some one died and somehow you didn't feel bad about it." "Ether in the brain," he concludes.

Before the next assault, Orpen thinks of his hands. He had wanted, he says, to be a famous pianist and play at Albert Hall. He compares the

This essay was written specifically for this volume and is published for the first time. The quotations from unpublished Hemingway manuscripts are included by courtesy of permission from the Ernest Hemingway Foundation.

175

digital dexterity required to "play" the machine gun with that needed by a pianist. Then he remembers sitting in the music room at home. His mother would listen while he played Chopin for her. "That's so sweet my dear," she would say. "Will you play some more. I just don't see any sense to Schönberg, my dear. Should I?"

The next assault leaves Orpen wounded, as does the next, and the next. In his delirium, he thinks the battle is a symphony for drums. He sees the men in the orchestra rise up and sink down, then run at his bayonet. Finally, Orpen dreams he's fighting in an ancient war, with shields, swords, and pikes. One of the combatants, a big man in a plumed helmet, roars, "Hold! We quench our thirst awhile." And the soldiers come toward Orpen. "Hail, O hero!" the big man cries, "For thou also kept a bridge well," and he holds out his mailed hand. Orpen grasps it and says, "How do you do?" "We fare well here O hero," the big man answers.

Orpen sees strange faces about him, and strange accoutrements. He knows that he is dead, because he once read a story like this. The big man tells Orpen that he is in Valhalla, the Hall of Heroes, higher than heaven, and that all the famous heroes are there: Lord Nelson, decorated with medals and gold brocade, Eric the Red, Drake, Raleigh, Sherman, Khan, Washington, Grant, Bonaparte, Ney, Crockett, Jackson, and Custer. In Valhalla these heroes all fight for the fun of it, and no one dies. "There is the fun of killing, but none of the drawbacks of dying."

Soon an absurd quarrel develops among the residents of Valhalla, and they fight it out with passion, and it appears, great enjoyment. Orpen hates the violence, but keeps this to himself. He feels certain no one will understand. "You had to pretend to like it."

At one point, George Washington rides up to Orpen and makes a silly joke. Orpen drives his bayonet into Washington's groin. Washington only laughs, says "Great fun," spurs his horse, and thrusts his sword into Orpen's chest.

Orpen withdraws and wanders moodily in a thicket. Then he stops for a time to rest. When he starts off again there is moonlight, and he finds steps leading down from Valhalla to heaven. He comes upon a country lane. "It looked much like the lane at home to Orpen with great elms meeting overhead. Moonlight dappled the dust of the road, and the night was warm." He notes that an arm of the sea juts close to the road, and as he passes, Orpen hears voices. "Plenty of bait and we'll start bright and early," he hears someone say. "They'll be running good tomorrow," another voice answers.

There are soft sounds of waves, and a glowing in the half dark. In this glow Orpen sees a little man walking in a garden with a woman. "This, sweetest one," the man says, "is my life. The garden, the roses, the smell of honeysuckle on the hedge, the warm night." "—and me beside you, Horatio?" the woman asks. "Yes, and you beside me," he says. But now the man (Lord Horatio Nelson) has on only a plain black suit.

Orpen turns away. "He seemed to know his way [to a door, for] without hesitation he turned the handle and entered. A woman smiled at him." "Mother," he said. "I've been a long way." "I knew you'd get here, son," she says. "Look!" Then the mother points across the room to the old concert grand piano. She tells Orpen his compositions are still there. "I've kept them just as you left them . . . waiting. There is the pen and ink." Orpen is delighted. "Now I can really go on with the symphony tomorrow," he cried. But he remembers. "I got to fight tomorrow in Valhalla—to cut to slice is the greatest joy of man." But his mother only smiles at him "like the mother of all wisdom." Nevertheless, he persists. "Today we slashed and slashed. I ran George Washington through as I battled down the road to you." He claims that "the joy of battle was in my heart." Still his mother smiles understandingly.

Orpen becomes angry. He insists that his mother believe he enjoyed the warfare. When she refuses, "Somehow, before he knew it he was on his knees before her and she was holding his head." Orpen confesses, "It wasn't wonderful, mother. It was horrible. I wanted to stay and do my music, mother. I don't want to be in Valhalla!" His mother strokes Orpen's head. "It was like being a boy again," Orpen thinks. His mother says, "I know son. I know."

Orpen's mother now reveals to him that all the heroes who had appeared to enjoy the fighting so much in Valhalla are living in peace at her home. They are all bored with fighting, his mother says; they only go up to Valhalla to welcome a new hero. There are many now, because of the War.

After his mother shows the medals she's kept for him, which were awarded to him for his hero's death, she promises Orpen he can stay home and work on his music. Now Orpen understands he's in heaven and is suddenly so happy that he dances. "It was a curious dance—great high leaps in grace note form with quaver duration. Orpen leapt high into the air— higher than ever before." Then he gets a pain in his chest—where George Washington stabbed him. After another, he's awake. The first words he says, as a small rectangular piece of shrapnel is removed from his chest, are, "Tell them I don't want to go back to Valhalla." A woman's voice replies, "No, you won't have to."

All the family characters are here. The diminutive father (dressed as Clarence most often was, in black), the heroic grandfather (embedded in Hemingway's psyche as his true father) in the person of George Washington, and the mother who welcomes her son home with love. This sense of "home" in the story of the wounded Orpen (the name suggests "orphan" and may also allude to the well-known British painter of sentimental wartime scenes, Sir William Orpen) is just what Hemingway lacked during his childhood in the Hall-Hemingway household. In the fictional world of "Orpen," the acts of war, even of heroes, are spiritually destructive. They engender hypocrisy, and are ultimately boring; they obstruct Orpen's return to his art, his mother, and to "home." Only when he rejects the life (and afterlife) of the hero does he receive the mother's blessing that Ernest never received from Grace.[4] As he wakes from anesthetic, Orpen hears a valediction to the arms of war.

In late February 1918, while working as a cub reporter for the Kansas City *Star*, Ernest Hemingway volunteered for service with the Italian Red Cross Ambulance Corps. (Defective vision prevented his joining the American forces.) After the long journey to New York for embarkation, the crossing on an old tramp steamer, and a week-long stay in Paris, he began his duties on the Italian Front, down on the Lower Piave River. A month later, a little after midnight on 8 July 1918, Hemingway was badly wounded by shrapnel from a huge Austrian mortar. Under enemy searchlights and machine gun fire (which wounded him again), he shouldered an Italian comrade back to the safety of the trenches. For this act he was awarded the Silver Medal for Valor, Italy's second highest military honor. (The Gold Medal went only to the dead.) As "the first American wounded on the Italian front," he became a celebrity, and for months convalesced in style at the new American Red Cross hospital in Milan. The doctors, competent and incompetent, were like fathers; the nurses were like mothers, sisters, or friends. One nurse was special. She was "nice," and Ernest fell in love with her.

Agnes von Kurowsky, 26 and on the rebound from a romance gone awry, was tall, gray-eyed, with short chestnut hair and a cameo neck. Concealed beneath the folds of her long, loose-fitting nurse's garment was the loveliest waist Ernest had ever seen. At first there were the usual impediments: "Gumshoe" superiors, inconvenient hours, a heavy patient load. But, after a while, Agnes sat by Ernest's bed in one of the hard-backed chairs and left his room only to make her hourly rounds. When the August nights were especially hot, she moistened a towel for Ernest's forehead, wiped his neck and chest with cool water, and, to alleviate the itching beneath his bandages, scratched the soles of his feet. To Ernest, Agnes's voice was soft and low, and at his request she sang amusing little songs for him that she learned at boarding school. Soothingly, she'd "put my head on that nice place—you know—the hollow place for my face—& go to sleep with your arm around me."[5] By November, Agnes von Kurowsky was his fiancée.

Back in Oak Park after the Armistice in the spring of 1919, Ernest worked hard to bring Agnes home. But she always refused. Finally, she wrote that she was breaking off their engagement and would marry someone else. The day he received her letter, Ernest wrote to his best friend, Bill Horne:

> But Bill, I've loved Ag. She's been my ideal, and Bill, I forgot all about religion and everything else because I had Ag to worship.
> Well, the crash of smashing ideals was never merry music to anyone's ears. But she doesn't love me now, Bill, and she is going to marry someone— name not given—who she has met since, marry him very soon, and she hopes that after I have forgiven her, I still start and have a wonderful career and everything. But Bill, I don't want a wonderful career and everything. That

isn't really fair. She didn't write "and everything." All I wanted was Ag. And happiness and now the bottom has dropped out of the whole world.[6]

This was the world Hemingway would recreate in *A Farewell to Arms*.[7]

The story of "Orpen" and *A Farewell to Arms* were written almost nine years apart: the first in Chicago in late 1920; the second mostly in Key West between 1928 and 1929. The "source" for each is Ernest's childhood. The driving force behind each is his search for "home." The opening paragraph of *A Farewell to Arms* establishes two motifs which come to control the book: the first, "home," is a quiescent point of observation. Movement dominates the scene.

> In the late summer of that year we lived in a house in a village that looked across the river and the plain to the mountains. In the bed of the river there were pebbles and boulders, dry and white in the sun, and the water was clear and swiftly moving and blue in the channels. Troops went by the house and down the road and the dust they raised powdered the leaves of the trees. The trunks of the trees too were dusty and the leaves fell early that year and we saw the troops marching along the road and the dust rising and leaves, stirred by the breeze, falling and the soldiers marching and afterward the road bare and white except for the leaves.[8]

There are two kinds of movement here: the current of life—the water, swiftly flowing, clear and blue in the channels; and the ironic, ugly, current of death—the stream of troops on the road, ". . . and under their capes the two leather cartridge-boxes on the front of the belts, gray leather boxes heavy with the packs of clips of thin, long 6.5 mm. cartridges, bulged forward under the capes so that the men, passing on the road, marched as though they were six months gone with child."

The first three books of *A Farewell to Arms* end with Frederic Henry on a train. At the end of the first book he has suffered his physical wound and is going "home" to heal. At the end of the second book he is leaving his new-found home and his beloved to return to war. At the close of the third book he is going home again, to Catherine, and believes he is finished with war. In each case a cruel irony intervenes. At the hospital, Frederic Henry heals one wound, only to open another—his love for Catherine. He returns to war from a sense of duty, a directive of conscience, and discovers that it outrages his sense of justice. He acknowledges the absurdity of war only to encounter, with the death of his wife and child, the absurdity of peace.

There are many "homes" in *A Farewell to Arms*. One, the house in Gorizia, is dominated by brutal boy-men who, pack-like at the mess, grin as the captain baits the priest. "Priest every night five against one," the captain jokes and explains his double meaning with a gesture. But it's actually five against two. Frederic Henry and the priest possess a morality of aesthetics. "Beautiful" acts mean good, "ugly" acts, evil. "Priest to-day with girls," the vulgar captain prods, looking at the priest and at Frederic Henry.

Frederic Henry is often with girls. But he does not like the officer's whorehouse, "where the girls climbed all over you and put your cap on backward as a sign of affection between their trips upstairs with brother officers." The priest commends the Abruzzi region to Frederic. It is where the priest's family lives and where he himself hopes one day to return. It is a home, "where it was clear cold and dry and the snow was dry and powdery and hare-tracks in the snow and the peasants took off their hats and called you Lord and there was good hunting." (All this is so reminiscent of the values Ernest saw in his sportsman-father, Clarence.) But though Frederic is drawn to the innocence of that pristine beauty, he doesn't go to the priest's Abruzzi. Instead he visits whores in Milan, Florence, Rome, and Naples. Frederic knows that the priest's home, his world of innocence, belief, and honor, is no protection against a persistently ugly heart. Speaking of his abuse of the priest, the captain says, "He can't do anything about it anyway." Frederic Henry sadly concurs: "We all got up and left the table."

Catherine Barkley, like the priest, has a home, even though it exists in the midst of brutality. In fact, it exists because of brutality. Miss Barkley's home is a British hospital in a villa built by Germans before the war. When Frederic Henry meets her, Miss Barkley is in the garden. Her wound is not obvious, but it is severe. "Miss Barkley was quite tall. She wore what seemed to me to be a nurse's uniform, was blonde and had a tawny skin and gray eyes. I thought she was very beautiful. She was carrying a thin rattan stick like a toy riding-crop, bound in leather.

'It belonged to a boy who was killed last year.'

'I'm awfully sorry.'

'He was a very nice boy. He was going to marry me and he was killed in the Somme' " (p. 18).

For Frederic Henry, the hospital is a place to pick up a nurse. With its marble statues, it reminds him of a cemetery. But there is no sympathy in this association. Frederic Henry is as insensitive and obtuse, as ugly with Catherine as the captain was with the priest in the mess. " 'Oh, darling,' she said. 'You will be good to me, won't you?' What the hell, I thought. I stroked her hair and patted her shoulder. She was crying" (p. 27).

Before his wounding, the hospital for Frederic Henry meant the hurt, the sick, the crippled. He felt no more about it, and no more for them, than he did for the statues in the hall. As for the lovely Catherine Barkley— if she were "crazy," all the better. He had no intention of falling in love with her. Of course, Frederic Henry had no intention of being wounded. But he was, and he went out of himself, "and out and out and out and all the time bodily in the wind" (p. 58).

In the ward of the field hospital, Frederic Henry has two visitors. The first, Rinaldi, gregarious, overbearing, and brusquely affectionate, comes in the afternoon. He calls Frederic Henry, "blood brother," hobo argot for homosexual lover. He claims he is jealous of Catherine Barkley and of the priest. He brings the drink of lovers, cognac, and he leaves it under the bed. He wants to kiss Frederic Henry; he calls him "baby."

Rinaldi and Frederic Henry are not homosexuals, and they know it. Their teasing shows their confidence in this. Speaking of Frederic Henry and the priest, Rinaldi jokes, "Sometimes I think you and he are a little that way. You know." Frederic Henry replies, "No, you don't." But for Rinaldi women are "goddesses" or "whores." There is comfort and safety—Rinaldi knows he is syphilitic—in masculine love.

The priest visits Frederic Henry at dusk. Supper in the ward is over; there are no lights on. The priest stands by the bed, "small, brown-faced, and embarrassed." Frederic Henry calls him "father." The priest has vermouth. But the cork is shoved down into the bottle as it is opened. Both Frederic Henry and the Arbuzzi priest are disappointed. The priest has practical gifts: mosquito netting and English papers. Frederic and the priest share a regret for the state of things. They talk of women and love. They agree, though Frederic Henry doesn't acknowledge the agreement, that love means sacrifice. And yet after the priest has gone, Frederic Henry thinks of the Abruzzi as a home only for the lone hunter.

The love of Rinaldi and the priest, like the field hospital itself, is incomplete. It's love of men only—even the nurses have beards. And Frederic Henry cannot heal there. The new American hospital, with its female nurses, awaits in Milan.[9]

Frederic Henry and Catherine Barkley speak a private language—very much like that used by Ernest in letters to his first wife, Hadley.[10] The tone creates an illusion of endless discovery, though with boundaries set and respected. It's their conspiracy of innocence. As they prepare for his operation, it's Catherine's turn to play:

> "Just start your prayers or poetry or something when they tell you to breathe deeply. You'll be lovely that way and I'll be so proud of you. I'm very proud of you anyway. You have such a lovely temperature and you sleep like a little boy with your arm around the pillow and think it's me. Or is it some other girl? Some fine Italian girl?"
>
> "It's you."
>
> "Of course it's me. Oh I do love you and Valentini will make you a fine leg. I'm glad I don't have to watch it."
>
> "And you'll be on night duty to-night."
>
> "Yes. But you won't care."
>
> "You wait and see."
>
> "There, darling. Now you are all clean inside and out. Tell me. How many people have you ever loved?"
>
> "Nobody."
>
> "Not me even?"

"Yes, you."

"How many others really?"

"None."

"How many have you—how do you say it?—stayed with?"

"None."

"You're lying to me."

"Yes."

"It's all right. Keep right on lying to me. That's what I want you to do. Were they pretty?" (111–12)

To Catherine and Frederic love is illusion, and, like any illusion, it either deepens or wears away. Yet for a time, love deflects pain and fear and makes sex possible when it is most needed. Their hospital sex sets things right in body and spirit and helps the healing begin.

But, horribly, there's death in this healing. It's Catherine's pregnancy. From the start, she speaks of it as a disease: "I did everything. I took everything but it didn't make any difference." Catherine is afraid to tell Frederic about the baby, and with good reason. A child is a hostage to fortune, and fortune is always bad. But isn't this pregnancy the current of life? Catherine asks innocently. "It's the natural thing."

Hemingway compares the house where the captain mocked the priest to the hospital where Catherine and Frederic Henry make love. Again there are the "haves" and the "have nots"—those with a morality of aesthetics and those without one. The "haves" are considerate, sensitive, tough. They learn their trade and do the best they can without thought of how their actions will appear. The "haves" are self-disciplined. They reject the temptation to be sentimental, self-indulgent. They seem composed, synchronized to a pleasing inner rhythm that makes them confident, appealing. They act to enhance life. The mustachioed Dr. Valenti, the major who finally operates on Frederic Henry, remarks on Catherine Barkley's beauty. "I will be a patient here myself" [he says]. "No, but I will do all your maternity work free." When Frederic offers him a drink, Valenti replies, "A drink? Certainly. I will have ten drinks. Where are they?"

The "have nots" are awkward, secretly insecure, sadly ridiculous. They affect a competence they do not possess. Like the bearded doctor who first examines Frederic Henry's legs:

"This is the young man," said the house doctor with the delicate hands.

"How do you do?" said the tall gaunt doctor with the beard. The third doctor, who carried the X-ray plates in their red envelopes, said nothing.

"Remove the dressings?" questioned the bearded doctor.

"Certainly. Remove the dressings, please nurse," the house doctor said to Miss Gage. Miss Gage removed the dressings. I looked down at the legs. At the field hospital they had the look of not too freshly ground hamburger steak.

Now they were crusted and the knee was swollen and discolored and the calf sunken but there was no pus.

"Very clean," said the house doctor. "Very clean and nice."

"Um," said the doctor with the beard. The third doctor looked over the house doctor's shoulder. . . .

"May I see the plates again, please, doctor?" [the bearded doctor said]. The third doctor handed him one of the plates. "No. The left leg, please."

"That is the left leg, doctor."

"You are right. I was looking from a different angle." (102–3)

Hemingway is recreating something of his own father here. (Clarence Hemingway, chief of obstetrics at Oak Park Hospital, always wore a full beard.) "I have noticed that doctors who fail in the practice of medicine have a tendency to seek one another's company and aid in consultation. A doctor who cannot take out your appendix properly will recommend to you a doctor who will be unable to remove your tonsils with success" (p. 102). When Ernest returned from Italy, Clarence sent him for work on his tonsils to a surgeon who nearly killed him.

The head nurse, Miss Van Campen, with her pietistic tone and presumptuous criticism, as though she had the right and the duty to set standards for people whose lives she could not hope to understand, is a model of Grace Hemingway. Her hatred of alcohol—for Hemingway, a useful tool for sustaining necessary illusions—echoes Grace's "never have it in the house." Miss Van Campen sins against charity and enjoys it. She tears at bandages stuck to the wound.

Still, in the world of *A Farewell to Arms*, the "have nots" are not essentially evil. (Miss Van Campen does add sherry to Frederic Henry's milk.) Most often they're just stupid and weak. According to a poem Hemingway would write to his fourth wife, Mary, during his time in Paris in 1944, they are the "Battle Fatigues" of life, those who mask their spiritual insufficiency with excuses and "thou shalt not."[11]

In *A Farewell to Arms*, the "haves" are conscious of time passing. There is an urgency in everything they do. It is not hysteria, born of fear, the business of the coward. The urgency in the "haves" clears their minds. They live in the valley of the shadow of death, yet do not despair. Just before Frederic Henry and Catherine Barkley part, when Frederic is about to depart for the Front, he recalls Marvell's poem, "To His Coy Mistress": "But at my back I always hear/Time's wingèd chariot hurrying near."

Like sexual intercourse, the pressure of time passing clears the mind: "My head felt very clear and cold and I wanted to talk facts." The hotel room had been their home. "After we had eaten we felt fine, and then after, we felt very happy and in a little time the room felt like our own home" (163). Then, suddenly, it is no longer their home, because the illusion is no longer required. With words "clear and cold," Frederic says, "I hate to leave our fine house." Catherine promises, "I'll have a fine home for you when you come back."

When Frederic Henry returns to the villa at Gorizia, it does "not feel like a homecoming." True, Rinaldi is as loving as ever, and despite his sickness, he is cheerful. He invites Frederic Henry to recreate the illusion of life as boyhood camaraderie, with drink the elixir and remorse the cardinal sin. But at supper, Frederic notices that the mess has changed. He senses that the tension, the hostility, has subsided. The men are tolerant, more domestic. The bread pudding is sweet to the men, and with it, they think of the sweetness and softness of home. They are all gentler now that they have been beaten, not by the Austrians, but by the sheer act of making war. All the violence, suffering, and death, ends not in victory or defeat, but in exhaustion and withdrawal.

Hemingway's metaphor for retreat is the river. At one point, Frederic Henry and Piani take refuge in a barn. While Piani searches for food, Frederic lies alone in the hayloft: "The hay smelled good and lying in a barn in the hay took away all the years in between. We had lain in hay and talked and shot sparrows with an air-rifle when they perched in the triangle cut high up in the wall of the barn. The barn was gone now and one year they had cut the hemlock woods and there were only stumps, dried tree-tops, branches and fireweed where the woods had been. You could not go back. If you did not go forward what happened?" (231).

The barn, the hayloft and the memories, Piani and the food he brings, make an island in the stream, but it will soon be washed away. The only escape from one current is to seek, and find, and be caught by, another. Frederic Henry finds his current in the Tagliamento:

> I ducked down, pushed between two men, and ran for the river, my head down. I tripped at the edge and went in with a splash. The water was very cold and I stayed under as long as I could. I could feel the current swirl me and I stayed under until I thought I could never come up. . . . There were no shots now. The piece of timber swung in the current and I held it with one hand. I looked at the bank. It seemed to be going by very fast. There was much wood in the stream. The water was very cold. We passed the brush of an island above the water. I held onto the timber with both hands and let it take me along. (241)

He will make his life, whatever life fate will allow him, with Catherine.

The motifs of "movement" and "home" in *A Farewell to Arms* are pervasive, but not easy to define. When Catherine and Frederic spend the hours before he leaves for the Front in the hotel, in a room full of red plush furniture and mirrors, Catherine lets her cape fall to the bed and says, "I never felt like a whore before." In the lines that follow Hemingway defines whoring. It's not sin, but an appetite for the crude, the transient, the selfish that makes the whorehouse, or the hotel, a mockery of home. After they make love, Catherine says, "Everything we do seems so innocent and simple. I can't believe we do anything wrong." And Frederic thinks, "My room at the hospital had been our own home and this room was our home too in the same way."

In fact, Frederic had always known what was wrong with the whorehouse and with whores. Even before he fell in love with Catherine, when he wasn't in love with anyone at all, Frederic knew that there was something awful about the singing coming from the Villa Rosa, and the whore with the thick, full lips and black eyes who "put out her tongue and fluttered it up and down." It was not what the captain of the finger games at the mess would recognize. But he, Rinaldi, and the priest would.

The whorehouse at the Front and the Hall-Hemingway house in Oak Park had for Hemingway a strange but telling association. Consider the essential vulgarity of his mother, the manipulation of his timid, acquiescent father, the pervasive sense of inadequacy and guilt stemming from the presence of Ernest Hall. Both Ernest's home in Oak Park and the whorehouse at the Front sinned against beauty and truth. Each was a house full of ugliness and lies.

Something else about the whorehouse, or the time spent with whores, makes Frederic Henry afraid. It's the excitement, the feverish excitement of obsession, to "resume again unknowing and not caring." The knowledge of time passing is tragic. But to make it disappear by force of will is obscene. Hence the final lines of the seduction poem Frederic Henry quoted earlier:

> Let us roll all our strength and all
> Our sweetness up into one ball,
> And tear our pleasures with rough strife
> Through the iron gates of life.
> Thus, though we cannot make our sun
> Stand still, yet we will make him run.

When one of the sergeants carries off a clock from the farmhouse occupied on the retreat, Frederic tells him to put it back. The sergeant, who will soon be dead, cannot steal time. Neither can Frederic Henry. The statues Frederic has mocked in the hall of the hospital because they possessed a simple, suggestive uniformity—the common ground of death—are recalled in the final lines of the book: "But after I had got them out and shut the door and turned off the light it wasn't any good. It was like saying good-by to a statue. After a while I went out and left the hospital and walked back to the hotel in the rain" (355). Catherine, now like the statues, is part of the past, that other country on whose border we live and, as we must, cross over in time. Time, which in Frederic's hospital world was "time-ashealer," as much a part of patient care as the work of doctor and nurse, now pursues and destroys.

Catherine Barkley's death was foreshadowed from the beginning of her pregnancy. There were obvious warning signs of trouble with childbirth—the too narrow hips, the talk of drinking beer to keep the baby small. Then all the little things that went wrong: it takes too long to get a cab to the hospital; Catherine is not allowed to wear the nightgown she has brought. She must wear that horrible johnny—"that looks as though it were made of rough sheeting." Then comes the technical language, masking the true danger—"The first labor is usually protracted."

Frederic is told he has plenty of time to get breakfast at the "café down the street at the square." Hemingway took the reader to this café another time. There is the light, the old waiter, the slopping of the wine. It is "A Clean, Well-Lighted Place." And Frederic—like the old man, the widower of that story who stays too late, and the older waiter—senses in the refuse cans, the nosing dogs, the dust and the dead flowers, that awful "nada."

When Frederic returns to the hospital, he is frightened by Catherine's room, empty except for her "bag on a chair and her dressing-gown hanging on a hook on the wall." The doctor's professional assurances set in high relief the desperation in Catherine's grasping for the gas. Eventually the pain and suffering reduce Catherine to a pleading child, drunkenly praising the doctor whose "wonderful" anesthetic is becoming useless. Frederic is reduced, too. He is back to being the child, Nick Adams, in "Indian Camp," too frightened to watch the Cesarean his father performs.

Eventually, Frederic Henry returns to the stream, to the current of fate that runs beneath all surface considerations, beneath even the current of life. It is the awful destiny that a man nurtured by fear comes to know. There is no reason for Catherine to die, Frederic tells himself, "She's just having a bad time. The initial labor is usually protracted." "But what if she should die? Hey, what about that? What if she should die?" Of course, Catherine does die, broken by a world that kills first "the very good and the very gentle and the very brave. . . ." (All this foreshadowed by the marching troops, at the start of the story, "six months gone with child.")

There is another story told by this ending to A Farewell to Arms—the story of Hemingway's childhood with Grace and Clarence and Grandfather Hall. But, unlike the Orpen story, here there is no wish-fulfilling dream. Frederic Henry has tried to make a separate peace. He has returned to home and love. But when Catherine's pregnancy comes to term, the tragedy begins. For a while, Catherine plays mother to Frederic at the hospital, as well as mother-to-be. Then she withdraws into the pain and suffering which antici-pate her death. Frederic, frustrated and impotent, sees himself in a mirror. He's the bearded, incompetent doctor in Milan, the one who couldn't tell the difference between left and right legs on an X-ray, just the "fake doctor with a beard." For Catherine's agony he can give her only anesthesia—with horribly sexual connotations—"Give it to me quick. *Give it to me!*"

By dying, Catherine denies Frederic her love. Like the "statue" she has become, her only home is the cemetery. The baby, symbol of the home Frederic and Catherine tried to create, is born with the umbilical cord around its neck, strangled in the womb. The specter of Ernest Hall appears in the bitterly cynical philosophy Frederic expresses when, considering coldly, he "realizes" that Catherine will die. The concept of a mocking, tyrannical god, the embodiment of selfishness, of will in the absence of love, is expressed in Frederic's parable of the ants.

> Once in camp I put a log on top of the fire and it was full of ants. As it commenced to burn, the ants swarmed out and went first toward the centre where the fire was; then turned back and ran toward the end. When there were enough on the end they fell off into the fire. Some got out, their bodies burnt and flattened, and went off not knowing where they were going. But most of them went toward the fire and then back toward the end and swarmed on the cool end and finally fell off into the fire. I remember thinking at the time that it was the end of the world and a splendid chance to be a messiah and lift the log off the fire and throw it out where the ants could get off onto the ground. But I did not do anything but throw a tin cup of water on the log, so that I would have the cup empty to put whiskey in before I added water to it. I think the cup of water on the burning log only steamed the ants. (350)

In the years between his wartime love affair and the writing of *A Farewell to Arms*, Ernest Hemingway tried to create a home with Hadley Richardson, who as much as Agnes von Kurowsky was the model for Catherine Barkley. The record of his success and failure appears in *A Moveable Feast*. Hemingway claimed that in Paris, in the Twenties, with Hadley, Bumby, and his devotion to work, he had found a home. But *A Moveable Feast* is much more fiction than history, and more "moveable" than "feast." In both *A Farewell to Arms* and *A Moveable Feast* the tone is elegiac. Each has the quality of failure, of a wistful looking back. In his yearning for home, Ernest Hemingway always looked well past Paris and Milan—back to the Hall-Hemingway household in Oak Park, Illinois, where he spent his first six years with an "heroic" grandfather, a timid, impotent father, and a mother who denied him her love.

Notes

1. See Peter Griffin, *Along With Youth: Hemingway, The Early Years* (New York: Oxford University Press, 1985), 3–16, 121–30.

2. See Jeffrey Meyers, *Hemingway: A Biography* (New York: Harper & Row, 1985), 478–79; and Kenneth S. Lynn, *Hemingway* (New York: Simon and Schuster, 1987), 389–90.

3. This and all subsequent quotations from Hemingway's story are derived from Griffin, *Along With Youth*, 222–24.

4. Ernest Hemingway to Grace Hall Hemingway, 5 February 1927, in *Ernest Hemingway: Selected Letters, 1917–1961*, ed. Carlos Baker (New York: Scribners, 1981), 243–44.

5. Agnes von Kurowsky to Ernest Hemingway, 16 October 1918; in Henry Serrano Villard and James Nagel, *Hemingway in Love and War: The Lost Diary of Agnes von Kurowsky, Her Letters, and Correspondence of Ernest Hemingway* (Boston: Northeastern University Press, 1989), 99–100.

6. Quoted from Griffin, *Along With Youth*, 114.

7. See Michael S. Reynolds, *Hemingway's First War: The Making of "A Farewell to Arms"* (Princeton, NJ: Princeton University Press, 1976), 181–219.

8. *A Farewell to Arms* (New York: Scribners, 1929), 3.

9. See Carlos Baker, *Hemingway: The Writer as Artist*, 4th ed. (Princeton, NJ: Princeton University Press, 1972), 108; and James R. Mellow, *Hemingway: A Life Without Consequences* (Boston: Houghton Mifflin, 1992), 379–81, 383.

10. See Griffin, *Along With Youth*, 144 *et passim*.

11. Ernest Hemingway, *88 Poems*, ed. Nicholas Gerogiannis (New York and London: Harcourt Brace Jovanovich/Bruccoli Clark, 1979), 107–13.

Index

♦